Max Décharné is a writer and musician. His books include *King's Road – The Rise & Fall of the Hippest Street in the World*, *Hardboiled Hollywood – The Origins of the Great Crime Films* and *Straight From the Fridge, Dad – A Dictionary of Hipster Slang*. A regular contributor to *Mojo* magazine since 1998, his work has also appeared in the *Sunday Times Colour Magazine*, the *Guardian*, *TLS* and *Bizarre*, among others.

In his music career, Max has released eleven albums and something in the region of thirty singles since 1989. He played drums with his friend Nikki Sudden before joining Gallon Drunk in 1991, with whom he toured the world. Since 1994 he has been the singer and principal songwriter with The Flaming Stars. He has also recorded nine John Peel Sessions and played shows all across the USA, Canada, Europe and Japan.

The Hipster's Guide to Rockabilly

Max Décharné

A complete catalogue record for this book can
be obtained from the British Library on request

The right of Max Décharné to be identified as the author of this work has been
asserted by him in accordance with the Copyright, Designs and Patents Act 1988

First published in 2010 by Serpent's Tail,
an imprint of Profile Books Ltd
3A Exmouth House
Pine Street
London EC1R 0JH
website: www.serpentstail.com

ISBN 978 1 84668 721 1

Designed and typeset by folio at Neuadd Bwll, Llanwrtyd Wells

Printed and bound in Great Britain by Clays, Bungay, Suffolk

10 9 8 7 6 5 4 3 2 1

The paper this book is printed on is certified by the © 1996 Forest Stewardship
Council A.C. (FSC). It is ancient-forest friendly. The printer holds FSC chain of
custody SGS-COC-2061

Mixed Sources
Product group from well-managed
forests and other controlled sources
Cert no. TT-COC-02227
www.fsc.org
©1996 Forest Stewardship Council

FSC

For Nikki Sudden,
who sang the Teenage Boogie on a Saturday night,
and was telling me nearly twenty-five years ago
to write something about Charlie Feathers.
Rest in peace, old friend

CONTENTS

INTRODUCTION

HOLD IT, FELLAS, THAT DON'T MOVE ME,
LET'S GET REAL, REAL *GONE* FOR A CHANGE...

Rockabilly came from the Southern states of America. I'm from England, but it always struck a chord with me. In the early seventies I was still at school, growing up near Portsmouth, the dockyard city on the south coast. The place always had a strong Teddy Boy contingent, who could still be seen in those days running the dodgem cars at the funfair down on the seafront – the same one that featured in 1973's fifties-era film *That'll Be the Day*, which, like the same year's *American Graffiti*, came with its own very useful double soundtrack LP of 1950s material. Fifties nostalgia was in fashion, usually in a family-friendly, watered-down version such as that being peddled on the TV sitcom *Happy Days*, which was itself inspired by *American Graffiti*. Books about James Dean seemed to be appearing at a rate of almost one a month, and many of the glam rock bands on British radio had hijacked a sizeable portion of their acts from the original fifties rockers. The word 'rockabilly' was hardly ever mentioned, but if you turned to the back pages of the *NME*, down among the small ads for hippy clothing, there was always one from a company called Orpheus, based in a

Gene Vincent, 1956

concrete brutalist car-park-cum-shopping arcade called the Tricorn Centre, Portsmouth. Orpheus would sell you Teddy Boy drapes, bootlace ties, drainpipe jeans and brothel creepers – all of which, in a time of split-knee loons, 30-inch flares and five-inch stack-heel boots, was something of a revelation.

I knew I liked rock'n'roll, but it wasn't always that easy

finding the original recordings when your main record outlet was the local branch of WH Smith. I'd been a piano player since the age of four, and a drummer since 1972, when I was twelve. A few months after getting my second-hand drumkit, I bought my first LP, a TV-advertised K-Tel compilation called *25 Rockin' & Rollin' Greats*. Sure, they crammed on far too many tracks a side, but it had Wanda Jackson doing 'Let's Have A Party', Gene Vincent & the Blue Caps with 'Be Bop A Lula', Roy Orbison's 'Oh! Pretty Woman' and even Johnny Kidd & the Pirates' majestic 'Shakin' All Over'. These were all the original cuts, but what I didn't know at the time was that the versions of Carl Perkins' 'Blue Suede Shoes' or Bill Haley's 'Rock Around The Clock' were later re-recordings. Still, it had a fair amount of roots rock'n'roll and even some rockabilly on it, and I would practise my drumming by playing along with both sides of the album.

I probably first heard the word 'rockabilly' on Mott The Hoople's single 'Roll Away the Stone' in November 1973, when Ian Hunter sang 'There's a rockabilly party on Saturday night' during the middle eight, but mostly the phrase rock'n'roll seemed to cover everything. Hunter was clearly a fan, as was Roy Wood, whose new band Wizzard could be seen regularly on *Top of the Pops* larking about in a selection of drape jackets, performing fifties-influenced songs like 'See My Baby Jive' (1973) and name-dropping the likes of Dion in their lyrics. In 1974 they went even farther with an album called *Introducing Eddy & the Falcons*, on which Wood wrote a selection of new songs, each in the style of a different fifties rocker. One of these ('I Dun Lotsa Cryin' Over You') was a remarkably close facsimile of the Elvis, Scotty & Bill Sun rockabilly sound, although at that stage all the Elvis songs I knew were those on his *40 Greatest* double LP which had come out the same year.

An occasional series in the *NME* at that time, called

Max Décharné

Junkyard Angels, attempted to hip the readers to rockers from the past, and in June 1974 Roy Carr used the slot to talk at length about Elvis's Sun sessions under the headline 'The Original Greasy Trucker', concluding with a couple of sentences that got right to the point: 'What I still can't comprehend is why, after all these years, RCA haven't collated all the "official" released Sun tracks onto one volume and released it with all relevant details as a collector's edition. After all, these are perhaps the most important rock records ever made.'

Someone out there seems to have been listening, because the following year, the first official LP collection of Elvis's Sun material appeared on RCA, with excellent sleeve notes by none other than Roy Carr. There may not yet have been much of a market for such a thing back in the US, but over in Britain it was much appreciated and long overdue. The rockin' scene had grown to such an extent in the UK that on 10 April 1976, the NME put Teddy Boys on the cover of the paper, accompanying a lengthy article inside by Tony Stewart profiling the rise of British bands like Crazy Cavan & the Rhythm Rockers, or the Flying Saucers, together with details of prime rock'n'roll pubs such as the Adam & Eve in Hackney, the Castle in the Old Kent Road and the rock'n'roll nights at the Lyceum Ballroom. The word 'rockabilly' was also bandied about, and there was a classic description of legendary 'King of the Teds' Sunglasses Ron Staples:

Sunglasses Ron is one of the movement's characters, almost a legend in his own time. Ron's a menacing beery-faced 32-year-old who always wears shades, a shabby brown drape and white crepes. His bootlace tie is looped through a swastika, and thick brass rings adorn all his fingers, which are usually firmly clutched round a pint of light'n'bitter. Originally from Newport,

Portsmouth's finest rockin' gear, 1974

he's had his photo in the papers almost as many times as Eddie Cochrane [sic], his Main Man. Living only for authentic rock'n'roll, he's not particularly impressed with reworkings of his hero's music. Not even The Who's version of 'Summertime Blues'. 'Well,' he says. 'I've just had a piss and *that* went down better.'

Ron was a familiar figure in the press in those days. The swastika tie was very likely down to him also moving in biker circles, at a time when Hell's Angels, and the early punks, often wore them in order to get a reaction out of straight society. The *NME* article was accompanied by numerous fine pictures taken by Chalkie Davies, including one of my home town's local legend, Pete Presley, the singer with Portsmouth rockabilly band Shazam. There was also mention of the current campaign

Max Décharné

German release of
'Jungle Rock', 1976

for a national rock'n'roll radio show on BBC Radio 1, which culminated the following month in a protest march of Teddy Boys organised by deejays Geoff Barker and Stuart Colman, and fronted by Sunglasses Ron. They won their show – it was called *It's Rock'n'Roll* – in a year when rockabilly really came out of the shadows and into the UK charts. Colin Escott & Martin Hawkins' landmark thirteen-part series of Sun albums on the Charly label, *The Roots Of Rock*, began being issued that year, and a twenty-year-old rockabilly single called 'Jungle Rock' by Hank Mizell, also reissued by Charly, surprised just about everyone by reaching the UK Top Ten, not least Hank himself.

I bought a copy of 'Jungle Rock' as it went up the charts, and I also bought Charly's follow-up release, 'Flyin' Saucer Rock'n'Roll' by Billy Lee Riley, largely on the strength of reading that it had Jerry Lee Lewis on piano. I also picked up the new T. Rex single, 'I Love To Boogie', and then saw in the *NME* that it was apparently 'borrowed' from Webb Pierce's 'Teenage Boogie', currently available on a new album called *Rare Rockabilly Volume One*, so I tracked down a copy of that and was duly blown away by what I heard. I still wasn't sure exactly how rockabilly differed from rock'n'roll, but that album, filled with obscure names completely unknown to me, convinced me that there were probably numerous singers out there who'd made astonishing records back in those days but had never quite had the breaks.

From 1976, if you were living in England, it was hard to keep track of the sheer number of rockabilly reissues that started to appear. Chiswick Records had put out Vince Taylor's 'Brand New Cadillac' as their first ever reissue, in 1975, and then when the same company started the Ace label, they gave the world another chance to hear all kinds of fine items like 'Tennessee Rock' by Hoyt Scoggins & the Saturday Nite Jamboree Boys (originally released in 1956), or unissued gems like Hal Harris's remarkable 'Jitterbop Baby'.

Of course, in 1977 punks and Teds were supposed to be knocking hell out of each other, and many of them were, but I was seventeen that year, and spent much of it buying the likes of Gene Vincent alongside records by the Clash, and Sonny Burgess at the same time as Richard Hell & The Void-Oids. It all sounded like it came from the same three-chord rock'n'roll spirit as far as I was concerned. Not everyone agreed. I remember going to see X-Ray Spex at a place called the Oddfellows Hall in Portsmouth in October 1977, just when their debut single, 'Oh Bondage Up Yours!', had been released. There were only about fifty people there, all of them my age, and when we left the building after the show, a sizeable number of the local Teds – full-grown men at least a decade older than us – were waiting across the street looking to batter some punks. There's no room in circumstances like that to try to explain how many Eddie Cochran albums you've got at home, it's easier just to run.

As for the original singles, if you were looking for a mint copy of a Sun 45 or 78 that had somehow survived the decades,

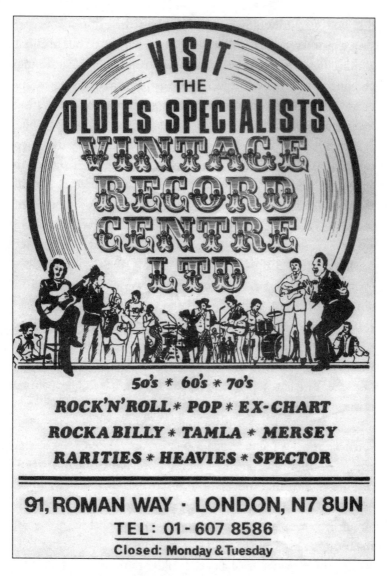

they certainly weren't likely to show up at my local record shop. Even up in London, one of the very few places likely to have them, outside of specialist mail-order record dealers, was the Rock On shop in Camden Town. Another was Vintage Records in Roman Way, near Caledonian Road tube station, run by a couple of guys called Mike and Pete, who also published one of the first guides to rare record prices. I probably first heard about Vintage in the *NME*, and found my way there some time in 1978 on a visit to London. It was a small shop, crammed full of rare vinyl of the 1950s and '60s, with a tattered original copy of the *Rebel without a Cause* poster pinned to the ceiling. Propped up on a shelf behind the counter the day I first walked in were two pristine Sun 78s that had just arrived in stock – 'Slow Down' by Jack Earls & The Jimbos, and 'Flyin' Saucer Rock'n'Roll' by Billy Lee Riley & His Little Green Men. It was barely two years since I'd bought the reissue of the latter on a Charly 45 brand-new for about 60p. Both of these 78s were priced at £5. I couldn't afford both, so I took the Riley. Over the next couple of years, I picked up originals of every other Riley single on Sun, plus most of Jerry Lee's singles for the label, along with stuff like 'We Wanna Boogie' by Sonny Burgess & the Pacers, 'Ubangi Stomp' by Warren Smith, 'Come On Little Mama' by Ray Harris, assorted Johnny Cash singles and a fair few others. The only problem was deciding what to leave behind during a visit. John Peel once told me about a similar shop in Dallas, when he was living there back in the sixties, called Ernstroms: 'I wish, now, I'd had a truck and just said, "Look, empty your shop into my van and I'll not trouble you again..."', and thirty years later, the music still comes tearing right out of those original Sun 45s like they were cut yesterday.

THE HOTTEST THING IN THE COUNTRY

The main reason I wanted to write a book about rockabilly is that I've loved it for many years, and in all that time, as different musical genres came and went, it seemed as if it never really received the respect it deserved. The history of rock music in general has been shaped by journalists from the sixties generation. Modern rock writing began with mid-to-late sixties magazines, staffed by people in their early twenties who grew up on the Beatles and the Stones, for whom the fifties were already ancient history – something that happened before they were old enough to care much about music. Hence, the work of the fifties rockers – even though barely a decade old at the time – was often depicted in those magazines as a quaint survival from another era, to be mocked and humoured like ear trumpets, horseless carriages and Granny's Victorian furniture. Nineteen sixty-two and the first Beatles recordings were seen as Year Zero, the invention of everything modern, and all that came before it some unmentionable embarrassment. As the years have passed, that generation of writers has continually shifted the goalposts, so that even though those same Beatles records are now approaching their half-century anniversary, as far as much rock writing is concerned, the Fab Four are still 'modern', and the fifties still back in the Dark Ages. Rockabilly, and much original rock'n'roll, has often been sidelined and ignored over the years because of this attitude.

Music books that have mentioned rockabilly in passing often seemed to think that running through the achievements of five or six of the best-known artists from Sam Phillips' Sun label was sufficient to cover the entire genre, as if these were the sole figures of note, and Sam's groundbreaking label had been the only game in town. This is about as useful as assuming that the whole complexity of the 1920s blues scene can be adequately dealt with by buying a Bessie Smith greatest-hits package. There were hundreds of labels, many thousands of performers who made it onto wax, and tens of thousands of recordings. The scale of activity was immense, yet rockabilly as a genre has still received remarkably little of the attention that it deserves. One book couldn't possibly mention every artist, still less every record, but the aim here is to give a picture of how the music developed, where and how it was made, and in what situations it was heard – the clubs, the radio and TV shows, and the films. This is the story of the music itself, rather than any individual performer, although Elvis rightly casts a giant shadow over its glory years.

So what exactly is rockabilly music? Essentially a mutant blend of uptempo country and hillbilly sounds combined with the backbeat of jump R&B, it erupted in numerous dance halls, bars and cheap studios across America in the wake of the massively influential handful of singles which Elvis cut for the Sun label in 1954 and '55. Rockabilly on its own ground is as pure, direct and unmistakable as the guitar blues of Robert Johnson or the rebel sounds of early Jamaican ska, perfect in its simplicity, but open to thousands of variations.

The story of rockabilly is largely one of individual recordings rather than stars. Most of the great performances were laid down by unknowns whose careers were over almost before the ink dried on their record contracts: one killer record, then a lifetime of low-paying straight jobs. Yet the first pure rockabilly record ever made launched its teenage singer on the biggest and most successful career trajectory the music world has ever known. When Elvis walked into Sam Phillips' Sun Studios in May 1954 to record his debut single – 'That's All Right'/'Blue Moon Of Kentucky' – he laid down the blueprint for the worldwide rock explosion of the 1950s, but also defined pure rockabilly for all time.

The term 'rock'n'roll' proved wide enough in the fifties to encompass everything from the R&B-flavoured, sax-and-piano-led sounds of Little Richard to the pure street-corner harmony vocalising of Dion & the Belmonts. Chuck Berry is for many the epitome of rock'n'roll, yet his records were reviewed favourably in Britain at the time by the rock-hating magazine *Jazz Journal* as an example of pure urban blues. Rockabilly, however, is a more elemental strain: less inclusive than rock'n'roll, but easier to define. Take the two sides of Elvis's 1954 debut single. Both were cover versions of songs from the mid-1940s. 'That's All Right' was a gutsy uptempo jump blues written and recorded by

Arthur 'Big Boy' Crudup. 'Blue Moon of Kentucky' had been the biggest hit recorded by Bill Monroe, the man who mapped out and defined his own genre of music: bluegrass. In the hands of a simple three-man band – Elvis, Scotty & Bill – these two songs, one black, one white, became 100 per cent rockabilly.

Although many of the original performers simply called their music rock'n'roll, and generally tell interviewers these days that they never, ever called it rockabilly back in the 1950s, the word 'rockabilly' surfaced in various song titles and band names of the time, yet no one could quite agree on the spelling. There were songs called 'Rock-a-billy Rhythm', 'Rock-a-billie Music', 'Rock Billy Boogie', 'Rockabilly Gal', and even – praise the Lord and let's have another bottle of whatever *they* were drinking – 'Rockabilly Bungalow'. The word seems to have been a particular favourite of the music industry, and was certainly in regular use from 1956 in the pages of the main trade paper, *Billboard*. In January 1957, reviewing the musical trends of the previous year, in the wake of the colossal success of Presley, Carl Perkins and others – all of whom were seen as basically country & western artists – the newspaper attempted to define for its readers how the word had come about: '... this resurgence of country talent in the pop play area was part of the whole so-called "rock and roll" surge in all fields and gave rise to the term "rockabilly", applicable to country artists who performed blues tunes and other material backed by the Big Beat.' In short, hillbilly music with 5,000 volts shot through it.

While the influence of the blues on rockabilly is clear, there was also a strong strain of traditional hill-country songs blended into the mix, going back to the pioneering 1920s sounds of people like the Carter Family, whose high lonesome sounds and simple instrumentation had evolved in turn from the folk ballads which came over with the first settlers many decades earlier.

The story of rockabilly is much like that of the blues in the 1920s and '30s – a tale of impoverished, unsung musicians making groundbreaking recordings which are only given proper recognition decades later. This was not music that was dreamed up by the major record companies or Tin Pan Alley songsmiths and aimed at the mass market. Rather, the majority of rockabilly recordings stand up as an accurate sample of what was heard at dance halls, roadhouses and high-school hops across the South: stripped down, pure, untainted by studio trickery or the kind of sugary, intrusive arrangements that the major labels were liable to inflict on their more successful artists. Most important of all, you could sing your own songs: in an age where the record company was king, and most singers were saddled with whichever tune the bosses thought would sell, the average rockabilly could mostly write about whatever he wanted: rockets to the moon, Asiatic flu, baboons doing the boogie, stuttering, you name it...

Charlie Feathers always said, when asked to explain why his music sounded the way it did, that it was just a feeling that gets a hold of you – it sounds that way because that's exactly the way it has to sound: deceptively simple, but devilishly hard to do right. Like punk, or ska, or sixties garage, if you try to make

Jerry Lee Lewis

it too fancy, you destroy the very essence of the music. Those that succeeded in capturing the authentic rockabilly sound hit on something elemental – as Jerry Lee Lewis once famously shouted at Sam Phillips during an argument in the Sun Studio that was being captured on tape, 'That's right! You're right! You're so right you don't even know what you're saying!'

Youthful enthusiasm, urgent rhythms and stripped-down

arrangements driven along by a slapping upright double bass; these were songs sung mostly by teenagers which dealt with all the essentials of the hepcat lifestyle: girls, cars, booze, dancing. Just like the punk explosion twenty years later, fifties rockabilly was a spontaneous outburst of spirited three-chord songs, in which the major companies had a stake, but there was still plenty of room for tiny record labels, primitive studios, fiercely partisan audiences and wild-eyed, driven performers who weren't planning much farther ahead than the following week. They were chasing something you couldn't ever quite catch up with, nail down or explain to your parents.

Lightning in a bottle, a tiger by the tail, a rocket in your pocket...

1 HILLBILLIES ON SPEED

In October 1954, when the relatively unknown Elvis Presley made his first and last appearance on country music's foremost radio showcase, *The Grand Ole Opry*, his primal rockabilly sound left most of the artists and audience horrified. Not only did he dress like a black pimp from the wrong side of town, but he'd also taken Bill Monroe's stately bluegrass waltz, 'Blue Moon of Kentucky', doubled the tempo and put an electric charge right through it. And anyway, couldn't he for God's sake stop his leg from shaking like that?

Wanda Jackson, the queen of rockabilly, who met a similarly unsympathetic reception a year later during her one and only Opry appearance, told me: 'They booed Elvis practically off, and he said the very same words as I did when he got off, "I'll never come back." And that's what I told my daddy.'

It's often been said that the fifties country establishment reacted with barely concealed disgust to the rise of this new upstart sound, yet the situation was much more complex than that. For all the undeniable blues, R&B and boogie-woogie strains running through it, rockabilly arose out of the mainstream of hillbilly music. Elvis's first proper tours of the South were support slots on package shows headlined by

1

established country stars like Hank Snow and Faron Young, he was written up in genre publications like *Country Song Roundup*, broadcast on country stations, and some of his early rockabilly singles on the Sun label were bona fide hits on *Billboard*'s country charts: 'Baby Let's Play House' reached number 5, while 'I Forgot To Remember To Forget' made it all the way to number 1.

This was back in 1955, when Elvis was known as The Hillbilly Cat or the King of Western Bop, a good half a year before 'Heartbreak Hotel' catapulted him to national stardom. The scale and speed of that success were truly remarkable: with the release of 'Hound Dog' (August 1956), Elvis racked up his fifth *Billboard* country chart number 1 in less than a year, at which point long-time hillbilly comedy duo Homer & Jethro responded with a fine rockin' downhome parody single called 'Houn' Dawg' ('You look like an Airedale, with the air let out'). Some of the old-time country stars may not have known quite what to make of him, but they still understood instinctively that he was one of their own.

In 1956, a month after 'Heartbeak Hotel' rewrote the rulebook, *Life* magazine called Elvis 'a howling hillbilly success'. Controversial word, 'hillbilly'. Even though the term had been applied to the white Southern rural community since around 1900, and to their folk music since 1924, many people then and ever since reacted against the label and what they saw as its stereotype image of a hay-chewing, moonshine-guzzling caricature. By the 1950s, the less contentious term 'country & western' was gaining acceptance, but even so, when Sam Phillips at Sun Records in Memphis put out a single by the Ripley Cotton Choppers in September 1953 – his first white release after a long successful stint of recording black R&B and blues – he flagged up the change to DJs and record buyers alike by issuing it with the word 'Hillbilly' stamped in red on the label. Of course, some rockabilly performers genuinely did grow up on farms or out in the hills, but that was by no means always the case, as Wanda Jackson says: 'See, in those days, what we'd call a country singer now was a hillbilly singer, and none of us liked that word. None of us were farm people, or hillbillies, so we were glad when it changed, but that's where The Hillbilly Cat came from, 'cause Elvis was dressing different, wearing his hair different and singing different songs, but he had that country flavour.'

FREE AND UNTRAMMELLED – THE ORIGINS OF THE HILLBILLY SOUND

Hanging a label on a type of music or a performer is often a misleading or inadequate business, but given that Elvis at Sun had come up with a genuinely new musical fusion, in many ways to call him The Hillbilly Cat was right on the money. A real gone hepcat from the hillbilly tradition, who'd taken a solid jolt of uptempo R&B and boogie and mixed it up with the raw-boned, high lonesome sounds from the hills of Virginia, Tennessee and Kentucky. Presley's first nickname gets right to the heart of where he was and what he was doing, and he was probably a lot less offended by it than some other early fifties mainstream singers who were saddled with supposedly descriptive nicknames: Johnnie Ray was billed as The Prince of Wails and the Nabob of Sob, while Mel Tormé famously hated being called the Velvet Fog, and who can blame him.

Certainly, a fair number of country performers from the 1920s onwards were irritated to have the hillbilly tag hung on them, but for every one that was, there were others who went along with the name, willingly or unwillingly. The first was veteran banjo player Uncle Dave Macon, born way back in 1870 in Warren County, Tennessee, an early star of *The Grand Ole Opry*. At his debut recording session he cut a number entitled 'Hill Billie Blues' (1924) – the first record to include the word 'hillbilly' in the title. The phrase was certainly in common usage by then. In 1900, a piece in the *New York Journal* had spoken of a 'free and untrammelled white citizen ... A hillbilly ... who has no means to speak of, dresses as he can, talks as he pleases, drinks whisky when he gets it and fires off his revolver as the fancy takes him.' The rise of the cinema then helped spread the word. Silent serial star Neva Gerber took the title role in the 1915 comedy *Billie the Hillbilly*, and just three months before Macon recorded his 1924 tune, a feature film appeared called *The Hill Billy*, starring Mary Pickford's younger brother Jack. (Whether the hillbilly image was helped or hindered by films such as these, or by later Hollywood offerings such as *The Hillbilly Goat* (1937) or *Hillbilly Blitzkrieg* (1942), is another matter entirely.)

In the music field, for about twenty years, the word was used extensively not so much in song lyrics but in band names. Al Hopkins, who recorded for trailblazing A&R man Ralph Peer in January 1925, arrived at the session without a name for his string band combo. When questioned by Peer, Hopkins is said to have replied, 'Call the band anything you want. We are nothing but a bunch of hillbillies from North Carolina and Virginia anyway.' As a result, their records were issued under the name the Hill Billies, and the success of their versions of songs for the Vocalion label such as 'Cumberland Gap' and 'Going Down The Road Feeling Bad' probably helped account for the names of later outfits such as The Newton County Hillbillies (who recorded for Okeh in 1930), the Kentucky Hillbillies (who anticipated the Stray Cats by fifty years in cutting a song named 'Runaway Boy' for the Brunswick label in 1931), the Crazy Hillbillies Band (who made 'Danced All Night With A Bottle In My Hand' for Okeh in 1934) or Gurney Thomas and His Hillbilly Pals, stalwarts of the King label in 1946. The word even crossed over into the blues idiom in 1935, when Blind Willie McTell recorded 'Hillbilly Willie's Blues' – a song with a very similar construction to the old hillbilly song 'Crawdad Hole'.

With the all-encompassing spread of radio from the early 1920s onwards, not only were white hillbilly musicians picking up on developments in the blues field, but there were also black artists paying attention to hillbilly music over the coming decades. The young BB King had a liking for artists such as Eddy Arnold, and Memphis blues singer Bobby Bland later told writers Colin Escott and Martin Hawkins: 'I used to listen to the radio every morning to people like Roy Acuff, Lefty Frizzell, Hank Williams and Hank Snow. I think hillbilly has more of a story than people give it credit for. We were taught that hillbilly wasn't the thing, but I guarantee they were wrong.'

If a percentage of song titles and band names was helping to popularise the 'hillbilly' label, the backwoods country-dweller image was also being reinforced by the style of dress adopted by some performers – battered hats, denim overalls and work shirts, as if they'd just taken a break from a day's labour down on the farm or at a logging mill out in the Appalachian mountains. The later rise of Hollywood's singing cowboys in the 1930s and '40s such as Gene Autry and Roy Rogers – with their elaborately hand-embroidered western apparel, which eventually became the default style of clothing for most country singers – has tended to obscure the original patched-and-threadbare, downhome look adopted by the first hillbilly performers.

Early song titles, too, took the hill-farming life, rather

than the wild west, as their inspiration. Fiddlin' John Carson, who made his first record in 1923 on the Okeh label and became one of the founding stars of the genre, kicked off with 'The Old Hen Cackled And The Rooster's Going to Crow'/'Little Old Log Cabin In The Lane' – a sure indicator of his frames of reference and his likely audience. Singing to the sole accompaniment of his own fiddle, which owed a heavy debt to traditional British and Irish folk music, Fiddlin' John recorded a bewildering variety of material; everything from 'It's A Long Way To Tipperary' (1926) to charming titles like 'It's A Shame To Whip Your Wife On Sunday' (1927), 'Old And In The Way' (1928), 'You Can't Get Milk From A Cow Named Ben' (1929) and 'Who Bit The Wart Off Grandma's Nose' (1929).

If Fiddlin' John played up the rural angle in his titles, he certainly wasn't the only one. Ever since the days of minstrel songwriter Stephen Foster in the mid-nineteenth century, the lives of Southern hill folk had long been providing inspiration for songsmiths, and many Tin Pan Alley writers of the North in the latter part of that century had concocted appealing images of country life despite never having witnessed it. Just as Foster had never seen the Suwannee River in Florida before writing 'Old Folks At Home' (1851) – and changed the spelling of its name to fit the metre of the song lyric – the city-dwelling writer of 'Mid The Green Fields Of Virginia' (1898), New Yorker Charles K. Harris, was equally unfamiliar with his song's location, as he later recalled: 'I had to enquire if there was corn raised in Virginia and if there were hills in Carolina. This information was given me by my office superintendent, Mr Blaise, a native Southerner, and my imagination did the rest.'

Where Harris and Foster led, others followed. From the 1880s, wax cylinders were the means of selling recorded music, but they suffered from the considerable disadvantage that they deteriorated each time they were played, and during the first decade of the twentieth century the likes of the Victor Talking Machine Company became well established marketing a wide variety of material on the more lasting medium of 78 rpm records. In among such items as 'Krausmeyer and His Dog Schneider' by Spencer & Holt (1904), or 'I'd Rather Be A Lobster' by Billy Murray (1907), we find the Victor Dance Orchestra recording something called 'Kerry Mills' Barn Dance' (1908), followed by the 'Haymakers Barn Dance' in 1909. Since, however, they also turned their hands to a tune called the 'Norsemen 2 Step' (1909), it can probably be assumed that their hillbilly credentials were about as genuine as their Viking ones.

Len Spencer cut a version of the future hillbilly fiddling standard 'Arkansas Traveler' for the Victor label in 1908, and in 1913 Edna Brown and James F Harrison recorded 'The Trail Of The Lonesome Pine', but all of these artists were mainstream Northern performers projecting a romanticised view of the South – or making fun of it – rather than authentic hill folk expressing themselves. Record companies were city-based businesses which had yet to make field trips out into the country, and the thought of heading south to record genuine hillbillies was an idea that doesn't seem to have occurred to anyone until 1923, when Ralph Peer of Okeh made a journey to Atlanta and turned up Fiddlin' John Carson. For the time being, the nearest that the record-buying public came to anything hillbilly-flavoured was the rube comedy-and-fiddle routines of Charles Ross Taggart, in which he told tales in an exaggerated hick accent of an unsophisticated Southerner at odds with the modern world. 'Old Country Fiddler In New York' (1914) set the pattern for a series which went on to include 'Old Country

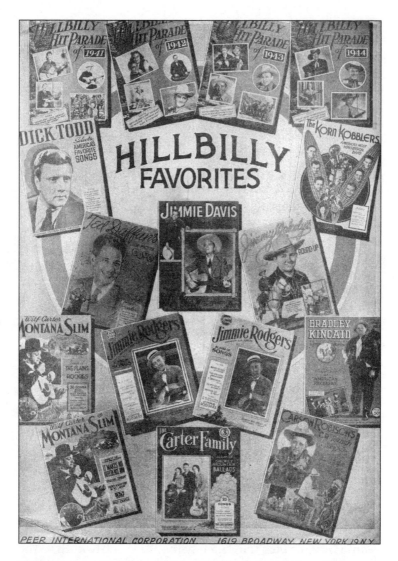

Fiddler On The School Board', 'Old Country Fiddler On The Phone' and 'Old Country Fiddler On Astronomy'. Quite what genuine country fiddlers of the time made of all this is anyone's guess.

This is not to say that authentic 1920s hillbilly performers weren't also capable of exaggerating or playing up to stereotypes of rural life. There's no mistaking the country flavour of titles like 'She Doodle Doed' (the Bouchillon Trio, 1925), 'Don't Sell Pa Any More Rum' (the Giddens Sisters, 1927), 'Throw The Old Cow Over The Fence' (Dr Humphrey Bates' Possum Hunters – the first string band to play on *The Grand Ole Opry* – 1928) or the decidedly pre-feminist 'She's Old and Bent But She Keep On Hoofin'' (Frankie Marvin, 1929).

In the event, once they dipped a toe in the water, the Northern record companies were completely taken by surprise by the sheer size of the market for hillbilly material. They'd only begun recording genuine hillbilly artists almost by accident, and looked down on its practitioners and its target audience just as they also looked down on the black record market. Indeed, the two were both regarded in a similar light, and from 1925 onwards the Victor record company had a separate series for each – the former labelled 'hillbilly', the latter 'race', both titles coined by star A&R man Ralph Peer – and as late as the Second World War the trade magazine *Billboard* was publishing a chart which showed combined race and hillbilly sales. The setting up of a separate series for what was generally called 'race' or 'sepia' material is hardly surprising, since the record industry seems to have run individual series for all kinds of ethnic groups at that time. US Decca, for instance, which started in the 1930s, had a designated imprint for almost every eventuality: Scotch, with singers like Sandy Macfarlane singing 'Granny's Highland Hame' (1934); Mexican, with the Orquestra Del Norte doing the 'Las Pajamas One Step' (1935); Cajun, with Leo Soileau's Rhythm Boys singing 'My Girl Don't Love Me' (1935); Irish, with Jack Doyle singing 'The Garden Where The Praties Grow' (1934); and a broad range of mostly Trinidadian artists on its Caribbean series such as The Lion with Gerald Clark singing 'Advantage Mussolini' (1936), and the superbly named Attila The Hun with 'The Horrors of War' (1938).

ARKANSAS TRAVELLER – THE FIRST HILLBILLY RECORDINGS

White rural hillbilly and black blues and jazz were each just another profitable niche market as far as the Northern city-based record executives were concerned, and although the first blues or jazz recording to be made by a black artist is generally acknowledged to be Mamie Smith's 'Crazy Blues' (August 1920, on which the ubiquitous Ralph Peer worked as engineer), it wasn't until two years later that an authentic hillbilly performer was recorded. Indeed, this came about only because Eck Robinson, the musician in question, made the journey up to New York on his own initiative and asked for a try-out. Robertson, a fiddle player from Arkansas, born in 1887, cut two tunes that day for Victor, 'Sally Gooden' and 'Arkansas Traveller'. Born at a time when Edison's wax cylinders were first being marketed, he lived long enough to appear at the historic 1965 Newport Folk Festival at which Dylan was booed for going electric.

The coming of radio at the start of the 1920s precipitated a remarkable collapse in record sales, as the public turned to the new medium for their listening entertainment. This led the record companies for the first time to seek out blues, jazz and hillbilly performers, whose respective audiences were found to be much larger than had been imagined, and proved themselves loyal record-buyers despite their poverty. Such was the early popularity of hillbilly material that some entertainers who had already had careers in mainstream popular music or the vaudeville circuit began performing tunes aimed at this section of the market. The most striking case is that of Vernon Dalhart, whose varied recording career already stretched back a decade before his 1924 cover of 'Wreck Of The Old 97', and his 1925 smash hit, 'The Prisoner's Song', marked him for life as a singer of hillbilly tunes. (The former song was given a proto-rockabilly treatment by Hank Snow in 1951, driven along by the upright bass of Ernie Newton and the twin guitars of Snow and Velma Smith, while the latter tune received a rockin' shot in the arm from Sun rockabilly Sonny Burgess in 1956 under the title 'Wings Of An Angel'.) Some of Vernon Dalhart's material was written by fellow hillbilly performer Carson Robison, born 1890, who later on, at the age of sixty-five, would cut a genuine 1950s rockabilly record for MGM – 'Rockin' and Rollin' With Grandmaw (On Saturday Night)'/'Hand Me Down My Walkin' Cane' (1956) – before dying the following year.

Dalhart's smoother, measured vocal style showed evidence of his parlour-singing origins, but the vast numbers of records and songsheets he was selling in the mid-1920s encouraged the record companies to put even more effort into finding out what kind of downhome talent might still be lurking out in them thar hills. Hopes were probably high, but even the most optimistic recording executive couldn't have predicted the seismic effects of the two world-class discoveries turned up by the busy Mr Peer over the course of a couple of days during his landmark field trip to Bristol, Tennessee, in August 1927. First he found the Carter Family; two days later he found Jimmie Rodgers. Between them, these two acts laid the foundation for virtually all the decent country music that has come along since.

JIMMIE RODGERS AND THE CARTER FAMILY

Jimmie Rodgers, the Singing Brakeman, had genuinely led a life of rambling, railroading and drifting before a combination

Jimmie
Rodgers

of his musical ambitions and his worsening TB curtailed his wandering in the mid-1920s. By the time he auditioned for Ralph Peer, he had his blues-influenced lyrics and guitar runs in place, welded to a unique high lonesome yodelling style. So influential was this yodelling that half the future hillbilly stars of the 1930s and '40s started out trying to imitate Jimmie's records like 'Blue Yodel (T For Texas)' (1927) or 'Waiting For a Train' (1928).

Rodgers was the giant star of early country music, selling records even in the depths of the Depression, when many other acts could barely get arrested. Jimmie absorbed everything – hillbilly, blues, jazz, Hawaiian guitar sounds, vaudeville and even sentimental parlour songs, but in particular his recordings are a classic example of the black blues influence on hillbilly music. He blazed a hardcore country career path that Hank Williams would follow two decades later, and he certainly helped shape the style and outlook of a good few rockabilly musicians – as recently as 1990 the Cramps laid down a superb version of Jimmie's 'Mule Skinner Blues' on their *Stay Sick!*

album – but Peer's other great 1927 find, the Carter Family, were arguably even more important in the development of what would become the roots rockabilly sound.

If you're looking for one song from those days which points the way forward to the primal rockabilly sound of the Elvis Sun sessions, then the Carter Family's 'Wildwood Flower' (1928) is a pretty good place to start. The line-up on Elvis's debut single in 1954 consisted of the man himself on vocals and rhythm guitar, Scotty Moore on electric guitar, and Bill Black on upright string bass. No drums, no overdubs, no unnecessary clutter at all. Now consider the classic 1920s Carter Family line-up – Sara Carter singing lead vocals and strumming rhythm on an autoharp, her husband A. P. Carter on occasional bass vocals, and A. P.'s sister-in-law Maybelle Carter on acoustic guitar. It's Maybelle who's the wild card here – a largely self-taught guitarist who evolved her own unique style known as the 'Carter Scratch', managing to hold down a bass line while simultaneously picking out a melody line, all with one hand. To put it another way, Sara's autoharp was equivalent to Elvis's rhythm guitar, but Maybelle was managing to be both Scotty and Bill all at once. Her daughter June, who later married Johnny Cash, once wrote of Maybelle's playing: 'She'd hook that right thumb under that big bass string, and just like magic the other fingers moved fast like a threshing machine, always on the right strings, and out came the lead notes and the accompaniment at the same time.'

To call her guitar technique influential is to seriously understate the case – she had an effect on the styles of everyone from Leadbelly to Merle Travis and all points in between – and recordings like 'Wildwood Flower' (1928) or 'I'm Thinking Tonight Of My Blue Eyes' (1929) need only a little more exaggeration in the bass to turn into first-rate acoustic rockabilly. Indeed, the second of these two tunes got religion and mutated into Roy Acuff's 'Great Speckled Bird' (1936) before having a change of heart and diving head first into the sinful world of the honky-tonks as 'The Wild Side of Life' (Hank Thompson, 1952). Listen to any recording of the latter song

by Charlie Feathers – a man who had pure-bred rockabilly music running through his veins throughout his entire career – and you'll see that the template set out by the Carter Family stands as one of the principal building blocks underpinning rockabilly music.

OL' HANK

The Carter family were certainly from the hills – they even came from a place called Poor Valley, in the shadow of Clinch Mountain, Virginia, not far from the Tennessee border – but they didn't dress up as hillbillies and resisted attempts to market them as such. The postwar giant of country music, Hank Williams, however, who performed in sharp-tailored suits far removed from any overalls-wearing hayseed cliché, had no problem using the word hillbilly when describing his music and the reasons for its success:

> It can be explained in just one word: sincerity. When a hillbilly sings a crazy song, he feels crazy. When he

The Carter Family
(l–r: Maybelle, A. P.
and Sara)

sings 'I Laid My Mother Away,' he see her a-laying right there in the coffin. He sings more sincere than most entertainers because the hillbilly was raised rougher than most entertainers. You got to know a lot about hard work. You got to have smelt a lot of mule manure before you can sing like a hillbilly. The people who has been raised something like the hillbilly has knows what he is singing about and appreciates it.

Hank, like the Carter Family, dealt in a pure, direct style of delivery that matched the power and honesty of blues singers like Robert Johnson.

Hank Williams
and His Drifting
Cowboys

Hank's plain-speaking yet lyrical world of love-gone-wrong and juke-joint Saturday nights – not to mention the hard-drinking, pill-popping chaos of his private life – laid down a pattern which would be followed by a number of rockabilly and rock'n'roll performers in the years to come. Some of his own performances have often been cited as foreshadowing rockabilly – particularly 'Rootie Tootie' (1947) – and the songs he sang were certainly popular cover material among the Sun rockers: 'My Bucket's Got A Hole In It' (1949) was given the grade-A rockabilly treatment by Sonny Burgess in 1958, 'Dear John' (1950) was handled in equally fine style by Warren Smith in 1957, and Jerry Lee Lewis regularly threw in effortlessly superb Williams covers during his time at the label. It's perhaps Hollis Champion's remarkable 1965 rockabilly throwback performance of the 'Long Gone Lonesome Blues' (1950), however, which really shows what could be done by jacking up the tempo on one of Hank's tunes. As the old saying goes, sometimes, if a thing's worth doing, it's worth overdoing...

Hank seems to have had no problem with the word hillbilly, and neither it seems did a considerable number of artists working with him in the C&W field during the immediate postwar years whose basic sound was shortly to be rocked up by the younger generation into a style known in some quarters as rock-billy, rock-a-billy or rockabilly. The Prairie Ramblers may have declared 'You Ain't Got No Hillbilly Anymore' in 1945, but they can't have been looking very hard. Three months later, the Delmore Brothers issued their landmark 'Hillbilly Boogie' for the King label's Hillbilly series, which was followed in 1947 by Hank Penny's 'Hillbilly Jump'. The year 1949 saw releases by Hillbilly Bill for Coral, while Carl Sauceman's Hillbilly Ramblers were recording for Mercury, and Hank Penny responded to emerging jazz trends by coming up with a track called 'Hillbilly Be Bop'. A particularly significant release was 'Hillbilly Fever', recorded in the very first week of the 1950s by Kenny Roberts, which has since been covered numerous times – not least by Jerry Lee Lewis at Sun. This was the song which Roy Acuff chose to kick off with in 1952 on the occasion of the *Grand Ole Opry*'s first national TV exposure – a fine rocking live performance which he introduced with the following words: 'Speaking of *Grand Ole Opry*, why everybody expects some pickin' and singin', well that's what we're gonna do for you here tonight, so we'll start off with a little bit of hillbilly fever. Take it away!'

Small wonder that Elvis was classed as a hillbilly hepcat only two years later. The energy of hillbilly hoedowns, coupled with a major dose of black jump blues and boogie-woogie rhythms, combined to produce a new kind of music made by people who sounded like they couldn't sit still if their lives depended on it. Years later, in 1979, a widely circulated bootleg appeared, containing early 1950s recordings made for Chuck Gregory's Speed label in Nashville. In a moment of genius, the anonymous compilers gave the LP the title *Hillbillies On Speed*, and if that phrase ain't as good a working definition of one strand of downhome rockabilly as you're likely to find, then you're probably looking in the wrong place.

2 DO YOU WANNA JUMP, CHILDREN?

Hillbilly music was just one of several important ingredients that gave rise to rockabilly, while the uptempo eight-to-the-bar rhythm known as boogie-woogie was certainly one of the others. A key figure in the development of that style was the black pianist Clarence 'Pine Top' Smith, from Alabama, who played everywhere from whorehouses to vaudeville theatres in his short life, sometimes backing popular blues performers like the duo Butterbeans and Susie, and who, on 29 December 1928, laid down a vocal-and-piano recording in Chicago for Vocalion which pretty much changed everything.

At a session three weeks earlier, Smith had recorded the same tune under the title 'Pine Top's Trouble', and sang the lyrics to match, but on the released version from 29 December, he tells

19

the listener right at the start, 'This is the "Pine Top's Boogie-Woogie"', and it was duly issued as such. Thus, the hard-driving, bass-heavy style of percussive piano playing, which had been evolving for some years, finally had both a name and a classic blueprint from which everyone else could take inspiration. Cow Cow Davenport had recorded a solidly boogie-style track in the same city six months earlier called 'State Street Jive', and in the months following Pine Top's session, the Vocalion label also recorded two other boogie performances in Chicago – Montana Taylor's 'Detroit Rocks' and Romeo Nelson's 'Head Rag Hop' – but Smith's track didn't just name the genre, it defined its essential form to perfection. 'Boogie-woogie' was a term that evidently caught on fast, since pianist Will Ezell could be found recording a track entitled 'Pitchin' Boogie', just a few months after Pine Top's death, for a different label (Paramount), and in another part of the country (Richmond, Virginia). Thereafter, it seemed as if almost everybody caught the boogie disease, and big band swing, hillbilly boogie, rockabilly and rock'n'roll would all owe a major debt to the basic boogie pattern laid down by Pine Top Smith and other trailblazing pianists such as Pete Johnson, Meade Lux Lewis, Jimmy Yancey and Albert Ammons.

Since record companies didn't start recording black music until 1920, it's very difficult to trace the emergence of the boogie style back before that date. Clues can be found, however, in the work of the Original Dixieland Jazz Band, the white New Orleans combo led by Nick La Rocca, whose recordings can fairly be assumed to be heavily influenced by the black jazz styles current in that city at the time. Of particular interest is their 1920 release, 'Bluin' The Blues', which is in many respects a boogie-woogie recording, played on brass and wind instruments, some eight years before 'Pine Top's Boogie Woogie', and prefigures the kind of orchestration that some of the big bands would later use, inspired by piano recordings,

Albert Ammons

during the height of the boogie-woogie craze of the early 1940s. Quite where the name for this style of music came from has been the subject of much inconclusive discussion over the years, but it may be worth noting in passing that the Victor label released a single by the American Quartet in 1912, when ragtime was king, entitled 'That Syncopated Boogie Boo'. The songwriting credit is to Lewis and Myer, which almost certainly makes it a Tin Pan Alley product, but the choice of words is intriguing.

Pine Top Smith didn't live to see the influence he'd have on music and on other musicians. A mere three months after his landmark recording session, he accidentally stopped a bullet let off by one David Bell, while watching a fight between two other patrons of a dance at the Masonic Lodge on Orleans Street in Chicago, and died aged twenty-five. Ten years to the month after his groundbreaking session, the music itself went national in a very public way when Ammons, Lewis and Johnson, together with vocalist Big Joe Turner, were featured at John Hammond's

21

groundbreaking 'From Spirituals to Swing' concert at Carnegie Hall in December 1938.

Boogie-woogie recordings had been made by a succession of black piano players throughout the 1930s, at a time when the piano, rather than the guitar, was arguably the more common instrument on which blues music was played. Most guitars were still unamplified in that decade, and therefore considerably quieter than a pounding barrelhouse piano, which was better at kicking up a storm above the noise of a dance hall or rent party. The driving eight-to-the-bar bass lines of boogie-woogie were purpose-built for the developing energetic dance-styles which would evolve into the jitterbug of the early 1940s. Music was becoming more frantic – an attitude reflected in the title of a song recorded by Count Basie in 1938, 'Do You Wanna Jump, Children?' – and the dance moves performed by black troupe Whitey's Lindy Hoppers, captured on film in pictures like *Keep Punching* (1939) and *Hellzapoppin'* (1941), are as wild and breathtaking as anything you're ever likely to see. The uptempo music that drove this forward had come a long way from someone, whether black or white, sitting on a front porch strumming an old acoustic or a banjo, and just as hillbilly performers had drawn on earlier blues styles back in the previous decade, they now began catching the boogie fever. Tempos were raised, bass fiddles began to be slapped rather than just bowed, and the distinctive new strains of hillbilly boogie, western swing and bluegrass all showed signs of the same urgency that would later come to underpin rockabilly and rock'n'roll – the urge to get real gone, to *jump*.

White jazz artists began moving into the boogie field in the late 1930s: Benny Goodman's Orchestra cut 'Roll 'Em' in 1937 and Tommy Dorsey's Orchestra covered Pine Top Smith's 1929 hit under the title 'Boogie Woogie' in 1938. They also started writing their own boogie tunes, such as the Ray McKinley Trio's superb 'Down The Road Apiece' (1940, featuring Freddie Slack on piano, and Doc Goldberg slapping that doghouse bass) or Woody Herman and His Four Chips' seriously rockin' 'Chips Boogie Woogie' (1940), while Gene Krupa and his Orchestra's 'Drum Boogie' (1941) was just one of his several ventures into the boogie field.

HILLBILLY BOOGIE

The first country musician out of the gate was Johnny Barfield, who cut a track called 'Boogie Woogie' in 1939. In the pop field, boogie-woogie really became a mainstream taste during the war years – with the likes of Bing Crosby and the Andrews Sisters enjoying smash hits with the form – but it was when hostilities ended in 1945 that hillbilly musicians really seem to have embraced the boogie influence. 'Hillbilly Boogie', recorded in January 1946 by the Delmore Brothers for the King label in Cincinnati, was a gorgeous, understated tune which transposed the usual boogie piano figures onto two guitars and matched them with subtle hill-country harmony singing. The distance from here to downhome rockabilly is pretty much no distance at all. Later that year, the Delmores followed up with 'Freight Train Boogie', an even bigger commercial success. Present on the latter recording was singer and harmonica player Wayne Raney, who also cut a series of hillbilly boogie tunes for King under his

"Gorn, you don't look like a real hill-billy singer to me," says the young cockney as he gives Tennessee Ernie Ford a close examination. But there's certainly no doubt in the minds of these girls. One of them, anxious not to miss a chance of getting close to Ernie, didn't even bother to take her pins out. . . .

Tenessee Ernie Ford meets British admirers

own name. Among many other entries in the hillbilly boogie field were Wally Fowler and His Georgia Clodhoppers' 'Mountain Boogie' (1947), Arthur Smith's hugely influential 'Guitar Boogie' (1948), Grandpa Jones and Cowboy Copas' 'The Feudin' Boogie' (1949), Bill Nettles and His Dixie Blueboys' 'Hadacol Boogie' (1949), the York Brothers' 'Motor City Boogie' (1950) and Hank Thompson's 'Humpty Dumpty Boogie' (1950). Hillbilly performers on the Capitol label seemed especially fond of the genre, issuing boogies by Cliffie Stone ('Jump Rope Boogie', 1951), Gene O'Quin ('Boogie Woogie Fever', 1951) and Merle Travis ('Lost John Boogie', 1951), not to mention the king of them all, Tennessee Ernie Ford, whose self-penned 'Shotgun Boogie' (1950) was followed by a string of similar boogie successes. The impulse even spread as far as the white gospel quartets which had been a mainstay of rural communities since the nineteenth century, resulting in such recordings as 'Satan's Boogie' (1949) by the Statesmen Quartet, whose widely respected lead singer, Jake Hess, would go on to sing at the funerals of both Hank Williams and Elvis.

As the above far-from-exhaustive sample might indicate,

a fair proportion of the hillbilly fraternity can be said to have gone boogie crazy in the immediate postwar years, helping in no small measure to lay the foundations for the rocked-up country sounds that brought forth rockabilly.

WHERE THE BLUE GRASS GROWS

Increased tempos and a more urgent rhythm also featured in another strand of hillbilly music which emerged strongly in the 1940s and came to bear the name of its most famous practitioners, Bill Monroe and the Blue Grass Boys. The bluegrass style, too, would play a key part in the development of rockabilly. Most significantly, one side of Elvis's debut single was a rocked-up treatment of the Blue Grass Boys' 'Blue Moon of Kentucky', which Bill Monroe's outfit recorded on 16 September 1946. By a strange coincidence, the original version of the other side of that Elvis disc, 'That's All Right', by Arthur 'Big Boy' Crudup, was recorded just ten days earlier, on 6 September 1946. (There seems to have been something in the air that month which proved a major influence on Elvis at Sun, because on 5 September, Bob Wills and His Texas Playboys, the kings of western swing, laid down a tune called 'Brain Cloudy Blues'. The writing credits of the latter were given to Bob Wills and his vocalist Tommy Duncan, and although it uses a couple of verses of Kokomo Arnold's 'Milk Cow Blues' (1934), when Elvis released 'Milkcow Blues Boogie' (1955) as his third single, it's mostly the lyrics and tune from the Bob Wills version he's following.)

With the solid blues influence in hillbilly and country music dating back to Jimmie Rodgers in the 1920s and farther beyond, the idea that Elvis was doing anything unusual in drawing on both black and white influences for his music is clearly a non-starter. What was radically different is the use he made of those influences, and how he put them across. Presley didn't so much cover songs as transform them.

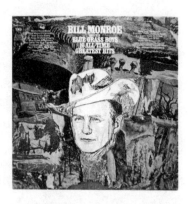

By all accounts, Bill Monroe was at first not remotely pleased that some nineteen-year-old Memphis hepcat had almost doubled the speed of his stately bluegrass waltz, 'Blue Moon Of Kentucky' (1946), and was performing it while flinging himself flat on the deck or doing knee-drops. After a month or so of consideration – or maybe royalty cheques – Bill was eventually moved to recut the tune himself at the newer speed. In truth, the song was one of the slower items in Monroe's repertoire. His 'Will You Be Lovin' Another Man?' (1946) and 'My Little Cabin Home On The Hill' (1947) are both very uptempo, with Bill's Gibson F5 model mandolin duelling with Lester Flatt's guitar, Chubby Wise's fiddle and Earl Scruggs's banjo, all driven along by the upright bass of Howard Watts. With that much rhythm, they had no need of drums, while the high mountain vocal harmonies and the intricate picking and fiddling on the Blue Grass Boys' classic 1946 and 1947 sides helped to define the bluegrass genre for all time. Bill Monroe's influence on the future rockabilly generation is clear: Gene Vincent and His Blue Caps covered Bill's 1945 song 'Rocky Road Blues' in 1958, while at that famous 1956 impromptu gathering of Sun rockabillies, the Million Dollar Quartet of Presley, Lewis, Perkins and maybe Cash – Johnny says he was there singing, others claim he left to go shopping before the tapes rolled – harmonised on at least four Monroe songs, including 'My Little Cabin Home On The Hill'.

Bob Wills

BOB WILLS AND THE RISE OF WESTERN SWING

If the postwar emergence of the bluegrass genre stirred something into the rockabilly pot, so did another highly popular variant of all things country, which came to be known as western swing. Chief practitioner of the style was Bob Wills, who with his Texas Playboys came to personify western swing in the same way that Bill Monroe stood for bluegrass. Having spent the 1920s hopping freight trains, doing radio broadcasts and appearing in medicine shows, Wills wound up at the start of the following decade in W. Lee O'Daniel's Light Crust Dough Boys, before splitting to form his own Texas Playboys in 1934. By this stage, the word 'swing' had become the accepted term for jazz, and gradually the hillbilly bands that reflected black jazz styles in their music were eventually referred to as western swing outfits. Refugees from the early line-up of the

27

Light Crust Doughboys went on to form not only Wills's own outfit, but also the very highly regarded Milton Brown and His Musical Brownies, whose career was suddenly cut short by the death of Brown himself in 1936 following a car crash. A crucial element in the latter band's importance in defining the western swing sound was the fact that they used a stand-up double bass, an instrument which would play a pivotal role in the sound of rockabilly.

SLAPPIN' THAT DOGHOUSE BASS

Nineteen-twenties jazz, blues and hillbilly recordings often either have no bass at all – as with the Carter Family recordings, where Maybelle plays bass and treble strings on her guitar to achieve a full sound – or else the bass notes are played on a brass instrument such as a tuba, as in the case of the wild, salacious 1928 recording 'Four Or Five Times', by the superlative black jazz orchestra McKinney's Cotton Pickers. A cheaper alternative to the tuba was to blow across the opening at the tops of stone jars or jugs, giving a variety of deep tones – a style popularised by outfits like the Memphis Jug Band, or Whistler's Jug Band, from Louisville, Kentucky. The latter band's recording career stretched from 1924, when they recorded songs like 'Jail House Blues' (later covered by Jimmie Rodgers as 'In The Jailhouse Now'), until 1931, when they cut a song called 'Foldin' Bed' for the Victor label. Astonishingly for an act of that vintage, excellent-quality film footage exists of the band performing this song live, not miming, while sitting on a front porch, and at the time of writing is available to view on YouTube. Watching this, it's possible to see how the bass parts are played on three different sizes of stone liquor jar, blending in with the rest of their line-up, which consists of just acoustic guitar and banjo. With these simple materials, Whistler's

Jug Band turn in a performance that rocks harder than most groups of any era could manage on whatever combination of equipment they choose, acoustic or electric.

Of course, some 1920s or early 1930s combos did use a double bass, such as hillbilly string band Seven Foot Dilley and His Dill Pickles (led by six-foot-seven-inch-tall guitar player John Dilleshaw), but often, as here, it was bowed, rather than slapped or plucked. Indeed, if you're looking for a genuine slice of slapping rockabilly-style doghouse bass in a 1920s recording, then try listening to Annette Hanshaw's 'You Wouldn't Fool Me, Would You?' (1929). Cut in Chicago, and featuring the finest white jazz singer of that decade, backed by the Columbia Orchestra, it reaches the halfway point before the bass player cuts loose in a style that wouldn't have disgraced Bill Black.

The western swing bands which evolved in the mid-1930s began featuring upright double bass in their line-ups (not to mention drums, but that's another story). You'll find one on records such as 'Give Me My Money' by the Blue Ridge Playboys (1936), and also on 'There'll Be Some Changes Made' (1937) by W. Lee O'Daniel, who'd changed the name of his band to the Hillbilly Boys – yep, there's that word again – in order to advertise his own company's product, Hillbilly Flour. For a western swing number really driven along by a definite slapped bass, however, check out the Crystal Springs Ramblers' record 'Fort Worth Stomp' (1937), with vocals by Link Davis, who'd go on to cut rockabilly records in his forties for the Starday label in 1956.

All this talk of bass, however, might suggest that the western swing sound was early rockabilly in all but name, which is very far from the case. The jazz influence remained paramount, and the use of steel guitars, trumpets, trombones, saxes and drums alongside more traditional hillbilly instruments like fiddles and banjos gave a big-band sound that was a long way from either the Carter Family on the one hand or the early acoustic Sun rockabilly sessions on the other. These western swing outfits were influenced by the work of black dance bands like those led by Cab Calloway, Count Basie, Louis Armstrong and Duke Ellington, among many others, not to mention predominantly white bands such as those of Benny Goodman, Will Bradley or Artie Shaw. As the 1930s progressed, the average size of such combos increased, and so did those of the western swing outfits. Whereas in jazz and in western swing it had been common to have a group of maybe six or seven musicians, by the end of the decade bandleaders were often fielding twice that number or more – Bob Wills at one time fronted a twenty-two-piece version of the Texas Playboys – and this trend was curtailed only by the coming of the wartime draft, which cut numbers drastically.

Bob's long-time vocalist was Tommy Duncan, whose laconic style was much imitated, and who went on to cut a version of 'Hound Dog' in 1953, three years before Elvis, not to mention a brief stab at getting down with the new generation in 1956 with 'Daddy Loves Mommyo'. As for Duncan's old boss, here's how Bob Wills reacted to the rise of Presley and his followers in a 1958 interview with the *Tulsa Tribune*: 'Rock and Roll? Why, man, that's the same kind of music we've been playin' since 1928! … We didn't call it rock and roll back when we introduced it as our style back in 1928, and we don't call it rock and roll the way we play it now. But it's just basic rhythm and has gone by a lot of different names in my time.'

DOCTOR RHYTHM & MR BLUES

Alongside western swing and bluegrass, anyone tuning their radio dial in the late 1940s would have run into equally uptempo types of black music. Names like 'jump blues' or 'rhythm & blues' were bandied around, the latter term coined by future Atlantic records producer Jerry Wexler while working for *Billboard* magazine. For instance, the 1945 recording 'Milton's Boogie', by jumping LA combo Roy Milton's Solid Senders, moves along at one hell of a pace, and proves beyond doubt that anyone wanting to play that old game of nominating the first ever rock'n'roll record is generally on a hiding to nothing. Roy's song, with boogie queen Camille Howard on piano, was cut a full six years before Sam Phillips in Memphis recorded that landmark, boogie-fuelled hymn to Oldsmobile engine power, 'Rocket 88' by Jackie Brenston & His Delta Cats, but they're close enough in spirit as to make little or no difference.

Roy Milton was out there playing nightclubs in Hollywood, but over in Chicago another black musician had just come up with a song destined to influence the 1950s rockabilly sound. Arthur 'Big Boy' Crudup, a Mississippi-born bluesman whose 'That's All Right' (1946) was covered by Elvis eight years later, recorded a long series of stark, gutsy blues songs for the Victor label from 1941 until 1954, featuring his own guitar, usually backed by just drums and bass. Elvis would go on to cover two more Crudup songs – 'My Baby Left Mc' and 'So Glad You're Mine' – and Arthur was known

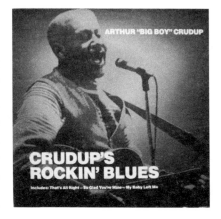

to be an understandably bitter man about the fact that he himself had not made much money from his songs as a result. The problem here was not Presley, however, but long-time Chicago A&R man Lester Melrose, the person who originally brought Crudup to Victor, and allegedly failed to pay him all the songwriting royalties he felt were due to him.

In an era when many writers sold their songs outright for a few bucks and a beer, and many influential radio and TV jocks would expect a cut of the songwriting credits in return for plugging the material, collecting your royalties or hanging on to the rights to your work was a hit-and-miss game at the best of times. Melrose, who was instrumental in the careers of numerous blues artists, including Tampa Red, Big Bill Broonzy and Memphis Minnie, once told folklorist Alan Lomax, 'I took my chances on some of the songs I recorded being hits, and I wouldn't record anybody unless he signed all his rights in those tunes over to me.' Presley's excellent cover versions certainly shone a lot of attention on the work of Arthur Crudup, and he was eventually tracked down and recorded again by Bobby Robinson's Fire label in 1962, before becoming a popular act on the college circuit during the 1960s blues boom. When Robinson found him, Arthur had been picking fruit for a living.

Another black musician who could be found selling enyclopedias in the 1960s to make ends meet, despite Elvis having covered one of his songs at Sun, was New Orleans musician Roy Brown. He'd written and sung a groundbreaking jump blues called 'Good Rockin' Tonight', released in September 1947, but the hit version had been a cover recorded by blues shouter Wynonie Harris in December the same year. Both versions pointed the way in no uncertain terms towards the rock'n'roll that would appear in the following decade, and it was this song which was laid down – alongside several others, of blues, hillbilly and pop origin – at Sun in September 1954 by

Elvis, Scotty & Bill (backed up by Memphis country musician Doug Poindexter on second guitar, according to Scotty's recollection). They were looking for a follow-up single in the wake of the local success of Elvis's debut 45, and since the latter had featured a jump blues on one side and a bluegrass tune on the other, it was natural that they'd look for a similar mix of styles on this one. Roy wasn't, on the face of it, a typical blues musician. His favourite singer when he started out had been Bing Crosby, and his early repertoire included cowboy and hillbilly numbers, but with 'Good Rockin' Tonight' he broke through into different territory altogether. By the time Elvis covered his song in 1954, in purely music business terms Roy's best days were already behind him. He'd successfully sued his label for unpaid royalties back in 1952, but the fifties were a decade of diminishing returns for him. As career trajectories in the blues – or rockabilly – go, it's a remarkably familiar tale.

Arthur Crudup and Roy Brown, like many of the other musicians mentioned in this book, never saw more than a handful of change from their music, but their records had a power and an influence far greater than many singers whose careers have been much more extravagantly rewarded by the business. Some people get the hits and all the money, others make world-class records yet wind up working in a gas station – there's no justice or logic to it. As long-time Memphis musician and producer Jim Dickinson was fond of saying, 'Hits are in baseball, singles are in bars, and your royalty lives in a castle in Europe.'

3 THE KING OF WESTERN BOP

ELVIS PRESLEY AND THE START OF IT ALL

When nineteen-year-old Memphis truck driver Elvis Presley linked up with guitarist Scotty Moore and double bass player Bill Black at Sam Phillips' Sun Studios in June 1954 to record the two songs which would form his debut single, 'That's all Right'/'Blue Moon Of Kentucky', they wrote the rockabilly rulebook from scratch. This historic moment has since been examined in books such as *Mystery Train* by Greil Marcus and *Last Train to Memphis* by Peter Guralnick, among many others. Even at the time, as the record began picking up airplay courtesy of Memphis radio wildman Dewey Phillips on his WHBQ show *Red, Hot & Blue*, while Elvis stirred up local audiences with a string of gigs around town, it wasn't easy for press commentators to know how to describe him. Sure, he came out of the hillbilly field, and even the idea of a white rocker wasn't that new – Bill Haley's slap-bass-propelled 'Crazy, Man, Crazy' had made it to number 15 in the *Billboard* charts in 1953 – yet most contemporary press reports from 1954 to '56 struggle to properly define the rockabilly music Presley was playing, or the force of nature that was his live show. Put simply, for all

Scotty Moore, Elvis, Bill Black

the rockabilly antecedents outlined in the previous chapters, nothing quite like this had ever existed.

In the confused scramble to pin down the rapidly growing phenomenon, journalists, press agents and deejays reached for the nearest approximate terms. On 14 October, 1954, three weeks after the release of Elvis's second single, 'Good Rockin' Tonight'/'I Don't Care If The Sun Don't Shine', local Memphis newspaper *The Commercial Appeal* played it safe with their terminology in an article about his forthcoming debut appearance on influential live Southern radio show *The Louisiana Hayride*: 'Elvis Presley, our homegrown hillbilly singer, is continuing his swift, steady stride toward national prominence in the rural rhythm field.'

He was quite often called The Hillbilly Cat that year, or the Memphis Flash, and by 1955 his early manager and booking agent, Bob Neal, seems to have been encouraging people to refer to Elvis as the King of Western Bop. Bob himself used the term when interviewing Elvis and Bill Black in a piece of taped radio publicity for an August 1955 show in Texarkana, and the following month a newspaper called the *Amarillo Globe-News* previewed a Texas show with the headline 'King of Western Bop Due Here Thursday'.

By the following year, Elvis had gone national with 'Heartbreak Hotel' and was causing pandemonium wherever he appeared, prompting one Florida paper, the *St Petersburg Times*, to dig deep into the dictionary for one of the more appealing attempts at categorising the King: 'The pied piper of rock'n'roll, a swivel-hipped, leg-lashing "entertainment bomb" blasted the downtown area into chaos all day yesterday. Screaming, fainting teen-agers lined the streets early to catch a glimpse of Elvis Presley, a rock billy gyrating singer who's shattered show business with his sultry style.'

That was in August 1956, with his Sun days behind him and 'Hound Dog' riding high in the charts, when Presley's recorded output had already moved into more mainstream rock'n'roll territory, yet the writers of this piece reached for the phrase 'rock billy'.

THE BOPPIN' HILLBILLY

Of course, the worldwide success of 'Heartbeak Hotel' meant that by now they were also trying to figure out exactly what to call Elvis in England. Writing in the November 1956 UK edition of top-selling film magazine *Photoplay*, journalist Eric

Random offered his thoughts on 'Presley: The New Svengali Of Song'. 'Personally, I want and need Presley like a hole in the head. But the facts must be faced. And they are that Mama Presley's son, otherwise known as "The Memphis Flash", "The Boppin' Hillbilly", and "The Cat" (on account of his cool looks, real gone clothes and crraazzy motions) is one of the biggest draws in American show-business today.'

In 1957, adverts for a show of his at the Olympia in Detroit were billing him as 'The Nation's Only Atomic Powered Singer', but Elvis himself seems to have been understandably reluctant to pin an exact label on what he was doing. There's a brief but fascinating audio interview recorded with Elvis in Jacksonville, Florida, on 25 July 1955, at a time when he was passing through the state as just one of a lengthy cast list of attractions on the All Star Jamboree Tour headlined by country star Hank Snow. The package featured a fine line-up of hillbilly and Opry favourites, including Faron Young, Slim Whitman and the lady who'd helped start it all, Mother Maybelle Carter and her daughters. This gives an indication of which market the twenty-year-old Elvis was being aimed at. His interviewer on this occasion was a woman called Mae Boren Axton, a Jacksonville schoolteacher who'd been employed to do some tour publicity, and who later that year would co-write 'Heartbreak Hotel' with Tommy Durden. She began by attempting to clarify Presley's style for her listeners, because although country fans knew where they stood with Hank or Maybelle, everyone could tell that there was something different about this new singer, but they couldn't quite pin it down:

MAE: You are sort of a bebop artist, more than anything, aren't you. Is that what you're telling me?

ELVIS: Well I never have given myself a name, but a lot of the disk jockeys call me a boppin' hillbilly, or bebop, I don't know what …

MAE: Sort of a combination of things …

This confusion had started the first day Elvis, Scotty Moore and Bill Black got together in the Sun studio with Sam Phillips on 5 July the previous year. Everyone knew that they had something, but were damned if they knew what it was. The story of this session has been retold so many times that it's almost taken on the status of myth, but it began as just an attempt on Sam and Scotty's part to try out a new singer. These days Scotty understandably feels he's pretty much said everything he can say about Elvis over the years, but luckily he was interviewed on tape by an unidentified reporter right in the middle of Elvis's Sun era, on 15 March 1955, midway between the release of their third single 'Milkcow Blues Boogie'/'You're A Heartbreaker' (8 January) and the fourth, 'I'm Left, You're Right, She's Gone'/'Baby Let's Play House' (25 April). Although the intial recording session which produced 'That's All Right' had taken place less than a year earlier, so much had changed in the intervening months that Scotty was already speaking about that day almost as if it were something from a completely different era:

When I first met Elvis, when he came to my house on that Sunday afternoon, he had on a pink shirt, pink pants with white stripes down the leg, and white shoes. And I thought my wife was gonna go out the back door. Again, just the shock, because people just weren't wearin' that kind of flashy clothes at the time. He had the sideburns and the ducktails – just a lotta hair. Bill and I were working together with a group called the Starlite Wranglers, what we referred to as just a regular juke joint or honkytonk band at the time, which there were many bands of that type around ... Bill was workin' daytime at Firestone, building tyres, and I was working for my brother who had a cleaning plant ... Elvis was drivin' a truck at Crown Electric at that time. I don't remember how long he worked there after we started performing, just in town, in those early weeks. Couldn't have been very long...

The teenage Elvis saw himself primarily as a ballad singer. Alongside all the gospel, hillbilly and rhythm & blues sounds he enjoyed listening to, he was also a great admirer of Dean Martin. Since his first casual visit on 22 August 1953, when Presley had called in at Sun's studio at 706 Union Avenue in Memphis and paid the small fee to record a couple of songs onto an acetate disc as a present for his mother, he'd taken to dropping in on occasion and talking to Sam Phillips' secretary, Marion Keisker, who ran the front office. The songs he cut that day ('My Happiness' and 'That's When Your Heartaches Begin'), and the further two he made on 6 January 1954 ('I'll Never Stand In Your Way' and 'It Wouldn't Be The Same (Without You)'), were all ballads, which he sang in a delicate but curiously affecting voice, a long way from future Sun rockers like 'Baby Let's Play House'. Nevertheless, Marion, who had recorded his first session, and Sam himself, who'd presided over the second, could see something in those simple performances in which Elvis sang to the accompaniment of his own guitar which made them think that the boy had potential.

As Scotty recalled in that 1955 interview, 'We went into the studio for primarily an audition … Bill and I only went in with him to have just some kind of meagre accompaniment with him, so he wouldn't be standing alone in the studio, you know.' Everyone involved seems to have seen Elvis as a ballad singer, and the initial choice of songs reflected that view. They laid down versions of 'Harbour Lights' – a song which had been recorded in 1950 by everyone from Bing Crosby to Guy Lombardo – and 'I Love You Because', a number 1 country hit in 1949 for its writer Leon Payne, who had started out as a member of Bob Wills' Texas Playboys. Both were fine performances for a young singer on his first day of professional recording, but then something entirely unexpected happened, which opened the door to another world. Scotty takes up the story:

> We went through two or three different songs, more or less takin' a break, havin' a coffee, or coke, and Elvis started clowning around. Just picked up his guitar and started kibitzing, singing 'That's All Right Mama' and clowning round the studio dancing, just cuttin' up in general, and Bill picked up his bass, started slappin' it, and clowning also … I joined in with just a rhythm vamp. Sam was in the control room, the door was open. He came out and said 'What're y'all doin'?' Said 'That sounds pretty good.' We said, 'We don't know…' He said, 'Well, see if you can do it again the same way. Let's put it on tape, see what it sounds like. Sounds pretty good through the door.'

And there it was: 'What're y'all doin'?', 'We don't know…' All they had was a teenage singer, one acoustic guitar playing rhythm, an electric guitar picking melodic figures and the rock-solid, warm tones of an upright bass being slapped along to provide a beat. No drums, at a time when western swing and jazz outfits had been using them for decades. Bill Haley's Comets already had a powerful snare drum backing up the rhythm of the bass, and the writer of the song, Arthur Crudup, had used a similarly prominent snare on the original 1946 version. This, however, was something else again.

Rockabilly, as it was defined and encapsulated by Elvis's first record, started out as primarily an acoustic music – for all the

'An appalling commercial freakshow' – *Picturegoer* magazine greets the Hillbilly Cat

use of electric guitar, and the prominence of drums on many later rockabilly singles. Listening to the surviving recordings of Elvis, Scotty & Bill performing live on *The Louisiana Hayride* in 1954 and 1955, this becomes even clearer, since the limitations of the mic set-up used by the radio engineers mean that most of the sound of Bill Black's bass is lost. The slap and click of the bass on early Elvis songs stood in for the drums and provided the beat, so to hear the Hayride versions of these tunes gives an idea of how they sounded with just the two guitars and Elvis's voice. More than ever, they sound like hillbilly or country songs, and line of descent is clear between this performance and such recordings as 'High Geared Daddy' (1947) by Tommy Little & The Sunrise Rangers or 'Hangover Blues' (1951) by 'America's Most Colourful Hillbilly Band', the Maddox Brothers & Rose. In the latter exuberant band, Fred Rose had been beating seven kinds of hell out of a doghouse bass since the late 1930s, and certainly influenced many musicians who came after him.

THE BEAT! THE BEAT! THE BEAT!

There's a famous televison clip from February 1959 of a young white Southern preacher railing against the influence of rock'n'roll as a prime cause of juvenile delinquency: 'I know the evil feeling that you feel when you sing it. I know the lost position that you get into in the beat. Well, if you talk to the average teenager today and you ask them what it is about rock'n'roll music that they like, the first thing they'll say is "*The beat! the beat! the beat!*"'

Yet those first few Sun singles had no drumbeat at all, but still managed to be completely incendiary. That preacher, of all people, would have known this, since he too had been a rock'n'roll singer before he'd been 'saved' in 1958. In fact, he knew it at first hand, because he was Jimmy Rodgers Snow, son of Hank Snow, and he himself had been a featured country artist on that same 1955 All Star Jamboree Tour which his father had headlined. He often roomed with Elvis on the road, and saw the effect that this new singer was having on the fans. Trevor Cajiao from *Now Dig This* magazine tracked Snow down in 1994 and asked him how different he felt Elvis was in 1955 to everything else that was going on. Snow replied, 'He was as different as daylight and dark, compared to the rest of country music.' Elvis had revealed himself as a big fan of Hank Snow on that trip (and would later cover one of Hank's biggest hits, 'A Fool Such As I'), for, as Jimmy Rodgers Snow points out, 'he was a country singer who added a beat and he put that vibrato to his voice with that slap-back echo which the Sun people came up with'.

That distinctive slap-back echo which Sam Phillips employed at Sun was indeed something new to country and hillbilly audiences, and was much imitated by other recording engineers in the effort to replicate the success which Elvis was having. For example, the large amount of echo used by Capitol's technicians in Nashville on 'Be Bop A Lula' (1956), the debut single from the original rock'n'roll bad-boy street gang, Gene Vincent & the Blue Caps, can be traced directly back to the sound of Presley's early Memphis recordings. RCA themselves, having signed the King, sometimes wound up producing muddy-sounding Elvis recordings that year as they experimented with various types of echo in the attempt to approximate that special sound which Sam knew how to capture.

Presley himself was asked about that unique Sun recording technique in a 14 May 1956 interview with an unknown radio deejay at the Sawyer Auditorium, La Crosse, Wisconsin (in which he also explains that his road band has been featuring drummer D. J. Fontana 'for about two or three months'):

INTERVIEWER: The first record you ever cut for the Sun label was *Blue Moon Of Kentucky*, wasn't it?

ELVIS: Yes. That's right.

INTERVIEWER: And I understand it had a real great response down there when it was first played by the DJs.

ELVIS: Well, it did ok but, uh, it kind of surprised me. I thought they would laugh me out of town.

INTERVIEWER: I noticed there was a very heavy echo effect in that, more than some of the others.

ELVIS: Yes, there was a lot of echo.

Although he was always unfailingly polite to deejays and the press, it's frustrating that Elvis didn't offer any further comments about Sam's recording methods.

'Blue Moon Of Kentucky' had been cut a couple of days after 'That's All Right', and in the interim deejay Dewey Phillips had aired the acetate of the latter on the radio, prompting so many phone calls that Elvis himself had been tracked down in a local cinema, the Suzore, while the show was still on air and brought over to be interviewed by Dewey at the Hotel Chisca, 272 South Main, where the programme was broadcast. 'I don't know nuthin' about being interviewed,' Elvis is supposed to have said beforehand, to which Dewey replied, 'Just don't say nothin' dirty, son.'

Sam and the boys knew full well they were on to something after that first night's reaction from local radio listeners, and when they convened in the wake of that to try to lay down a suitable flip-side for the track they'd already cut, according

Sam Phillips

to Scotty Moore, the final choice of song was as much of an accident as the other had been.

> We had the one song – we didn't know what we had. We knew it was different, so now the problem was to get something for the other side, in the same vein … Again, during a break, Bill Black started clownin', singin' 'Blue Moon Of Kentucky', in a high falsetto, *a la* Bill Monroe, and he was slappin' the bass, and Elvis joined in, started singin' it with him, and I think we all knew immediately when this happened that it might be what we was lookin' for. We kind of stopped, figured out where to start and stop, and put it on tape, and that was it.

So there you have it. Both sides of a 78 or 45 release on Sam Phillips' distinctive yellow label, catalogue Sun 209, released on 19 July 1954, just days after they were recorded. A rocked-up version of a bluegrass waltz that initally left Bill Monroe deeply unimpressed, coupled with a boppin', countrified reworking of an urban jump blues number that eventually caused Arthur Crudup to wonder where in the damn hell his royalties had got to. But it wasn't Elvis's job to pay Arthur's royalties – that was down to the song's publishers and the collection agencies. As the singer of a cover version, in an era when covers were the norm, Elvis would have received only his performer's cut, but it's not as if he stuck his own name on the writing credits, in marked contrast to several wealthy 1960s and '70s mainstream rock bands when they made their names covering old blues tunes.

SONGS OUR DADDY TAUGHT US

Ever since the early part of the century, when sheet music sales were the measure of a tune's success, a pop tune was just that – popular with all kinds of singers, from people at home gathered around the piano all the way to the leading artists in all fields, whether jazz, country, blues or mainstream pop. When the hit song 'Stardust' came along in 1927, no one could have predicted that it would eventually be recorded by a staggering list of people including Bing Crosby, Billy Ward & The Dominoes, Louis Armstrong, Billie Holiday, Django Reinhardt, Frank Sinatra and many hundreds of others. It was still common in the UK charts of the late 1950s to have three or more separate versions of the same rock'n'roll tune fighting it out for the top spot, and even within the confines of the *Billboard* country & western charts, 1948 had seen the song 'Signed, Sealed and Delivered' make the listings in versions by four separate artists: Cowboy Copas, Bob Atcher, Texas Jim Robertson and Jimmy Wakely. Songs were part of the currency, and in that era, a great many singers didn't write their own material. As a working musician, you learned to cover songs right at the start of your career, because crowds at dance halls and juke joints wanted to dance to the hits of the day, and if you couldn't do a fair approximation of them, you weren't likely to be asked back.

Musicians tend to take whatever they find, wherever they can find it, and will adapt a tune to whatever style they choose. For instance, without covers, the history of ska, rocksteady and early reggae would be very different, and of all the early hillbilly singers who started out as virtual clones of the recently deceased Jimmie Rodgers – blue yodels and all – none had more cause to be grateful to that legacy than future country giant Ernest Tubb. Rodgers' widow Carrie helped secure Ernest a record deal and would even travel with him and introduce his shows. Tubb's son Justin – who would cut rockabilly tracks for Decca in the mid-1950s – later told Robert K. Obermann that his father had asked her, '"What can I ever do to pay you back for what you've done for me?" And she told him, "Just pass it on." And that's I think, what he did for the rest of his life. He passed it on.'

This is exactly the phrase which Keith Richards has used when asked how he feels about all the guitarists who have imitated him over the years, usually pointing out that he'd absorbed plenty from the likes of Chuck Berry and Elmore James, and all he was doing was passing it on. Elvis at Sun took inspiration from a wide variety of performers, both black and white, blues and pop, hillbilly and R&B – if it sounded good to Elvis, Scotty & Bill, they tried it, transformed it and passed it on in turn.

Pretty soon, it would seem that every rockabilly with a cheap guitar would be conjuring up thinly disguised rewrites of 'That's All Right', 'Good Rockin' Tonight' or 'Baby Let's Play House'. In trying to be Elvis, they turned out an endlessly inventive series of variations on a classic theme, since rockabilly, like the blues, can stand all sorts of interpretations as long as you resist the impulse to clean it up and knock all the guts out of it.

Sam Phillips knew exactly what he was doing with Elvis at Sun, and the best of the rockabillies who were trying to capture a little of the magic that Sam had found turned out to be the ones who valued feel over perfection, and let a few rough edges show through. It was all about the spirit, and not necessarily about whether you were always in tune. As the fine Memphis writer Robert Gordon (not the rockabilly artist of the same name) noted, when describing the unworldly genius of the boss of Sun Records: 'I heard Sam Phillips once say, "Producing? I don't know anything about producing records. But if you want to make some rock'n'roll music, I can reach down and pull it out of your asshole." Yessir, Sir.'

4 GET WITH IT

CHARLIE FEATHERS – IN THE FOOTSTEPS OF THE KING

I saw Charlie Feathers play only once, on 9 September 1990, which turned out to be his last ever show in London. He'd been seriously ill for quite some time, and the rumour went around that he'd agreed to make the trip as a way of raising money to set against medical bills. Before he sang the first song, he said: 'Last time I was over here, I was sick. I went back home and I spent over three years in the hospital. I'll probably go back into hospital when I go back. I know I will. I don't know how long I'm gonna be in it. I hope I'm not in it long...'

When a show starts out with a statement like that, from a musician who's seated, and will spend the entire gig sitting down, some might think the chances of a wild show would be slim. But the performance he gave at that ballroom on Fulham Broadway that night was a revelation, and it remains the finest pure rockabilly I've ever witnessed: just the man himself on vocals and acoustic guitar, his eldest son Bubba on electric, with the sparsest of backing from double bass and one snare, played by two musicians from British band, the Firebirds.

Right from the start, Charlie had total control of the situation, telling the band to 'back on down here now' after just one bar of the first song, *lowering* the volume in order to increase

49

Charlie and his son Bubba
rocking the Fulham
Hibernian, 1990

the song's power, and when he opened up with his undimmed singing voice above that classic rockabilly instrumental line-up, it was perfect: a masterclass in how to create downhome 1956 Memphis rockabilly three and a half decades after the event. Over the years I'd heard a lot of reports of Charlie's various appearances over here, in which he apparently talked a lot more than he sang, and cut short songs only halfway through. None of that matched up to what he delivered in 1990. This, unmistakably, was the real deal.

IT'S JUST THAT SONG

Charlie was one of many young Southern musicians who'd started out in the wake of The Hillbilly Cat's astonishing 1954 debut, determined that they too had something to offer. It's hard to overstate the influence of the songs which Elvis recorded in little over a year at Sam Phillips' studio. Those, and his early tours in the deep South, unleashed a tidal wave of musicians who also craved a little of the action. Many beat a path to Sam's door; others were picked up by a dizzying variety of largely small, ill-funded labels across the country. Indeed, the sheer number of people who were moved by the sight and sound of Sun-era Elvis to haul their teenage selves into a studio over the next few years and start wailin' is astonishingly large.

What is even more remarkable is the sheer quality of the work produced, often on shoestring budgets and frequently with little hope that their record's distribution would make it farther than the city limits. For every hepcat lucky enough to have landed a deal with a major company like RCA or Columbia, there were hundreds more recording in storefronts and garages for the kind of one-off outfits who listed only a PO box number as their address on the label. In between those two extremes, however, were some whose work was of consistently high quality, issued by record companies with a real feel for the genre, yet who somehow never made it through to the Hot Hundred and *American Bandstand* level of fame.

Charlie Feathers went right to the source – he started out on the Sun label back in 1955 – and became one of many who never broke through into the big money despite cutting some killer rockabilly singles, whose career can't be measured in terms of record sales or TV appearances. Elvis might have gone from 'That's All Right' to motion pictures in a little less than two years, but Hollywood never came knocking at the door for Charlie back in the fifties. Rockabilly back then had precious few national, let alone international, stars, yet the numbers involved and the wealth of talent displayed in the genre were remarkable. There were certainly many singers in those days who were better paid for their work than Charlie Feathers, but not many could match the quality of his recordings.

Over the years, when mainstream writers have addressed the subject of rockabilly, they have often given the impression that the field consisted almost entirely of a handful of the better-known performers at Sun Records. The book *Mystery Train* by Greil Marcus (1975) says that: 'Rockabilly was squeaky

Charlie Feathers, a country singer of no special talent or even much drive.'

Considering the large number of superb recordings Charlie left behind over the years – from the uptempo hillbilly of 'Peepin' Eyes' (1955) via rockabilly killers like 'Tongue Tied Jill' (1956), 'Bottle To The Baby' (1956) or 'That Certain Female' (1973) to the heartbreaking country of 'The Man In Love' (1958) – it's ridiculous that Marcus writes him off as a 'failure' with only 'one great song' who then disappeared, and as for Charlie's voice, it was surely one of the finest in the entire genre. Mind you, Marcus also goes on to say that 'collectors call the likes of Alvis Wayne and Johnny Burnette geniuses, but their aggressive stance is never convincing and the flash is always forced'. That'll be the same Johnny Burnette who, performing with his brother Dorsey and guitarist Paul Burlison as the Rock'n'Roll Trio, laid down some of the purest examples of flat-out, life-enhancing rockabilly ever recorded. Anyone who can casually dismiss the likes of 'Train Kept A Rollin', 'Tear It Up' or 'Lonesome Train' (all 1956) is very close to admitting they don't much care for the whole genre in the first place.

REAR BACK AN' HOLLER

If Elvis, Scotty & Bill wrote the rockabilly rulebook with their first single, then Charlie Feathers exemplified it all the way from the mid-1950s up to his death in 1998. He had a voice like no other, an endlessly flexible instument that could swoop and hiccup in all the right places, and nail a song to the wall with a remarkable combination of subtlety and power. Charlie never beat the songs to death, he let them stretch out and unwind.

In the sleeve notes to an album called *Charlie Feathers Volume Two* (1979), issued on his own label, Charlie had this to offer about his style of music and his methods of recording; using capitals, bold type and italics for emphasis:

> Now I liked bluegrass, ya know Bill Monroe, and Hank Williams, *but* bein' raised up on the farm like I was, I *couldn't* pick bluegrass, but I added *what I could*, and started **doing** these licks, and it was MY type a music. *Rockabilly* is got a **blues** about it. It's got some **black** in it, you can *rear back an' holler* WELL. It's like someone sittin' around talkin' to theirselves their minds *so occupied*. I always thought that when you're recording something, you wanted to get *exactly* what the man is doing out there... breathing, slapping his leg, patting his feet, clapping his hands, and that you *sometimes* got to mic a guy in *more* than one place. THAT is *true sound*. THAT is the *sound* of THIS man.

Memorably described by Peter Guralnick as a 'sometime ambulance driver, stock car racer, shuffleboard hustler, and rockabilly legend', Charlie Feathers was born on 12 June 1932, in Holly Springs, Mississippi. Having moved to Memphis, he began recording at Sun in October 1954, when Elvis was electrifying the label, but Sam Phillips seems to have viewed Charlie primarily as a country artist, rather than a rocker. Both sides of his debut single, 'Peepin' Eyes'/'I've Been Deceived' (April 1955), and the follow-up, 'Defrost Your Heart'/'A Wedding Gown Of White' (December 1955), were fine examples of Sun's downhome country style, sparse and affecting, but quite removed from the rockabilly sides Elvis was cutting. Unissued material recorded during Charlie's time at Sun was also in the Hank Williams and hillbilly mould, such as 'Honky Tonk Kind'. A couple of tunes, though, like 'Corrine Corrina' and 'Bottle To The Baby', were definitely on the rockin' side, and when Charlie broke away from Sun in 1956 and headed across town to cut a single for rival Memphis label Meteor, he came up with one of the most perfect examples of a double-sided rockabilly statement you're ever likely to hear.

On 'Get With It'/'Tongue-Tied Jill' (June 1956), Charlie moved away from the fiddles and steel that had sometimes adorned his Sun cuts and teamed up with Jody Chastain on double bass and Jerry Huffman on electric guitar, who also joined in with the songwriting and meshed with Charlie's own acoustic guitar and that remarkable voice. This was the

Charlie Feathers and His Musical Warriors

classic rockabilly lineup which Elvis, Scotty and Bill had pioneered two years before, and the opening lyrics of 'Get With It' spelt it out for the listener; he tells the guitarist to pick the tune and the bassist to start slapping and establish the beat, so that Charlie himself could join in on rhythm guitar and cut loose. You want to play some rockabilly? Just follow the instructions.

'Get With It' was a reworking of 'Corrine Corrina', which he'd cut at Sun but Sam hadn't released (by all accounts prompting Charlie to go over to Meteor out of frustration), while 'Tongue-Tied Jill' was a virtuoso example of Charlie's unique stuttering and moaning vocal style. *Billboard* magazine's reviewer called the result 'country blues with the deep bass and souped-up vocal', noting that Charlie's voice 'carries a lot of true feeling', and *Cash Box* reckoned it was 'another of the "Presley" type r & b-western-pop rockers that can go in any category ... Feathers is good and the platter is strong'.

The fact that Feathers left the world's greatest rockabilly label in order to cut his best sides, in a year when other rockers were beating down Sam's door in the rush to get in, is just one of the many contradictions in Charlie's career. He then promptly acquired a drummer, Jimmy Swords, and switched over right away to a third label, King Records up in Cincinnati, who had a distinguished hillbilly and blues pedigree. Reporting this development, local Memphis paper the *Commercial Appeal* had no doubts how to describe the band's music, even if they weren't quite sure how to spell his name,

referring to the contract signed by 'the rock and roll trio of Charley Feathers'. The recorded results of that move were magnificent: 'One Hand Loose', 'Everybody's Lovin' My Baby', 'I Can't Hardly Stand It', and a reworked version of 'Bottle To The Baby', all featuring textbook rockabilly bass and relentlessly simple beats on a snare. With these, and the Meteor single, Charlie's place in the rockabilly firmament was more than assured. What's astonishing is that he then went on to cut superb examples of the genre decades later, such as 'Stutterin' Cindy' (1968) and 'That Certain Female' (1974), which on audio evidence alone sound much more like the product of a time when the pre-army Elvis was wearing his gold suit than the years in which the likes of 'Hey Jude' or 'Kung Fu Fighting' were topping the charts.

TODAY AND TOMORROW

Charlie's original 1950s recordings, together with some remarkably authentic later performances, such as the searing version of 'Tear It Up' recorded for a TV show in Houston in 1979, justifiably brought him great renown among rockabilly fans as the years went by. His tendency to tell journalists and audiences stories of the Sun days which placed him right at the forefront of many rockin' innovations, however, caused a controversy that dogged him in the pages of rock'n'roll magazines all the way through to his obituaries.

During a visit to England in 1984, Charlie informed the crowd at Bristol Town Hall that he was the one who had come up with the original arrangement for Elvis's version of 'Good Rockin' Tonight'. He also asserted in various interviews over the years that he'd been responsible for the latter's radical reimagining of 'Blue Moon Of Kentucky' back in 1954, not to mention his claim to have helped develop Sun's remarkable

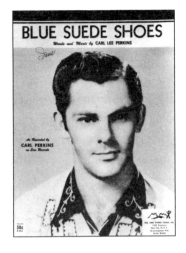

slap-back echo system. Other veterans of the 1950s Memphis rockabilly scene, including Sam Phillips, often recalled things differently.

All this has unfortunately tended to obscure the genuine contribution to the genre made by one of the purest rockabillies of them all. In much the same way, when the great blues pianist Jelly Roll Morton sat down in marathon sessions at the Library of Congress with Alan Lomax in 1938 to sing and talk on the record about his early days in pre-First World War jazz, he laid claim to all sorts of musical innovations which have since been hotly disputed, but that in itself can't disguise the scale and importance of Morton's music.

With Charlie's talent, he could have been forgiven for thinking that if Carl Perkins could reach number 1 in the national charts with a slice of downhome Memphis rockabilly like 'Blue Suede Shoes' (1956), then his own top-notch recordings ought to put him in films and on TV just like Carl. Hadn't Sam taken Perkins out into the street outside the Sun studio and handed him the keys to a brand-new Cadillac on the strength of that record's sales, saying 'Here y'are boy, it's all yours'? Charlie never saw the kind of material success that Carl enjoyed, let alone that of Elvis. But you need a serious amount of luck, as well as talent, in the music business, and it really doesn't hurt if you've also got a money-hungry operator like 'Colonel' Tom Parker out there hustling for you seven days a week.

By 1956, when Charlie Feathers was cutting his classic

sides for Meteor and King, Elvis was already showing up in mainstream fan publications in England, such as the glossy book *Your Record Stars*, which informed its readers that the 'rocking-and-rolling hill-billy' was now 'riding the luxury train like a man who owns the railroad company'. In truth, Charlie was probably way too rootsy for anything like this kind of stardom. He had his own style – what *Billboard* once called his 'heartbreaking ... back-shack type blues' – and his own way of doing things, which he stuck to, come what may, throughout the years. For better or worse, you could tell he wasn't likely to rumba in a sports car, or do the clam, any time soon.

When Charlie died in 1998, his *New York Times* obituary noted that he had kept going in the sixties despite lack of commercial success: 'He persevered, and eventually European rockabilly fans discovered him. After the broadcast of a British television documentary, he did a concert at the Rainbow Theatre in London in 1977 that was recorded by EMI; this raised his stock considerably, but by then he was classified as an oldies performer.'

If there's one annoying word that the US music business has been throwing around almost since the end of the fifties, it's 'oldies'. *Rolling Stone* magazine founder Jann Wenner, writing about the Beach Boys in 1967, said: 'On "She's Goin' Bald" they throw in, *a la* Frank Zappa, a speeded up "sha la la la la la" [sic] from the mouldy-oldy "Get A Job".'

'Get A Job' by the Silhouettes, one of the best vocal group hits of the fifties, was just ten years old at the time. Two years later, writing in the same magazine, Jan Hodenfield reviewed the 1969 Rock & Roll Revival Show at Madison Square Garden as if all the performers involved were already drawing their pensions ('Now in their late twenties–early thirties...'), and managed to describe the hits of The Coasters as 'mouldy minstrel show standards' (that's Lieber & Stoller's 'Searchin' and 'Yakety Yak' he's talking about). Since the music of the first generation of rockers was casually dismissed like this – ironically at a time when many unfairly neglected vintage blues performers were just being rediscovered – it's probably not surprising that by the 1970s the Sun Studio was a tyre warehouse, that other landmark studios such as Stax in Memphis and Gold Star in Los Angeles were torn down in the decades that followed, and that the original fifties rockabillies had to come to Europe to get some recognition. Charlie Feathers may have been an 'oldies' performer to some in the US, but he certainly wasn't in England, either in the nineties or back in the seventies, when the UK's greatest deejay John Peel called him in to record a session for Radio 1 in 1977, during the week that the Sex Pistols' 'Pretty Vacant' was released.

It had been a mighty long road, but public recognition of sorts did eventually come to Charlie Feathers in his home country. The month before that magnificent 1990 show in London – and over twenty years since record collector Breathless Dan Coffey had gone over to the US to get Charlie into Select-O-Hit Studios in Memphis to cut 'Stutterin' Cindy' (1968) – the man himself had been back in his home town making an album. The location was the Sam C. Phillips Recording Service, and the record was for a major label, of all things, at a time when Elektra was commissioning solo records from artists such as boogie pianist Johnny Johnson and zydeco accordionist Boozoo Chavis, as part of their *American Explorer* series. Recorded over just four days in August 1990, featuring fellow Sun veterans Jimmy Van Eaton, Stan Kesler and Roland Janes, it came accompanied by a ringing endorsement from another former stalwart of the label, Johnny Cash: 'Charlie Feathers has never been given the credit or recognition he deserves. I will always be a Charlie Feathers fan.'

Charlie wasn't Elvis, but Elvis wasn't Charlie, and that's the whole point. His story stands for the many who set off down the rockabilly path in the wake of the King's early records, and wound up blazing a righteous trail of their own.

5 ROCKIN' UP AT SAM'S PLACE

SUN RECORDS, SAM PHILLIPS AND THE MEMPHIS
ROCKABILLY HIT FACTORY

On 12 July 2000, a seventy-seven-year-old former radio
engineer who'd made a tidy sum investing in stocks of the
fledgling Holiday Inn hotel chain back in the mid-1950s took
his first ever plane trip across the Atlantic. Sam C. Phillips was
appearing onstage at the National Film Theatre in London,
being interviewed in conjunction with a showing of the
excellent feature-length documentary, *Sam Phillips – The Man
Who Invented Rock'n'Roll.*

This was an occasion I couldn't miss. Like the majority of
those in the audience that night, I'd initially learned most of
what I knew about Sam and his label, Sun Records, from the
works of two English writers, Colin Escott and Martin Hawkins,
who'd travelled to Memphis in 1971 to find out the story first
hand. New in town, they'd opened up the phone book at the
last page and started looking for names, which is how they
came to speak first to singer Malcolm Yelvington. It wasn't such
a bad place to start. Back in 1954, Sun single number 209 was
Elvis's 'That's All Right'/'Blue Moon Of Kentucky', 210 was his

'Good Rockin' Tonight'/'I Don't Care If The Sun Don't Shine', and number 211 was 'Drinkin' Wine Spo-Dee-O-Dee'/'Just Rollin' Along' by Malcolm Yelvington and the Star Rhythm Boys.

At the time when Escott and Hawkins began their researches into Sun's history, Elvis was not only the hottest ticket in Vegas, but was enough of a star to pull in the still-record figure of one *billion* TV viewers worldwide for his 14 January 1973 concert special, *Aloha from Hawaii*. By contrast, Malcolm Yelvington had been out of the business since 1958, having returned to his former trade of pipe-fitting and welding, and when the writers tracked him down, his music career must have seemed a long way in the past, as he told them: 'I guess I can say I started in recording at the same time as Elvis. That's something, isn't it! He got his first record out in the summer of '54 and I got mine in the fall … It sold a few – I can't remember exactly – around Memphis. If you got one of 'em you got more'n I got.'

The world wasn't exactly beating a path to his door at the time of this interview, but the work that Escott and Hawkins were doing, researching and writing a book which appeared in 1975 as *Catalyst: The Sun Records Story* – and also their parallel activities during that decade – putting together thoroughly annotated record reissues of the Sun catalogue of hundreds of tracks recorded by Sam Phillips (including many previously unissued) – eventually helped create a market for surviving Sun artists to come over to England. So it was that more than a decade after first hearing Malcolm Yelvington on a Sun compilation in the 1970s, I found myself at a North London rockin' pub venue, the Clay Pigeon in Harrow, on 3 April 1988, watching the man himself, just a few months short of his seventieth birthday.

Standing on the tiny stage wearing a black stetson and matching black western suit, Malcolm Yelvington sang superlative versions of his Sun and Meteor recordings to an audience of a couple of hundred rockabillies who knew every last word of every song. He had never left America before, was clearly delighted with his reception, and after the show happily signed the picture of himself and the Star Rhythm Boys in my copy of *Catalyst: The Sun Records Story*. By then, Escott and Hawkins had already updated their landmark book once, issuing it in 1980 under the title *Sun Records – The Brief History of the Legendary Record Label*, and would go on to expand it into its definitive form in 1991, as *Good Rockin' Tonight – Sun Records & the Birth of Rock'n'Roll*. Anyone looking for the authoritative history of Sam's label would be well advised to seek out any or all of them.

OUT TO GET GUTBUCKET

If Sam Phillips had done nothing else except record Presley's five Sun singles, that in itself would be a major argument for the significance of his label in the story of rockabilly, but of course he did so much more. Sun is unquestionably the most important rockin' label of them all, and has long been recognised as such, so that its artists have been generally tracked down and interviewed to a much greater extent than those who recorded elsewhere. Yet Sam Phillips recorded much that was not rockabilly. He started with the blues, R&B and boogie-woogie, tried a little gospel and vocal harmony material, a side order of hillbilly and straight country, and eventually wound up issuing mainstream pop recordings and even the odd novelty record. Through it all, though, from when he first opened for business in 1950 under the name Memphis Recording Service, up until he gradually lost interest after 1957, and began leaving more of the day-to-day studio work to Jack Clement, Sam's guiding principle was to capture a performance, a moment – that unique quality which he felt each artist of any worth could bring to a song. As Sam himself put it, shortly before his death: 'I wanted the sound you'd get from hearing [the musicians] play on the stage, even though we were in the studio. I wanted them to feel we were in this together ... I just went out to get gutbucket, and in the main, we did that, and that set us apart from a lot of other great labels.'

He didn't necessarily care if there were mistakes, rough notes or tuning problems. If a recording had that essential spark, then that was better than a hundred other supposedly 'perfect' takes, in which every note was played and sung correctly, yet no one sounded remotely like their life depended on it. Sonny Burgess, who with his band The Pacers cut some of the wildest rockabilly ever recorded at Sun, had this to say when I asked him about Sam's method of working in the studio:

> He didn't try and tell you *how* to play, or what to play or anything else. He simply listened, and he had this great ear, a feel. If it felt good, then Sam would put it out. You know, it didn't have to be perfect. Look at 'Whole Lotta Shakin''. J. M. Van Eaton gets off on the drum lick there – somewhere in that song he's off – but it felt so good that Sam didn't care, he put it out anyway, sold about ten million records. I think that was really Sam's

Sam in the studio with
Jerry Lee, on the cover of
a Sun Special edition of
UK rockin' magazine, *Now
Dig This*

thing, he had this great feel for the music. I always told
him he shoulda been a musician, he had the looks and
everything. Now Jack Clement, he'd kinda point you
in a direction. But Sam's way worked best. Sam had
more hits.

Sam himself spent the best part of half a century after he
sold Elvis's contract to RCA being asked to explain his success
and his motivations, and just what it was that had made his
relatively small independent record company produce so many
hugely influential artists. There were no guarantees back in
January 1950 when he set up in business that a man already
working a day job as a radio engineer broadcasting from the
Hotel Peabody in Memphis would even recoup the costs of
building his own modest studio – especially as his intention
was to concentrate on recording the wealth of black talent in
the area. Yet, as he told an interviewer in 1970, 'I felt music
in general was becoming stereotyped,' and following his own

65

instincts, he succeeded in leasing R&B, blues and boogie masters he'd cut to labels such as Modern/RPM and Chess. Tracks such as B. B. King's 'She's Dynamite' (1951), for example, jumped like a juke joint on Saturday night, and then of course there was the groundbreaking sound of Ike Turner and his Kings of Rhythm knocking hell out of a song called 'Rocket 88', (often touted as the first ever rock'n'roll record, it was released in 1951 under the name of Jackie Brenston & his Delta Cats). Recordings like these showed that Sam was on to something very special, and by 1952 he was releasing material on his own Sun label.

WORKIN' FOR UNCLE SAM

There were more blues and R&B hits, such as 'Bear Cat' by Rufus Thomas (1953), and the superb harmony singing of the Prisonaires – a group of inmates on day-release from the Tennessee State Penitentiary in Nashville – whose magisterial 'Just Walking In The Rain' (1953) was later watered down and sold in the millions by Johnnie Ray. And then, in 1954, along came Elvis, and the rockabilly floodgates opened, as Sam told *Billboard*:

> After Elvis hit, many white persons of varying backgrounds, but equally deprived of opportunity in their opinions, came to the studios to be heard because they were met with the informality that they were raised up in and with. It was, I believe, this way that such persons as Jerry Lee Lewis, Carl Perkins and Johnny Cash came to my studios ... They were rough, but willing to be polished. They created a new breed of excitement and expressions. They were fearless and willing to put up with the criticism any new artist with changes has to

Carl Perkins

take. The abuse for all must have been hard for them to take. But they were message sellers and they had their messages to sell. They have all stood the test of time.

Elvis kicked the doors down in 1954, and then on 22 January 1955, Carl Perkins came in and cut 'Turn Around' and 'Movie Magg'. He'd been playing for Sam for the last few months, but this was his first releasable proper session, and the following month Carl's debut single appeared on Sam's short-lived subsidiary label, Flip, with 'Country Vocal' written on the label. It didn't even merit a review in *Billboard*, just a listing in the C&W section under 'Other Records Released This Week'. By July, however, a deejay at WTJS, Jackson, Mississippi, named Fred Brooks, was happily telling the trade press that Carl's single was 'garnering a lot of spins in West Tennessee', which probably meant a lot to one particular resident of Jackson,

Carl Perkins. No one at that stage could have predicted what a monster hit Carl's next single, 'Blue Suede Shoes', would turn into. For anyone who thinks you might need vast amounts of equipment to record a multi-million seller like that, here's Carl talking to Trevor Cajiao about the technical side of those sessions: 'I can't remember but three microphones, most of the time there were just two, two microphones ... And I remember he used to turn my amp right in the corner and sometimes he'd put a pasteboard box on it with a hole cut in ... Sam was inventive, to do what he did with what he had ... Those old Sun records had a slight roar or somethin' about them that I still hear on 'em today.'

Right after Carl's debut at Sun came another artist who would also score heavily for the label, Johnny Cash. He hit the jackpot with his very first release, 'Cry, Cry, Cry'/'Hey Porter', which was issued on 21 June 1955, but took a while to slowly climb up the charts, and *Billboard* then picked it out as one of the week's best buys:

> While this disk has been available two months, it is only now beginning to shape up as a left-field threat. Starting off nicely in the Nashville and Memphis trade areas, it has continued to grow there and has begun to spread. Richmond, Dallas, New Orleans and Little Rock are the other territories where Cash has now established himself.

Once again, tying in with the fact that Elvis's first fan base was centred in Texas, Tennessee and nearby states, the gradual spread of Johnny Cash's success demonstrates how much of a largely Southern phenomenon rockabilly was in the beginning. In those far-off days before huge radio conglomerates and wall-to-wall music television combined to homogenise taste

across the nation, it was still very possible to have a purely regional hit. Rockabilly artists could sing in their own local accents and use regional slang and terminology, and still not have to worry about alienating their listeners, which is why you occasionally heard vocalists cutting loose with a slice of pure hog-calling, 'Aaaah suey!', as if they'd just that minute come in from the farmyard. Elvis himself sang 'meet me in a hurry, behind the barn' on 'Good Rockin' Tonight' – not a phrase that your average Manhattan teenager was likely to be using in 1955. Perkins and Cash were encouraged by Sam just to be themselves, and he captured the music which they were making in the juke joints around Memphis pretty much just as it stood, releasing it in the hope that if it sounded good to him, then there were likely to be others out there who understood, regardless of if they'd grown up dirt poor in the country like those two singers. In the event, even Sam must have been taken aback by the extent to which that music crossed regional and national borders.

Once Sun had launched Elvis, Perkins and Cash in quick succession, it's hardly surprising that people from all over the South were beating a path to his door, such as Jerry Lee Lewis and his father Elmo, who showed up one day in November 1956, having sold dozens of eggs in order to raise money for the trip. Jerry, too, would hit the big time, only to lose it all and then claw his way back by means of a string of remarkable records and what has been accurately described as 'the greatest live show on earth'.

TAKIN' CARE OF BUSINESS

That Sam had achieved something quite remarkable with the avalanche of raw talent which came knocking at his door in those early years was soon acknowledged. Two years to the day from when Dewey Phillips first aired Elvis's 'That's All Right' on his *Red, Hot & Blue* show in Memphis, *Billboard* summed up Sam's business situation in a front-page article about diversification in the record industry:

> The most outstanding record label operation, currently owned by an indie broadcaster, is Sun Records, the Sam Phillips firm. Phillips, who owns WHER, Memphis, negotiated a plum $40,000 deal for himself with RCA Victor on Elvis Presley last winter, and hit the charts barely a month later with two new artists, Carl Perkins and Johnny Cash. Phillips owns Hi-Lo Music, and has an arrangement with Hill & Range on certain material.

People often ask why Sam sold Presley's contract less than two years after discovering one of the most remarkable performers in the history of popular music. As is clear from the above description of his immediate post-Elvis business interests, he not only used that money to help give Perkins and Cash the promotional push required to turn their records into national, rather than regional, hits, but was also already investing in radio stations and music publishing companies. That one crucial deal helped bankroll Sun's rockabilly explosion of the next three years. Until Elvis came along, Sun was a small

label leading a hand-to-mouth existence. The money generated by selling his contract to RCA helped secure Sun's future, and at the same time laid the foundations for Sam's business empire; he'd eventually own a string of radio stations across the South, and bought shares in the fledgling Memphis hotel company which had been incorporated in 1954, Holiday Inn.

These investments bought Phillips long-term security, but it was his record label which brought him worldwide fame. At Sun, and his subsidiary label Phillips International, he not only provided a launch pad for a list of remarkable, groundbreaking stars such as Elvis, B. B. King, Johnny Cash, Howlin' Wolf, Jerry Lee Lewis, Ike Turner, Carl Perkins, Charlie Rich and Roy Orbison, but also coaxed the finest results out of scores of hugely talented artists who never quite got the breaks in terms of record sales. Names like Ray Harris or Jack Earls wouldn't have sold out large venues back in the 1950s, but Sam captured something of their primal rockabilly spirit on tape in a way which has since made their original 45s sought after and very highly valued as some of the wildest examples of the genre. Ray's 'Come On Little Mama' (1956) is a frantic screamer of a song, powered along at breakneck speed solely by Wayne Cogswell's unhinged guitar playing and Joe Reisenberg pounding hell out of the drums. It sold pretty well in Memphis, but was probably way too primitive to have a chance in the national charts, and in any case Sun was a small company with limited promotional money, and couldn't give everyone the big push at the same time.

To gain an idea of what Ray Harris was up against, on the very same day that Sam issued 'Come On Little Mama', he also put out the following classic rockabilly releases: 'You're My Baby'/'Rockhouse' by Roy Orbison & the Teen Kings, 'Ubangi Stomp'/'Black Jack David' by Warren Smith, and 'I Need A Man'/'No Matter Who's To Blame' by Barbara Pittman. (Another fine rocker, 'Love Crazy Baby'/'I Feel Like Rockin'' by Kenneth Parchman, was given a catalogue number but never released.) This was just what Sam launched onto the market on 24 September 1956, and to round them all up now in playable condition would cost you hundreds of pounds. Some months the in-house competition was even more fierce. Several former Sun artists have since complained that once Jerry Lee Lewis started selling, Sam would put all his promotional clout behind the Louisiana wildman, and other singles were pretty much left to fend for themselves, so you can only sympathise with the nine other people who had their Sun singles released on 9 April 1958, the day that Jerry's 'High School Confidential' appeared. The Killer was just coming off the back of two consecutive million-sellers – 'Whole Lotta Shakin'' and 'Great Balls Of Fire' – and his new single was the title song of a motion picture, so Sam justifiably expected it to take off like a rocket. Within months, the debacle of Jerry's English tour would deal a hammer blow to his career which took years to make right, but that didn't stop some first-class rockabilly singles such as 'Right Behind You Baby'/'So Young' by Ray Smith and 'Drinkin' Wine'/'I Done Told You' by Gene Simmons getting lost in the shuffle because of sharing a release date with 'High School Confidential'.

Yesterday's chart positions matter less and less as time goes by, and the quality of the music laid down in Sam's tiny 35-foot by 18-foot studio at 706 Union Avenue, Memphis, speaks for itself, to the extent that these days some of the best-loved Sun material includes a fair proportion that was not even issued in the 1950s. Carl Perkins was embarrassed to the end of his days by the eventual release of a song of his called 'Her Love Rubbed Off' (1957), a magnificent untamed howl of a song which changes brilliantly between major and minor keys, in which the band appear to be just about in control of the mayhem, and very likely three sheets to the wind. Carl later claimed to not even remember writing or recording the song, perhaps on account of what sounds very like some engagingly basic Anglo-Saxon terminology he appears to be employing in the song's later stages. Given the amount of alcohol generally consumed by Carl and his band at their sessions, it's not surprising he may not have recalled playing certain songs which remained unissued for three decades.

ONE-CUT WONDERS

The informal recording atmosphere at Sun, in which artists were free to try their hand at all sorts of material, and if it wasn't working, move on, could mean that many different titles were recorded in the same evening. These days, the pampered elite of the rock business lucky enough to still have a major label deal often disappear into the studio for the best part of a year, only to emerge triumphantly with nine whole songs (overdubbed and polished to within an inch of their lives). Back then, you could cut more tunes than that in a matter of hours. Take the case of Jerry Lee Lewis, who was with Sun from 1956 to 1963; when Bear Family Records rounded up his material for the 1989 box-set *Classic Jerry Lee Lewis*, they were able to include a whopping 246 songs – considerably more than most artists cut in a lifetime. Given that he was principally being

Johnny Powers

recorded as a singles artist, that shows how widely he ranged during his sessions, and how much freedom he was given. As Sonny Burgess told me: 'I think Jerry Lee must have recorded everything in the world. Jerry Lee, the type he was, if he didn't get it in one, two or three takes, he go on to something else. We were almost that bad. We got a lot of stuff that we did one cut on and we'd say "No, that don't sound good…"'

The speed at which things happened could be breathtaking. Sonny and the Pacers cut both sides of a single the first day they arrived at Sun. The same thing happened to Johnny Powers. He landed a deal with the label in 1959, having already written and recorded many very fine songs up at United Sound Studios in Detroit, including the classic 'Long Blond Hair' (1957), which appeared on George Braxtons' Fox label. It's one of the paradoxes of Sun's history that prime home-grown Memphis rockabillies like Johnny Burnette & the Rock'n'Roll Trio failed their audition for the label, and the likes of Jimmy Wages recorded for Sun but never had a single issued, despite cutting frantic recordings such as 'Miss Pearl' and 'Mad Man'. With all their rockabilly credentials, these people didn't make it through the selection process, and yet in August 1959 that glorious yellow label was stamped onto a throwaway novelty single by Sherry Crane called 'Winnie The Parakeet'. Still, the following month, Sun issued 'With Your Love With Your Kiss'/'Be Mine, All Mine' by Johnny Powers (on the same day as 'Little Queenie'/'I Could Never Be Ashamed Of You' by Jerry Lee Lewis). I asked Johnny how he'd come to sign a contract with the label, and he told me he'd cut a demo up in Detroit, a copy of which had been taken by his manager, Tommy Moers, to an Alabama disc jockey, who'd aired it on the radio, where it went down a storm:

> The phones lit up like crazy, and the guy called Sam Phillips. I was playing a gig someplace, and my manager flew me down there, and checked me into a hotel, the Peabody Hotel, and we went over to the studio and started cutting right away. I was like, wow, this is something else... I'm kinda disappointed, you know. I walked into the studio, I was so nervous, because, you know, Elvis recorded there, now here I am, lucky guy, getting a contract with Sam. No rehearsal, it was like, 'You know, I wish I'd had time to go over it with the band.' There were a lot of mistakes made.

The songs which Johnny cut that day – both sides of the single, plus others which surfaced years later, including the great 'Me And My Rhythm Guitar' – were recorded in conjunction with some of Sun's best studio musicians, including Jimmy Van Eaton on drums, Brad Suggs on guitar and Charlie Rich on piano. The credits usually also list Billy Riley on bass, but Johnny's not so sure:

> Well, you know, I have a question on that. It sounds a

little silly – it may have happened, but I didn't see him. You know, 'With Your Love, With Your Kiss', and 'Be Mine All Mine', there *was* no bass. There was the foot-pedal of the drums. I didn't see a bass player. I mean, I could be totally wrong, but I just remember three guys… Maybe they overdubbed the bass [laughs].

SOME CATS JUMPED OUT AND THEY FORMED A BAND

Billy Lee Riley and his group, the Little Green Men, functioned for several years as the de facto house band at Sun, playing on numerous sessions. When they weren't backing other people, Billy and his outfit laid down some flat-out stormers of their own, in particular 'Flyin' Saucers Rock'n'Roll' (1957) and the double-sided monster 'Red Hot'/'Pearly Lee' (1957). Billy had arrived at Sun in 1956, along with engineer Jack Clement. They'd cut Billy's first single, 'Rock With Me Baby', elsewhere, intending to issue it on their own Fernwood label, but wound up licensing it to Sam instead, and both of them were offered a job at Sun on the strength of it. Riley's band also turned out to be a huge asset to the studio. His drummer was Jimmy Van Eaton, who, as Escott and Hawkins have pointed out, eventually played on an incredible 173 of the 330 songs issued on Sun during his time at the label. The band's guitarist was Roland Janes, who went on to appear on most of the classic Jerry Lee Lewis Sun material, his superb solos usually introduced by the Killer's cry of 'Roland boy!'

Billy Riley himself had the exasperating experience of standing in the office at Sun in 1957 listening to Sam cancel orders at the pressing plant of his own 'Red Hot' in order to use all the available capacity for copies of Jerry Lee's fast-selling 'Great Balls Of Fire'. 'Red Hot' was shifting pretty well, but it was sacrificed in order to help Jerry Lee's second hit take off

Billy Lee Riley

nationally. Some say that Sam didn't really want Billy taking his fine band on the road too much, because he needed them there in the studio at 706 Union Avenue, backing all the other acts, and there's probably some truth in that.

On balance, it's understandable that money was tight and that some excellent recordings failed to get the right promotion. The sheer scale of the rockabilly activity at Sun from 1955 onwards is breathtaking, and for much of the time the business side of it was mostly down to just Sam himself, with his assistant Marion Keisker in the front office, and Jack Clement also handling certain recordings after 1956.

Then there were all those who really should have made it but didn't – such as Warren Smith, who cut five absolutely flawless singles for Sun, and left even more material in the can good enough to have bought him a string of Cadillacs and a mansion to rival Graccland. His two 1956 relcascs, 'Rock'n'Roll Ruby' and 'Ubangi Stomp', would have been enough to fix his reputation among the greats, but to follow that with the double-sided killer 'Miss Froggie'/'So Long I'm Gone' in 1957, then

Roy Orbison's Sun rockabilly material repackaged to cash in on his 1960s success

the frantic 'Got Love If You Want It' in 1958, was remarkable. Interestingly, Sam didn't really see Warren as a rockabilly singer at all, commenting, quite rightly, that Smith had one of the finest country voices he'd ever recorded, as can be heard on many of his Sun recordings, including his final single for the label, 'Goodbye Mister Love' (1959). One of his most effective performances stayed in the can for twenty years, and yet has become one of those most associated with him, 'Red Cadillac And A Black Moustache', which he cut in 1957.

If Warren Smith was a natural ballad singer who could turn around and rock with the best of them, so too was Roy Orbison, who also left behind some wild material in the Sun vaults, and whose singles for the label, 'Ooby Dooby' (1956) aside, never found sales that matched their quality. Of his time at Sun, Roy later recalled that Sam 'wanted everything up, everything fast, everything with all the energy that was possible'. Although he'd eventually find lasting fame with slower material, Roy's powerhouse performances of songs such as 'Domino', 'Rockhouse', 'You're My Baby' and 'Mean Little Mama', featuring his own excellent guitar work, are vintage slices of Sun rockabilly. Roy's original band, The Teen Kings, fell apart relatively soon after he joined the label, so that when he, like many other Sun artists, began playing package tours organised by Bob Neal, Roy was backed by Sonny Burgess and the Pacers. The two of them frequently opened for Johnny Cash, and as Sonny explained the situation to me, it's clear that some of the artists on Sun had a great deal in common, and got to know each other well on those lengthy tours:

Bob Neal was Johnny Cash's manager, and when Elvis left him in '56, he had Johnny Cash and Jerry Lee. And he took over, started booking us. Roy Orbison's Teen Kings had left him, so he started riding with us. We had an old green stretch limo, Cadillac. We was down to four pieces then. He must have rode three hundred thousand miles with us, never bought a nickel's worth of gas. We'd get a room. There was only four of us, so we'd bilk a motel room, two guys in each bed. He'd go and get him a rollaway bed and roll in that damn little old room with us. You know, you're walkin' on beds, almost, it was that little. Yeah, but he was a great guy, though, I really liked Roy. Played a real good guitar and sang great. Took his glasses off and said, 'Don't let me get too close to the edge of the stage, 'cause I can't see, and if I get too close I'll fall off the stage.' He thought girls didn't like a guy in glasses. Don't know if that was true or not. That was his theory. He'd pull 'em off, couldn't see nothin' without 'em. He had them coke bottle glasses, y'know, thick ones. He was a good guy.

WHO LOVES THE SUN?

That sense of camaraderie didn't last, as one by one the original artists left Sun for other labels. Carl Perkins departed for

Columbia Records in February 1958, and Johnny Cash followed to the same label in August, by which time Jerry Lee's career had taken one hell of a beating at the hands of the UK press, and Orbison had also defected to RCA Victor. Rockabilly wasn't really Top Ten chart material any more either by 1958 – in fact, 1956 had been by far the best year for that – and sugar-coated, grinning boys-next-door were simpering their way regularly onto Dick Clark's *Bandstand* show, paving the way for further horrors in 1959. Sun was still cutting rockabilly, that's for sure, and some of it was even released, like Ray Smith's 'You Made A Hit' (1958), but a lot of equally good rocking material stayed in the can, such as Tommy Blake's 'You Better Believe It' (1958), Eddie Bond's 'This Old Heart Of Mine' (1958) or Warren Smith's 'Uranium Rock' (1958). Of course, this was nothing new, since classic rockabilly tracks such as Carl Perkins' iconic 'Put Your Cat Clothes On' (1957), Jack Earls & the Jimbos 'Crawdad Hole' and 'Let's Bop' (both 1956) or Ray Harris's 'Lonely Wolf' (1957) all sat on the shelf until the 1970s. The fact is, Sam just had far too much quality material for one medium-sized indie record company to effectively launch onto the market, and the window of opportunity for rockabilly success opened and closed within a couple of years of the emergence of Elvis. By 1957, Sam was already building up his radio and publishing empire, and had even started a new subsidiary label, whose name, Phillips International, gives some indication of his ambitions, as the following *Billboard* news item from August that year shows:

SAM PHILLIPS TO GO GLOBAL WITH NEW INTERNATIONAL LABEL – Sam Phillips, proprietor of Sun Records, is preparing to launch a new label within the next three weeks. Label will be called Phillips International, and will be an adjunct of the (Sam C.) Phillips International Corporation. Phillips, who is also owner of several radio stations in Tennessee, and who is credited with the creation of the rockabilly craze thru his discovery of such artists as Elvis Presley, Johnny Cash, Carl Perkins and Jerry Lewis [sic], intends to make the new label more general in its repertoire scope, and aims at worldwide distribution.

Times and trends had changed, and pure-bred rockabilly was becoming marginalised. By 1960, Sam had moved out of the old studio at 706 Union Avenue and opened up in a custom-built, $750,000 place at 639 Madison, but the remarkable amount of material recorded in that modest original location by Sam during those few short years has fed, since the early 1970s, a massive reissue programme, despite the label's habit of wiping and reusing tapes back in the 1950s for reasons of economy. Sun Records remain central to the development and success of rockabilly music, and, in the end, it comes down to Sam giving people the chance to do just what they were doing naturally in the honky-tonks, to get down and wail, without worrying a song to death or second-guessing the life out of it. As he himself told *Billboard* the year before he died: 'It wasn't that I was afraid of changing someone's style, I just felt like I wouldn't have what we could do best if we put a real tuxedo on someone who loved a truly good pair of overalls.'

6 LIKE IT SAYS ON THE LABEL

OTHER VARIETIES OF ROCKABILLY RECORD COMPANY

Head across Memphis from Sun in 1956 and you'd pretty soon have tripped over one of the other landmark rockabilly labels, Lester Bihari's Meteor Records. With a more rootsy, downhome sound than Sun usually aimed for, their rockabilly 45s are now some of the most sought after on the planet. Star of the show was Charlie Feathers, but recordings by the likes of Bill Bowen, Junior Thompson and Brad Suggs were also superb.

Meteor was a small operation. Other great rockabilly independents like Starday/Dixie were a step up in terms of size and distribution, and then came the majors, such as US Decca, Mercury or Columbia, all of whom consistently managed to issue first-class rockabilly. It makes sense to talk about Meteor Records right after a chapter about Sun, since a great many of the people who recorded for the former also worked for the latter, or were even sent along to Meteor personally by Sam Phillips because he didn't have time to record them himself. Although the faces might well have been familiar, there doesn't seem to have been any real rivalry between the two labels; Meteor was a much smaller operation, which in business terms

Lester Bihari in front of Meteor Records with an unknown woman

wasn't a serious competitor to Sam, and never came close to achieving the national success of a Carl Perkins or a Jerry Lee Lewis.

Like Sun, Meteor started out specialising in black music. A news item in the 20 December 1952 issue of *Billboard*, titled 'Lester Bihari Sets New Meteor Label', announced:

> Lester Bihari, who, up to now, has been associated with his brothers' Modern and RPM diskeries as Memphis rep, handling pressing and distribution, is branching out on his own with a new R&B label, Meteor. Bihari, who will continue to headquarter in Memphis, has signed Elmo James, ex-Trumpet warbler, whose first release is 'I Believe' and 'I Held My Baby Last Night'.

That particular Elmore James record would prove to be a hit, but when the label folded five years later, it also turned out to have been their biggest success, and most of Meteor's other releases showed little sign of breaking out nationally. When Elvis began causing waves around Memphis in 1954, Lester Bihari made his first moves into recording local white musicians. Indeed, although he'd been running a label for nearly two years, these were actually his first proper attempts at recording anything, since nearly all of what he'd issued so far were discs that had been cut elsewhere. His own studio, at 1794 Chelsea Avenue in Memphis, was in very poor shape, and needed a fair amount of repair work undertaken by two future Sun label mainstays, Quinton Claunch and Bill Cantrell, before it was in a fit state for the recording of Bihari's first hillbilly success, 'Daydreamin'', by Bud Deckleman & the Daydreamers (1954).

From here, it wasn't too much of a jump to dipping a toe in the rockabilly market, which they did with the aid of a Sun refugee, Malcolm Yelvington, working under an assumed name to avoid contract disputes. Calling himself Mac Sales, Yelvington cut the single 'Yakety Yak'/'A Gal Named Joe' (1955), the first song of which had been supposed to be his second single on Sun, following 'Drinkin' Wine Spo-Dee-O-Dee'. Frustrated with its non-appearance, Malcolm simply headed across town to Meteor and recut it. 'Yakety Yak' was easy-rolling, good-natured rockabilly of the best kind, and later proved the highlight of Yelvington's 1980s comeback shows in England.

Having taken the plunge, Lester Bihari then released a string of absolute rockabilly classics over the next twelve months: 'All Messed Up'/'Sleepy Time Blues' (1955) by Jess Hooper with the Daydreamers; 'Mama's Little Baby'/'Raw Deal' (1956) by Junior Thompson with the Meteors; 'Tongue-Tied Jill'/'Get With It' (1956) by Charlie Feathers with Jody & Jerry; 'Don't Shoot Me Baby (I'm Not Ready To Die)'/'Have Myself A Ball' (1956) by Bill Bowen with the Rockets; 'Charcoal Suit' '/'Bop, Baby, Bop'

(1956) by Brad Suggs with the Swingsters; and 'Rock, Roll And Rhythm'/'Lonesome Rhythm Blues' (1956) by Wayne McGinnis with the Swingteens. These are now some of the most sought-after vinyl records of all time, and it's not hard to see why. If you're looking for the sound of no-nonsense, hillbilly-to-the-bone rockabilly, exactly as it would have been played in the West Memphis honky-tonks circa 1956, then this is as good as it gets.

What's remarkable is that Lester Bihari himself was not really a producer in the classic sense, and his studio itself left some musicians distinctly unimpressed. Steve Carl, whose excellent 'Curfew'/'18 Year Old Blues' (1958) was the label's swansong, later recalled Bihari showing them his echo chamber, which turned out to be the bathroom, and was infested with snakes. In the light of this, it's not surprising to learn that Carl actually cut his record himself in Minneapolis, and brought the tapes to Bihari. By the time it was issued, the label was no more.

Along the way, although their distribution was poor and their output nowhere near as extensive as Sun's, Meteor managed to issue some of the best of Memphis music, both black and white. Unlike Sam, they never really gave up releasing R&B and blues material, and the run of rockabilly listed above was closely followed by releases from former Sun R&B stars Little Milton and Rufus Thomas. Never a natural record businessman, Lester Bihari effectively closed up shop after 1957 and went back west to work for his brothers, but he and his artists captured something very special in that studio on Chelsea Avenue during rockabilly's epic year, 1956.

For a long time afterwards, if you wanted to hear those Meteor recordings, you had no alternative but to track down some of the impossibly rare original singles, until in the 1970s the bootleggers got involved, culminating in a 1979 album called *Hillbilly Bop – Memphis Style*, which rounded up the best of the label's rockabilly output. Whoever put it together here in England seems to have done so in a hurry – one Wayne McGinnis tune mistakenly appeared twice, credited as two separate songs, and the Charlie Feathers classic 'Get With It' was listed on the back cover as 'Get On With It'. On the front, just to give that authentic, Memphis-in-the-fifties look, was a blurry B&W photo of an electricity pylon and some fields near Harrow in North London. For all that, until the legal issue of these tracks happened a decade later, this album was a godsend for anyone wanting to hear the real deal. I ran into a copy in the Alleycats record shop in Norwich in '79, and apart from Charlie Feathers, at that stage I'd never heard of any of the artists on the record, but it knocked me out. The sheer quality of what was in the grooves makes it still one of the best rockabilly compilations of the era, although the full story was only really revealed with the appearance of Ace Records' magnificent two-CD collection, *The Complete Meteor Rockabilly & Hillbilly Recordings*, in 2003.

AIN'T JUST WHISTLIN' DIXIE

If the downhome, gutbucket sounds of the Meteor artists exemplify rockabilly at its finest, then so too does the output of Harold 'Pappy' Daily's Starday label, and its subsidiary, Dixie.

Meteor was a relatively small label, albeit with ties to larger concerns out in Los Angeles, but Starday was an example of the type of company that was several steps up the ladder in terms of size and organisation. They released far more records than Meteor during those days, but this was partly because they were also running a custom service, separate from their main label, whereby musicians from all over the country could send in tapes they'd recorded and have them pressed up and released on Daily's Dixie subsidiary. This was a very different situation

SONNY FISHER   U.K. Tour 1980

Singles:
NS 94 Pink & Black/Sneaky Pete 45rpm
NST 59 Rockin' Daddy/I Can't Lose 78rpm

UK Representation:
PAUL BARRET
0222 704279

to that at Sun, where pretty much everything Sam Phillips released was recorded by him or his co-workers at his own studio. Much of the more obscure material released by Pappy Daily came to him already recorded, the product of numerous different studios. In this way, however, a fascinating cross-section of rough-and-ready rockabilly material saw the light of day either on label names of the artists' own choosing or on Pappy's Dixie subsidiary, and if the bands proved to be more than usually talented, then they might also appear on Starday itself.

If Sun and Meteor were Memphis through and through, Starday at the outset was very much a Texas outfit. The label was founded by Pappy Daily and Jack Starnes in Houston in 1952 – combining parts of each of their surnames. Pappy had been in the music game in one form or another since 1931, and his credits included production work for the 4 Star label, and discovering the likes of Eddie Noack and also the Maddox Brothers. Having founded Starday, Daily soon bought out Starnes, and then went into partnership with Don Pierce. These two jointly ran the label until 1958, when Daily went off to start his own label, D Records. In the interim, Daily had discovered country star George Jones (whose producer he remained for decades to come), but along the way this operation managed to release some of the best rockabilly around.

Starday moved into the market early, issuing Sonny Fisher's 'Rockin' Daddy' in the spring of 1955. In fact, they'd already put out 'Who Put The Turtle In Myrtle's Girdle' by the Western Melody Makers in June 1954, which was a cover name for Texas rocker Sid King, who later found fame on Columbia with his band the Five Strings. If the latter song was borderline rockabilly, there was no mistaking Sonny Fisher's intent. He released four singles on Starday in 1955 and '56, all of which were full-on examples of the genre, the most perfectly formed of which was arguably 'Pink & Black' (1956), a bass-slapping song of praise to pink Cadillacs, pink-and-black shoes and high-school babies. Equally classic in its way was 'Don't Be Gone Long' (1956) by twenty-four-year-old Bob Doss from Dangerfield, Texas, co-written by Doss and Starday's phenomenal guitarist, Hal Harris. It's difficult to see just how much national airplay they were hoping to gain for a song about holing up in a bedroom with your girlfriend for hours on end, not wanting her to leave for more than a few minutes ('don't be gone long or your dog'll find another bone'), but as rockabilly evocations of unbridled lust go, it's up there with the very best.

Perhaps Bob Doss stood little chance of breaking through to the wider market, yet by the end of that same year, Pappy Daily was even thinking internationally, attempting to bring Texas rockabilly to far-flung places like Australia and Japan. In October 1956 he and Pierce signed a deal with the W&G Record Processing Company in Melbourne to manufacture and distribute from Starday masters in Australia and New Zealand, and another similar deal for Japan and Okinawa. Two months later they entered into a five-year joint agreement with Mercury Records, so Daily was certainly thinking big at that point.

It's tempting to think of hepcats in Shinjuku having the

chance to pick up a copy of downhome gems like Rocky Bill Ford's 'Mad Dog In Town' (1956) and Benny Joy's 'Spin The Bottle'/'Steady With Betty' (1958), or grooving to the berserk guitar solo on Orangie Ray Hubbard's 'Sweet Love' (1957), but in truth, most of these fine records barely left the South, let alone the country. Hubbard, for instance, was from Barbourville, Kentucky, and his big break came as a result of a competition, as he later told Randy McNutt:

> A man came to town from Nashville and staged a talent contest with the local radio station, WBVL. The winner got to cut a record for Dixie records, a subsidiary of Starday. Well, I won. Took 'em a year to put out 'Sweet Love', the record I had cut at the station. It was rockabilly, man. The record went big in my part of the country. I was just a poor country boy who thought it was great to be recognized in his hometown. I was only about nineteen.

That single was one of Starday's package deals – in fact, Orangie Ray Hubbard was on only one side of the single, and the flip went to another artist, David Lundy, whose self-penned tune was listed somewhat eccentrically on the label as 'If I Had A Nickle For Every Time Your Untrue' [sic]. Similarly, J. C. Sawyer's excellent rocker 'Goin' Steppin' (1958) appeared on one side of a Dixie release, with Howard Bingham's 'Baby Love' on the other side. Among the many other incidental highlights of the Starday/Dixie catalogue, there's the infectious sound of

'Sweet Rockin' Mama' by the Hi-Tombs (1960), the lip-curling put-downs of 'You're So Dumb' by Mack Banks & His Drifting Troubadours (1956), and the hillbilly-flavoured barn dance rocker 'The Cats Were Jumpin' by John Worthan (1958). Then there were artists like 'Groovey' Joe Poovey, whose singles 'Move Around' (1958) and the Jerry Lee Lewis-influenced 'Ten Long Fingers' (1959) have long been sought after by collectors, as has the work of Rudi 'Tutti' Grayzell.

Born in Saspamco, Texas, in 1933, Rudi had been cutting rockin' material for Capitol, and had worked with Elvis on the *Louisiana Hayride,* before showing up at Starday in 1956, where he recorded the self-penned haircut hymn 'Duck Tail', along with several other fine rockers. When interviewed in the 1980s by Dan Davidson, Rudy had nothing but praise for his old label boss, and some memorable words about his old pal Elvis and his singular effect on women:

> Pappy was tremendous! A great man. Pappy stood behind me all through the Starday years. He told me, 'Rudy, you've got a message in there somewhere and we're gonna find it!' … Baby, I performed with Elvis for about a year and a half before he became famous. I knew he was great, but I didn't know *how* great! I had a lotta pictures of him and me together but gave most of 'em to chicks. You showed a picture of yourself with Elvis to these dolls and baby, you were IN! Elvis, baby, the chicks were tearin' off their brassieres for him to sign 'em! He was the one who really started callin' me Rudy *Tutti,* so I billed myself that way for a few years.

As mentioned earlier, Starday had locked themselves into a mutually beneficial deal with the much larger Mercury company, and some records such as Rudy Grayzell's 'Let's

Get Wild' (1957) or Sleepy La Beef's wonderful 'All The Time' (1957) appeared on the joint Starday/Mercury label. Pappy Daily sold up his interest in Starday and then formed his own D label, based in Houston, Texas, which began issuing singles in May 1958, among them premium rockabilly material such as Jimmy & Johnny's ultra-tough 'Can't Find The Doorknob' (1958), Les Cole & the Echoes' easy-swingin' 'Be-Boppin' Daddy' (1958) and Dave Edge's rockin' tribute to marital discord, 'Wham Bam' (1959).

HEPCATS ON MERCURY

Mercury Records themselves were one of the big boys, having carved out an impressive reputation in the immediate postwar years. Although based in Chicago, they'd managed to corner a solid slice of the country market, with artists such as the Carlisles and Johnny Horton, so rockabilly was a natural progression for them, and they issued some important examples of the genre. Eddie Bond's version of Sonny Fisher's 'Rockin' Daddy' appeared on Mercury in March 1956, just as Elvis's career was taking off like a rocket, and then one of their regular country artists, Curtis Gordon (a regular star of the *Dixie Barn Dance* on WKAB, Mobile, Alabama), reinvented himself as a full-blown rockabilly wildman with the road-race anthem 'Draggin'' (May 1956), complete with home-made hot-rod noises and some of the best slap-bass of the fifties. Eddie Bond & the Stompers then came back with an even wilder bass-driven monster, 'Slip, Slip, Slippin'-In' (June 1956), a frantic tale of after-hours lovin' that was pure rockabilly all the way down the line. Eddie himself later gave Barry M. Klein his own definition of the music:

Rockabilly is nothing but country, you can't really call

rockabilly 'rock and roll' because it ain't – it's really fast country – if I was going to say that's a fast song, like really and truly the great Hank Williams Sr was doing it when he did 'Move It On Over' and Johnny Horton when he did 'Honky Tonk Man'. All of them certainly were country songs, but they were still considered rockabilly because they were fast country songs.

Mercury went on to issue some fine rockers from Conway Twitty, as well as Dave Diddle Day's cracking 'Blue Moon Baby' (1957, later covered by the Cramps), and scored a rare international rockabilly hit with Jimmy Edward's 'Love Bug Crawl' (1957). One of their very finest was Thomas Wayne's howling stop-start rocker 'You're The One That Done It' (1958). 'Tune is a rockabilly sort,' commented *Billboard*'s reviewer, and how right they were. Wayne's full name was Thomas Wayne Perkins, and he was the brother of Luther Perkins, guitar player in the Tennessee Two for Johnny Cash.

'You're The One That Done It' (which seems to have influenced Allen Page's excellent 'She's The One That's Got It' on Moon Records, recorded later that year) was in fact a pick-up from Memphis indie label Fernwood, which had issued it earlier the same month, and it was probably felt that the record would have a better chance with Mercury's finances and distribution behind it.

DECCA RECORDS – BARKING UP THE RIGHT TREE

There was certainly something to be said for the financial wisdom of signing with a major. Decca, for example, was a big industry player with a history in the US stretching back to 1934, who had already proved with Bill Haley that they knew how to bring rockin' sounds to worldwide attention. Once again, this was a company with a country pedigree – their roster in the year that Elvis first showed up at Sun included Bob Wills and Red Foley – so the move into rockabilly with Roy Hall's 'Whole Lotta Shakin' Goin' On'/'All By Myself' in October 1955 was no great stretch. Roy's version of 'Whole Lotta Shakin', although not the original, predated Jerry Lee Lewis's definitive take on the song by nearly two years. Born in Big Stone Gap, Virginia, in 1922, Hall had hillbilly and country credentials dating back a fair few years when he made the successful transition to rockabilly, as *Billboard* noted: 'Webb Pierce's pianist takes a stab in the vocal field and shows a highly distinctive, flavorsome voice, showcased in two rock'n'roll type entries.'

Seemingly encouraged by the response, in 1956 Roy covered 'See You Later Alligator' and 'Blue Suede Shoes', but really hit the rockabilly jackpot with another single 'Three Alley Cats'/'Diggin' The Boogie' (September 1956); the former song being a magnificent exercise in hipster jive-speak,

BUDDY HOLLY & THE CRICKETS   MCA RECORDS

powered along by a rock-solid snare drum. I first encountered Roy Hall's recordings in 1976 when I found a copy of the groundbreaking compilation album *Rare Rockabilly Volume One*. I'd been buying fifties rock'n'roll for several years, but this was the first time I'd ever bought an album with the word 'rockabilly' in the title. As I soon found out, there'd been enough great rockabilly issued on US Decca in the 1950s to make a superb twenty-track album, and the series continued for three more very useful volumes over the next couple of years.

Highlights of Decca's rockin' output included Don Woody's exuberant 'You're Barking Up The Wrong Tree' (1956), featuring razor-sharp guitar work and some of the finest dog imitations on record (although he's run a close second by hillbilly veteran Rex Allen's 1958 Decca release, 'Knock Knock Rattle'). Woody left in the can the excellent 'Make Like A Rock And Roll' and 'Morse Code', both of which surely deserved a release at the time. Jackie Lee Cochran's blistering 'Mama Don't You Think I Know' (1957), with Jimmy Pruett whipping hell out of the piano, could easily have been the Hillbilly Cat himself, and the label also issued three top-notch singles by Texas wildman Johnny Carroll, cut at Jack Tiger's studio in Dallas in 1956. Of course, the most successful Texas rockabilly of them all, Buddy Holly, had all of his records issued on Decca, or on its subsidiaries Coral and Brunswick, including rockabilly classics such as 'Blue Days – Black Nights' (1956) and 'Rock Around With Ollie Vee' (1957).

Among the other sought-after rockabilly tracks issued on the label are those by a former school friend of Buddy Holly's, Terry Noland (born Terry Nolan Church in Abilene, Texas, in 1938), in particular his debut for the label, 'Ten Little Women'/'Hypnotised' (1957). Terry was one more teenage rocker who'd been blown away by an early Elvis gig, as he told Howard Cockburn and Trevor Cajiao:

> One day Elvis Presley came to town and my older brother, Bob Church, he said 'Hey! There's someone I want you to see'. So we went up to where Elvis Presley was appearing that afternoon, at the Pontiac House, and I sat on his pink Cadillac and watched him perform. And, y'know, that was just what I wanted to do. I was about sixteen or seventeen then.

The Holly connection went deeper than just school. Terry Noland was managed by Holly's own manager and producer, Norman Petty, and recorded his debut single at Petty's studio in Clovis, New Mexico. 'Hypnotised' was covered by The Drifters, while 'Ten Little Women' was then recorded by Vegas lounge king Louis Prima. In writing the latter song, with its talk of 'ten little women all in a row, all of them hollerin' Go Daddy-O!', Terry was very much in the rockabilly tradition of one-man-and-his-harem songs. Other notable examples include Link Davis's 'Sixteen Chicks' (1956), Jerry Irby's 'Forty Nine Women' (circa 1956), which helpfully points out that 'you can lose five women and still have forty-four', and the even more ambitious '99 Chicks' by Ron Haydock & the Boppers (1959).

One of the best loved of all the Decca rockabilly singles is the 1957 recording 'Cast Iron Arm', which was issued on the Brunswick subsidiary. The singer was Johnny 'Peanuts' Wilson, the former guitarist in Roy Orbison's Teen Kings, and the song, co-written by Orbison, was a humorous tale of a guy with a popular girlfriend and a mean left hook, in which the music comes to a dramatic halt so that the diminutive

Wilson can tell the listeners how he walloped a rival in the head. Briefly released in the UK, that particular pressing has long been one of the rarest rockers of the 1950s.

COLUMBIA RECORDS – AIN'T I'M A DOG

Another of the major labels which successfully joined the rockabilly business was Columbia, both on its main imprint and also through its subsidiaries Epic and Okeh. Yet again, its output in the field was so extensive that it was the subject of an early series of rockabilly reissue albums in the 1970s, commencing with *CBS Rockabilly Classics Volume One* in 1977. Columbia had long been issuing hillbilly and country recordings, and began to move into the new market very early on with the likes of 'Rock Me' by Little Jimmy Dickens (January 1954) or western swing veteran Leon McAuliff's cover of 'Sh-Boom (Life Could Be A Dream)' (August 1954). The following year they were right in the middle of the action, with a young Texan rockin' band of their own, Sid King & the Five Strings, not to mention Rose Maddox singing 'Wild, Wild Young Men', and country star Marty Robbins covering 'That's All Right'. By the end of that year, they'd latched on to teenage rockabilly sensations The Collins Kids, and from then on the company unleashed a phenomenal string of outright rockin' classics. There was Jimmy Murphy, from Republic, Alabama, who seemed to be attempting to beat his acoustic guitar into submission by sheer force of will on singles like 'Sixteen Tons Rock'n'Roll' (1956), and *Town Hall Party* regular Freddie Hart, who brought a similar nervous intensity to 'Dig, Boy, Dig' and 'Snatch It And Grab It' (both 1956). Freddie and Jimmie sounded positively relaxed, however, when lined up next to Cliff Johnson's full-on performance of his own 'Go 'Way Hound Dog' (1957), two minutes and seven seconds of what *Billboard* called 'rockabilly that professes satiation with rockabilly music'. Cliff's music career had already lasted three decades by this point, but he certainly delivered the goods here.

Ever since the King Of Western Bop started singing about hound dawgs, the rockabilly world had been awash with records about canines, or people who behaved like them. A fine entry on Columbia was the 1957 recording 'Ain't I'm A Dog' by 'Mr

Ronnie Self onstage at WRNL, Virginia

Frantic', Ronnie Self. He had already delivered a great single that year, 'Big Fool', but reached true rockabilly immortality with his 1958 recording 'Bop-a-Lena', a one-hundred-mile-an-hour rampage through most current words in the teen language, set against a band who appear to be racing each other to the finish line. If you're looking for frantic, it really doesn't get much more frantic than this. Ronnie left a fair few songs in the vaults, including choice items such as 'Beat Broke & Blue', 'Waitin' For The Gin To Hit Me', 'Ugly Stick', 'Hair Of The Dog' and 'Go Go Cannibal'. Columbia was running adverts at the time telling record retailers that 'Ronnie's got an ever growing and devoted following who'll be snapping these showcase numbers up like fresh doughnuts'. He deserved nothing less. Born in Tin Town, Missouri, Ronnie died in 1981, aged forty-three, after a hard life of serious drinking and a near-fatal wreck, but his records have sure as hell outlived any amount of doughnuts.

On the face of it, Ronnie Self did a lot better than most, spending time at two majors (Columbia, then Decca), reaching the lower end of the national charts with 'Bop-A-Lena', and even seeing records issued in Germany on the Phillips label in 1958. Yet whether you were on a one-off custom label of your own as part of Starday's package deals, or given the backing of a large company, the real message was in the grooves, and most of those who recorded the songs went back to their day jobs shortly afterwards, perhaps with the bonus of being tracked down and rediscovered by European collectors several decades later.

7 IT CAME FROM THE GARAGE

FROM CHEAP STOREFRONT RECORDING STUDIOS TO THE CAPITOL TOWER

Whether you were dodging the flying bottles when playing local juke joints, tearing it up on TV shows like the *Town Hall Party*, or knocking them dead at the drive-in, you still needed to cut some wax. Just how and *where* you could do this was the question.

Back in the 1920s, Ralph Peer was able to set up his portable equipment in hotels and warehouses and record the likes of the Carter Family straight to disc, completely live and with no possibility of overdubbing. The essential process hadn't really changed much in the intervening years, except for one major innovation – reel-to-reel magnetic tape recorders. These had begun to come into use in the late 1940s, with Bing Crosby an early champion of the technology. Over in England, future rock'n'roll producer Joe Meek astounded his friends as a schoolboy around 1950 by building his own tape recorder from scratch. By the time Sam Phillips founded Sun Records at the start of the fifties, tape machines were a vital part of his equipment, and the way was clear for him and many other like him all over the South to set themselves up in all kinds of makeshift rooms, recording the wealth of upcoming rockabilly talent that would appear in the wake of Elvis. As Phillips later told Escott and Hawkins:

> I had a Presto portable tape recorder, a PT 900 … Before that I had a Crestwood tape recorder, a little amateur thing. The second one I got at the same time was a Bell recorder. The Bell was in a red case and the Crestwood was in a beige case. I'll never forget them. I was real proud to get the Presto. Man, that was big-time for me!

A report in *Billboard* on 16 February 1956, headlined 'Tape Recorder Sales Jumped 50% in '55', tracked the spread of this technology, and noted that the 'greatest percentage increase was racked up by higher priced units'. Clearly, people weren't just buying them for their own amusement – some, like Sam, were trying to use them to make a living.

Take the example of motel owner, songwriter, former bluegrass musician and sometime moonshine-distiller Jack Rhodes, who bought himself a Magnacord tape machine and a microphone in the early 1950s, and set up a demo studio in a couple of rooms behind the kitchens at his Trail '80' Courts motel in the hamlet of Mineola, Texas, to record local talent. Jack was a fine songwriter, who'd go on to write 'Woman Love' (1956) for Gene Vincent (the B-side of 'Be Bop A Lula'), not to mention country standards like 'Silver Threads & Golden Needles', and he wasn't the only musical talent in the family – his stepbrother Leon Payne wrote and sang the original versions of 'Lost Highway' (1948) and 'I Love You Because' (1949). Encouraged by the success of having a song he'd written on one side of an early Jim Reeves hit in 1953, Jack went on to pitch songs at a variety of labels, eventually making a good connection with Capitol Records' key A&R man, Ken Nelson.

Much of what Jack wrote was then cut by Ken in Nashville and at the Capitol Tower in Hollywood, but the remarkable thing is just what a superb rockabilly sound Jack was getting when he demoed those songs with local musicians in that little space behind his motel in Texas. Quite simply, these excellent recordings, made on minimal equipment in the sparsest of settings, capture the rockabilly spirit in a way that few have equalled either then or since. Nearly all of Jack's demos remained unissued until 2004, when Ace Records compiled a selection of them on a CD entitled *Gene Vincent Cut Our Songs*. Freddy Franks can be heard singing 'Red Blue Jeans & A Pony Tail' and a version of Carl Perkins' 'Everybody's Trying To Be My Baby' with a slapping double bass a sole accompaniment, and the results are magnificent. The same can be said for Johnny Dollar's original demo of the song 'Action Packed', and his very fine 'Lovin' Up A Storm', to name just a couple of the artists captured by Rhodes on these intimate but fully rounded recordings.

MEANWHILE, BACK IN THE JUNGLE

A similarly warm and high-quality sound was achieved in a garage in Chicago the day that Hank Mizell laid down his phenomenal 'Jungle Rock' (1958) – destined to become one of the rockabilly genre's only true international hit records (albeit two decades after its original release). Gene Parsons, who ran a tiny local label called Eko, recorded the session in the garage of his house, and Hank stuffed paper into his guitar in order to achieve the desired sound. The results were astonishingly full and powerful, and even *Billboard*'s reviewer – well used to evaluating the results emanating from far more expensive set-ups – complimented the production in their 10 November 1958 edition: 'A persistent jungle blues item would make a good swingin' dance fare. It's all about the jungle denizens doing the rock. Good sound and rhythm.'

That something so simple yet so gutsy could wind up on BBC1's flagship *Top of the Pops* programme in 1976, with dance group Pan's People strutting their stuff along to a twenty-year-old monaural downhome rockabilly track, is one of life's more pleasant surprises. Someone tracked down ol' Hank to tell him he was up there in the UK Top Five, fighting it out with the likes of 'Fernando' by Abba and 'Save Your Kisses For Me' by the Brotherhood of Man, and found that he was currently working – you've guessed it – in a garage.

Stuffing your guitar full of paper was one thing, but what if, as a performer, you took hold of the studio controls yourself and threw all the normal procedures right out of the window? In the summer of 1958, Jerry Lott (aka Marty Lott, aka The Phantom) showed up with his band and his manager at Gulf Coast Studios, in Mobile, Alabama, and proceeded to tear up the rulebook, recording a stone-cold masterpiece of rockabilly mayhem entitled 'Love Me'. As he later told Derek Glenister:

> The song was wild, I'm tellin' ya. I was runnin' around clappin' my hands, screamin', 'Let's go'… the drummer lost one of his drum sticks… the piano player screamed and stood up and knocked his stool over… the guitar

player's glasses were hangin' sideways over his eyes, he looked like he was hypnotised!

Jerry had booked the date in order to record a far more conventional tune, 'Whisper Your Love', unmindful of the fact that you need two songs to make a single:

I hadn't even thought about what I was going to put on the other side! It wasn't any problem at all... I put all the fire and fury into it that I could utter... and I wrote 'Love Me' in about ten minutes. Me and Johnny Blackburn (my manager) worked the controls in the studio, as we didn't want it to sound like a commercial record, that was for sure!

Jerry recalled that his manager then sat on the tapes for over a year, without securing a release, so that Jerry himself got hold of the masters and caught a Greyhound bus all the way to Hollywood in search of a deal. He wound up convincing Pat Boone, of all people, to help him get a deal with Dot Records, a well-funded subsidiary of Paramount Pictures Corporation. Hence one of the most berserk records ever cut in a studio during the 1950s finally saw a release in early 1960, when the prevailing trend was for saccharine-sweet teen idols, all because the man who'd made a mint singing watered-down covers of Little Richard records thought it was a solid-gone smash. Pat even came up with a promotional gimmick: Jerry would be renamed The Phantom, and wear a mask at all times. Thus, the record was listed in full-page trade adverts taken out by Dot in the spring of 1960, right alongside other new singles they had to offer, including 'Am I That Easy To Forget' by Debbie Reynolds and 'Summer Set' by Lawrence Welk. 'The Nation's Best Selling Records', ran the tagline. If only it had been true in Jerry's case. 'A wild vocal which attempts to outdo Presley at the latter's wildest. Sleeve shows The Phantom with a blindfold over his eyes,' said *Billboard* on 29 February. They didn't know the half of it.

Jerry Lott had kicked off his only record with a blood-curdling, distorted scream, which then led into the full-on attack of a band seemingly bent on destroying their instruments in the shortest time possible. In a parallel universe, it should have been a Top Ten smash, and certainly demonstrated one of the great truths of recording rockabilly music (or any other kind of music worth the name, for that matter): spirit is everything. As Sam Phillips, the absolute master of capturing world-class rockabilly on tape, told Martin Hawkins in 1982:

> It has an awful lot to do with the atmosphere under which the artist is working ... You have to have a good song, of course, but atmosphere is nearly everything else ... Generally I didn't go for overdubbing. Still don't, even if they get 94 tracks. I understand all the techniques and all the bullshit but I just don't see the spontaneity. I'm not trying to go back in time and I don't say that you shouldn't overdub the occasional instrument. Sure. I'm not against improvement or new techniques but I feel that you can have too many crutches, too many shots, too many opportunities ... Today I see and hear too much of the lack of the real soul that has to come with knowing 'This is it'. I like the originals, I like things that I know are there because somebody feels, 'I can do it. It might take one take, or four, or whatever, but I can do it myself, *right here and now.*'

These words ought to be nailed up prominently in every recording studio across the planet. Sam was speaking at the

Hasil Adkins

outset of one of the most dismal, technology-obsessed decades the music business has ever seen, when in many cases all the instrumental sounds on a record, including drums, weren't played any more, but faked on a keyboard. For the whole history of recorded music, ever since the Edison wax cylinders of the late nineteenth century, the main process had involved capturing a live performance in a studio, but by the 1980s you could mostly counterfeit anything, and it showed. It wasn't so much about the performance, more a matter of computer programming, which is fine if you want to be Kraftwerk, but a disaster if you're trying for some rock'n'roll.

THE *WILD* SIDE OF LIFE

Of course, if you take the feeling-over-technology approach to extremes, you may well find that most record labels will refuse to have anything to do with you, which was for a long time the fate of legendary Madison, West Virginia wildman Hasil Adkins. In the late 1950s and on through the '60s, he pitched his self-written, home-recorded blasts of rockabilly mayhem like 'I Wanna Kiss Kiss Kiss Your Lips' and 'The Hunch' at any and every company he could think of, but the response was generally along the same lines as this 1961 formula letter from long-time Capitol Records producer Ken Nelson: 'We are sorry … that we cannot find a place for you in our talent roster. We appreciate your interest in Capitol Records.'

Hasil would have to wait decades for recognition: The Cramps covered his song 'She Said' in 1981 (on the B-side of their single 'Goo Goo Muck'), stirring considerable interest, and then in 1986 Billy Miller and Miriam Linna formed Norton Records specifically so that they could release Hasil's 'Out To Hunch' LP. Other hollering wildmen of the 1950s were luckier, such as Gene Maltais, who cut his double-sided monster 'The Raging Sea'/'Gangwar' (1958) in the front room of a TV soundman in Manchester, New Hampshire, on an Ampex portable tape recorder. Backed by the Gibson String Band – his regular crew when playing gigs at a local joint called the Riverside Boat Club – Gene gave it all he'd got, the vocal distorting off the scale as he screamed his way through the chorus. He'd cut a couple of rockabilly singles before, including one for Decca in '57, on which he was backed by the Anita Kerr Singers, but this was in a whole different league – a live-to-tape experience that's the next best thing to having Gene and the boys parked in front of your sofa and howling. They barely pressed enough copies of 'The Raging Sea', released on his own Lilac label, to cover the local area, but if you're looking for primal, front-room rockabilly that jumps right out of the grooves, this is a good place to start.

The majority of rockabilly recordings of the 1950s sound so fresh and gutsy precisely because they were cut in a limited time, in small spaces, with the band all crowded together, and everyone trying to just get down and *wail*. They were putting on a show, just as they'd usually done every night of the week at juke joints, school hops or store openings. The only difference was that this time the show was for the engineer (and maybe a few friends who'd dropped by the studio to watch), but the teenage band were usually seasoned performers who'd been learning their craft at gigs and on local radio for anything up to a decade before cutting their debut disc. Any musician will confirm that nothing sharpens you up like playing numerous gigs, and many of these one-off singles recorded by bands that came out of nowhere display remarkable musicianship and a real sense of a band gelling together organically, because of all those years they'd already put in on the bandstand. Compare that, for instance, to the situation in the 1990s, when some indie bands found themselves signed after playing just three or four gigs, and would cut a single right away for a major label. Small wonder they might rely on every piece of studio trickery to 'fix' the parts of their recordings that didn't work, or just build the whole three-minute track as a laborious construction, layer upon layer, in a process taking months.

As a deejay in the UK, John Peel championed new music and new bands for four decades, but throughout his time at Radio 1, he insisted that if you wanted to record a session for his show, you had to come in to the BBC Maida Vale studios and cut four or five tracks pretty much live in one afternoon, with a break for tea, then a couple of hours to mix it all down. There's no room to hide in a schedule like that, and if your records relied on months of studio fakery rather than performance, then there wasn't much point in showing up, and John probably wouldn't have asked you anyway. For John, as for Sam Phillips, it was the performance which counted – something indefinable which a particular artist had that set them apart, and how they put it across – and it's no coincidence that when the first high-profile gig of the 1970s rockabilly revival took place in London (a stellar line-up of Charlie Feathers, Warren Smith, Jack Scott and Buddy Knox at the Rainbow, Finsbury Park, on 30 April 1977), John called them all in four days later to record a Peel Session.

AGAINST THE GRAIN – LEE HAZLEWOOD

The business of capturing that elusive sound on tape, the excitement and the sheer guts of an electric guitar turned up loud, was something which occupied the minds of many of the mavericks drawn into the business during the Elvis Sun era. One such was future star Lee Hazlewood, who'd been working as an early-morning deejay at KTYL in Mesa, Arizona, and in 1956 began writing and producing rockabilly records. Lee started his own small record label at this time, called Viv, releasing singles such as 'How About Me Pretty Baby' by Jimmy Johnson with Al Casey & the Arizona Hayriders – a fine rockin' track that moves along to a 'Mystery Train'-style rhythm – but he really hit paydirt with a record called 'The Fool' by Sanford Clark. Both of these singles appeared in the early summer of 1956, produced by Lee, and also written by him under his wife's name, in case the radio station employers objected to one of their deejays playing their own record. Reviewing 'The Fool', *Billboard* commented that 'with proper exposure, this might catch on', and catch on it did, being picked up at once and reissued by the Dot label, climbing right up the charts to become a genuine national hit. Not bad for something cooked up behind a barber shop in Phoenix, Arizona, in a tiny studio called Ramsey Recording, whose console was so small that its dust cover was a cigar box. Hazlewood later told Rob Finnis about the session that produced his first hit:

> Connie Conway played 'drums' with one brush that we found in the studio, and a Campbell's tomato soup box over a drum stool ... but [it took] nearly three weeks, on and off, to get Sanford's voice on it. It wasn't his fault, it was just me trying to get a sound on it, 'cause we didn't have echo chambers so we tried all kind of combinations

of 7½ and 15ips tape echo on little machines, stretching them and plugging them into each other 'till we got something like I wanted it.

Lee Hazlewood, together with his guitar buddy Al Casey, was behind another low-budget rockabilly classic the following year, the storming 'Snake Eyed Mama' by Don Cole, in which the piano break is introduced by a delirious yell of 'Take off your gloves and *play*', but Lee really found a gold mine in 1958 when he locked into a string of worldwide hits with Duane Eddy. In the light of his problems achieving the right kind of echo effect when making 'The Fool', and unable to convince the studio owner to invest in any new equipment, Lee took inspiration from the farms in the neighbourhood. He spent some time shouting down the tops of a selection of large empty grain silos, finally paying two hundred dollars for the one that produced the correct echo, and then set it up in the car park by the studio, with a speaker at one end to relay the sound and a cheap microphone at the other. Hey presto, a full-bodied, cavernous echo to complement the twang of Duane Eddy's guitar.

A JACK TO A KING

Up at Syd Nathan's King Records studio in Cincinnati (where rockabilly classics by Mac Curtis and Charlie Feathers were cut), the natural sound of the room itself greatly aided the recording process, as King's star A&R man Henry Glover told Rob Finnis:

It had a very high ceiling, maybe 24 feet, and the control room protruded into the studio in a V-shape like the bridge of a ship so the engineer could see in front and to the side of him … Everything was done at one time, there was no multi-tracking; you would continue making cuts until you got every instrument, every voice, on the ¼ inch tape and that was considered your final mix … The drum sound in those days was generally gotten by releasing the snares completely and you'd put a heavy object like the drummer's wallet – or Syd Nathan's wallet – on the snare and the really hard-driving backbeat was actually a rimshot.

If you were working with a room that didn't have much in the way of natural ambience, you relied very heavily on echo, and the most famous type to emerge from those days was the 'slap-back' tape-echo effect developed by Sam Phillips at Sun, for use in his own modestly-proportioned studio. Sam's place was tiny, but his genius in selectively using echo and in knowing where to place the handful of microphones enabled him to create a sound that half the nation's studio engineers were trying to copy by 1956.

GET A ROOM

Small-room studios, with everyone gathered around just barely avoiding knocking into each other, certainly helped shape the essential rockabilly sound of the 1950s, but it's not as if good results weren't achieved in some of the larger places too. Gene Vincent & the Blue Caps still turned in blistering performances once their sessions had moved from the smaller confines of Owen Bradley's studio on 16th Avenue South in Nashville in 1956 to the larger spaces of Capitol's newly built home studio on North Vine Street in Hollywood, at the Capitol Tower, from June 1957 onwards, but the former location was probably more suited to capturing the rockabilly sound.

The Screamin' End –
Gene Vincent

Owen Bradley had been recording country acts like Red Foley at the Tulane Hotel in Nashville, but when that was torn down, he opened his own studios early in 1955 on what later became Music Row. Much has been written about Owen recording acts in his prefabricated 'Quonset hut' studio; the kind of huts originally developed during the Second World War for use by the US Navy, inspired by the Nissen huts used in Britain. These buildings found many uses after the war – a 1946 edition of *Billboard* informed readers that a 40 × 100 foot Quonset hut would be used as a hog barn at Michigan's Kalamazoo Free Fair – but while it's tempting to imagine a parade of 1955–56 rockabilly talent going hog wild in a similar building, in fact Gene and most of the others Bradley recorded that year actually did their sessions in Bradley's main studio building on 16th Avenue South, not in the quonset hut behind it. Not only did Gene and the Caps cut their wildest sides at Bradley's – everything from the million-selling 'Be Bop A Lula' to flat-out screamers like 'Pink Thunderbird', all featuring the awesome guitar playing of Cliff Gallup – but this was also the place where Buddy Holly recorded his magnificent debut single, 'Blue Days Black Nights' (1956), and where the likes of Johnny Carroll, Johnny Horton and Roy Hall laid down rockabilly tracks. Brenda Lee certainly cut sessions at the Quonset hut, but Don Woody, the man who wrote her rockabilly belter 'Bigelow 6-200' (1956), recorded his excellent Decca sides such as 'Morse Code' (1956) and 'Barking Up The Wrong Tree' (1956) in the same studio as Gene had used.

In moving to Captiol's new studio at the Capitol Tower, Gene Vincent found himself in a larger venue which had been purpose-built to accommodate a whole orchestra (just as the main rooms at London's Abbey Road had been when that studio complex opened in 1931). The Tower opened in 1956, and its studios boasted special underground concrete echo chambers designed by Les Paul, which had been sunk thirty feet below ground level, giving a rich, controllable reverb. Nevertheless, the space was designed more with Capitol star Frank Sinatra than any of the upcoming rockabilly generation in mind. It was here that Sinatra recorded albums such as *Frank Sinatra Sings For Only The Lonely* (1958), featuring the lush string arrangements of Nelson Riddle, but in that same year the studio also hosted sessions by Wanda Jackson, when she cut rockabilly classics like 'Let's Have A Party' and 'Mean Mean Man'. She can be seen in the Capitol studio recording the former song on the cover of Ace Records' fine compilation *Queen Of Rockabilly* (2000), with upright bass player and rockabilly singer Skeets McDonald in the background. 'I was just rehearsing at that point,' Wanda told me when I showed her the picture, 'so I was probably walking around showing them the songs.' Pointing to her own guitar in the picture, with her name painted on it, she said, 'That guitar has become kind of famous, too, in its own right, and I still have it, and it still sounds *wonderful*. I had new strings put on it recently, and it sounds so good. I promised the Hall of Fame I'd let 'em have it *if...*' (At the time of the interview, Wanda had just been nominated for the Rock'n'Roll Hall of Fame. In 2009, she was duly elected.)

Aside from Skeets McDonald, someone else who backed Wanda on some of those early sessions with producer Ken Nelson at the Capitol Tower was sometime rockabilly and future country star Buck Owens, who made one important contribution to the recording process which Wanda still remembers:

> He played rhythm guitar most of the time. Buck is very special with me because of those early days. I was singing 'Silver Threads And Golden Needles', probably at my first session, but I don't remember. Ken Nelson was stopping me, he was wanting something, 'smooth out that line', you know, or something, and I was getting really frustrated, 'cause I didn't know what he meant and it wasn't the way I was feeling it. And I walked over to Buck and I said, 'Buck, what do you think about this song?' He said, 'I think it sounds like Wanda Jackson.' And that's all it took. I said, 'Ken, this is the way I'm doing the song' [laughs].

Which is really all the advice you need, as Sam Phillips said in the earlier quote. A studio will get you so far, and so will musical ability, but in the end it just comes down to that feeling: 'I can do it. It might take one take, or four, or whatever, but I can do it myself, *right here and now.*'

8 BOUND FOR GLORY

THE EARLY ROCKABILLIES WHO BROKE INTO THE BIG TIME

If you were looking to reach the national US charts with a pure-bred rockabilly record, 1956 was almost the only year in which you were likely to succeed. This was a brief interlude when the major record labels hadn't a clue why Elvis was successful but they all wanted a piece of the action, just as the record industry was to scrabble around desperately for a short while in 1963 signing up almost any guitarist with a Liverpool accent, and did it all over again in 1977 chasing bargain-bin Johnny Rotten impersonators.

Still, even a headless chicken with a chequebook is going to get it right some of the time, and the upside of all this confusion among the majors was that some genuinely wild performers were caught in the net. Two years later such rockers would have been told to go away and come back when they looked a little more like a matinee idol and sounded a lot less Southern and a hell of a lot less wild. In 1956, however, all bets were off, and so the likes of Eddie Cochran, the Johnny Burnette Trio and Gene Vincent all wound up with major-label deals, and Carl Perkins, the son of dirt-poor Tennessee sharecroppers, found himself with a number 1 record in the pop, R&B and country

charts. In fact when Elvis's label RCA saw Carl's self-penned, downhome rockabilly original, 'Blue Suede Shoes', start selling relentlessly in all three available markets, they wondered whether they'd signed the wrong guy.

Life magazine – a mainstream publication aimed squarely at adults rather than teenage rock'n'roll fans, which at its peak had a print run of 8,500,000 copies per issue – made a lengthy pictorial assessment of the situation in August 1956, by which time The Hillbilly Cat's 'Heartbreak Hotel', and his *Ed Sullivan* appearances, had changed the landscape for ever. This was significant, if only because even major rock'n'roll stars hardly ever merited a passing mention in that publication during the 1950s, so it works as a useful test of how conservative, adult society apparently viewed the new music at the time. In an article entitled 'Elvis – a Different Kind of Idol', *Life* printed superb black & white shots of Presley onstage in Jacksonville, Florida, together with others showing what they termed his 'mimics and critics'. An action shot of Capitol Records' new signing was captioned 'Closest facsimile of Presley is shouter Gene Vincent who recorded the fast-selling "Be-Bop-A-Lula"', while an onstage shot of Sun's new hit-maker playing his guitar was captioned, 'Strongest rival of Elvis in his field is Carl Perkins, 23, whose "Blue Suede Shoes" was a best seller'.

Yet the urge to make fun of the new phenomenon was ever

present, and space was given to pictures of a hostile journalist posing with a guitar and wearing a tatty mop on his head as a wig, a Seattle deejay playing 'Hound Dog' to the bemused canine inmates of a local dog pound, and some entries in a letter-writing competition run by Boston deejay Norm Prescott, offering genuine hairs taken from the King's sideburns in New York, 'where their removal from Elvis was witnessed by a notary public'. One winning entry read, in its entirety: 'Dear Sir, I would like some Elvis Presley hair because I'm bald.'

The article concluded with pictures showing Florida religious groups listening to sermons on 'Hotrods, Reefers and Rock'n'Roll' – which sounds more like a call to arms than a warning – and of well-groomed kids praying for Elvis's soul: 'teenagers in front rows led in prayer that salvation be granted him'. Clearly, it was open season on Elvis by this stage. Meanwhile, record company executives across the US were also praying – that they could find someone just like him, and quickly.

Yet contrast the attitude shown above towards rock'n'roll with that handed out by the same magazine a couple of months later in a lengthy profile of country music and the *Grand Ole Opry*, which gave it a full measure of respect, with no hint of an adverse comment: 'Today hillbilly music, dolled up with the new name of "country music," draws all classes of listeners. This year some 50 million country music records will be sold, which is 40% of the total sales of all single popular music records.'

Essentially an extended article about the *Opry*, it admiringly quotes some Hank Williams lyrics, while the photos include fine portraits of Roy Acuff, Little Jimmie Dickens, Hank Snow, June Carter, Webb Pierce, Marty Robbins, Ray Price and other WSM regulars. There's even a group shot of almost the entire cast of the show, lined up on the stage of the Ryman Auditorium, in

which the likes of Jim Reeves, Faron Young, Kitty Wells, Ferlin Husky and Ernest Tubb surround the *Opry*'s veteran announcer, 'Judge' George Hay. Yet a further examination of this and other illustrations reveals a reasonable amount of rockabilly crossover, just as the *Billboard* C&W listings that year included a fair few rockabilly singles. In particular, standing among all the other stars at the Ryman, was a man who was a year into his contract with Sun Records and whose new single, 'Train Of Love'/'There You Go', appeared that same month – Johnny Cash.

Cash was proud to refer to himself as a Memphis rockabilly in his 1997 autobiography, and certainly lined up with the rock'n'rollers in a year when the country music establishment was running scared, very much threatened by the rise of rock. Despite the confident tone of this article, a solid portion of the record sales boasted of in that earlier quote would have been those of Elvis, who'd had nine records in the *Billboard* C&W Top Twenty that year, and by 1957 many established country stars were tentatively trying to record in the rock'n'roll style in an effort to get in on the act. In truth, as detailed in earlier chapters, there wasn't a whole lot of distance between the two types of music, and even the description given by *Life*'s writers – 'the first earmark of country music is a strong, contagious beat, accented by slapping the bass strings' – is as near as damn it a definition of rockabilly. Yet country was deemed respectable in these quarters, while anything suspected of being rock was apparently juvenile, a threat and probably in need of religious intervention.

TEAR IT UP – THE ROCK'N'ROLL TRIO

Still, in 1956 Elvis was hotter than a pistol, and anyone who looked or halfway sounded like him was in there with a chance. Impersonating the King was a start, but having grown up with him was even better. It certainly didn't hurt Johnny Burnette & the Rock'n'Roll Trio. When interviewing the band during one of their triumphant appearances in the summer of '56 on the *Ted Mack Amateur Hour* TV show, shortly after they'd recorded their album, the host was careful to mention the fact that they'd originally 'driven up from Memphis in an old jalopy', and that guitarist Paul Burlison had previously worked alongside Elvis:

MACK: You know several of our contestants have said, coming from Memphis, they knew Elvis Presley. Did you boys know him?

BURLISON: I knew him, Mr Mack. I used to work with him at Crown Electric Company, Memphis, Tennessee.

MACK: Is that so? What'd you do with him?

BURLISON: Well, I did electric work, and he did the truck driving.

MACK: What kind of truck driver was he?

BURLISON: Oh, he was a good truck driver, but always had his hair real long. Always needed a haircut.

MACK (laughing): Oh now, c'mon, he ain't gonna like that...

Reviewing their double-sided killer 'The Train Kept A-Rollin'/'Honey Hush' on 13 October 1956, *Billboard* praised the 'lively, uninhibited warbling in the Presley groove by Burnette, with solid guitar backing'. Burnette's Trio had lately been getting exposure touring on a rock'n'roll package in August which also included another artist who was being described as a potential new Presley: Gene Vincent.

WILD CAT

Interviewed in 1957 in Vancouver by deejay Red Robinson, Gene recalled that Capitol Records had run a contest the previous year to find a new Presley, and out of 250 entrants, 234 sang Elvis songs. Gene had won singing a song of his own, which would shortly send him right to the top.

Back in June, *Billboard*'s reviewers had initially devoted more attention to the tune on the other side of Gene's debut single, entitled 'Woman Love' (written by Jack Rhodes in his back room at the Trail '80' motel), but they were in no doubt about whose influence was in evidence: 'Gene Vincent is Cap's entry in the general scramble to find another Presley. This side is a blues, in the extreme high-tension style popular currently.'

As for the other side, they merely commented: 'Another blues in the same extreme style – this one additionally gimmicked with echo.' The gimmick obviously worked. The song was the one that had landed Gene his record deal, 'Be Bop A Lula', and two weeks later they were highlighting it as one of the week's best buys, saying 'not many of those trying to move in on the money-making tracks of Elvis Presley are succeeding. Vincent is a notable exception'. By August, 'Be Bop A Lula' was up there in the Top Twenty with the likes of 'Hound Dog' and 'Don't Be Cruel'. As for how to categorise Gene, it's interesting to note that the same magazine the following year mentioned his manager Ed McLemore as handling Gene, Sonny James, Buddy Knox, Jimmy Bowen 'and other rockabilly artists'. In fact, in Gene's last-ever interview, given in 1971 to David Simmonds at Radio London just a few weeks before his death, he was particular about the terminology: 'What *you* call rock'n'roll, we called rockabilly then.'

Gene had a pretty good run at it for a couple of years, with most of his releases getting national attention, despite the fact that he was increasingly surrounded by a chart scene that favoured dull-as-ditchwater pretty boys over his and the Blue Caps' street-gang menace. For Carl Perkins, though, the big time was almost over before it had properly started, owing to the disastrous 1956 car crash in which he and his band were involved on the way to promote 'Blue Suede Shoes' on the Perry Como TV show. Carl had been riding the crest of a remarkable hit, as *Billboard* commented on 16 February 1956, in the review section 'This Week's Best Buys in Country & Western Records':

> Difficult as the country field is for a newcomer to 'crack' these days, Perkins has come up with some wax here that has hit the national retail chart in almost record time. New Orleans, Memphis, Nashville, Richmond, Durham and other areas report it a leading seller. Interestingly enough, the disk has a large measure of appeal for pop and r.&b. customers. Flip is 'Honey Don't'.

That spring, just as things turned horribly from good to bad for Carl Perkins, several other contenders were coming through. Texas rockabilly outfit Roy Orbison and the Teen Kings laid down a string of outstanding tracks for Sam Phillips at the Sun studio during March and April, including 'Ooby Dooby', 'Go Go Go' (aka 'Down The Line'), 'You're My Baby', 'Rockhouse' and 'Domino'. Meanwhile, down in Dallas on 26 April, Johnny Carroll and his Hot Rocks recorded 'Hot Rock' and 'Wild Wild Women' for US Decca at Jack Tiger's studios, and over at RCA, Janis Martin, billed by the label as 'The Female Elvis', released 'Drugstore Rock'n'Roll'/'Will You Willyum'. On 11 May, Janis cut a new song in New York called, pointedly, 'My Boy Elvis'.

Of these, Roy Orbison was to score a significant hit when his two-sided rockabilly debut for Sun, 'Ooby Dooby'/'Go Go Go' was issued on 1 May, selling over a quarter of a million copies and reaching number 59 in the national pop charts. What the reviewers called 'Orbison's spectacular, untamed quality' and 'impressive primitive flavour' were apparently generating 'plenty of loot in the rural sectors'. Not bad for someone who'd eventually hit the megastar league singing ballads. As for Janis Martin, the Elvis angle was being heavily pushed in the press, and her chart positions seemed to indicate that it was working:

> Singing something like 'a female Elvis Presley', Miss Martin has begun selling in a way that has some happy resemblances to young Presley. First reports were from the South and were very good; now however she is being exposed by more and more pop disk jockeys, North and South, and is appealing to a wide segment of the record-buying public.

In truth, the Presley resemblance was circumstantial at best, but this seemed to be what the industry was looking for at the time, and shows how quick the press were to pick up on any supposed link to the King. As for Johnny Carroll, he certainly cut some wild rocking tracks for Decca that year, which at least had the muscle to ensure that his singles would receive some attention. He also had a go-getting manager prepared to hustle up an entire feature film showcase for Johnny and the Hot Rocks, yet somehow all this didn't result in the frantic ringing of cash registers in the way that it should have. The press even charged him with not sounding *enough* like The Hillbilly Cat, when they reviewed 'Tryin' To Get To You' on 19 May: 'Carroll invests it with energy and personality, but he does not seem to have assimilated the Presley sound and style yet.'

Overall, their writer preferred the other side, Carroll's cover of Warren Smith's recent Sun hit 'Rock'n'Roll Ruby', which had been written by Johnny Cash. Meanwhile, Cash himself had come through very strongly, to the extent that his single 'So Doggone Lonesome'/'Folsom Prison Blues' (released right at the end of 1955) spent much of that spring in regional Top Five charts alongside former or current Sun artists Presley and Perkins, whose 'Heartbreak Hotel' and 'Blue Suede Shoes' were going head to head for the top spot. Cash was even big enough by the spring of 1956 that a venerable country performer like Ernest Tubb felt the need to release a cover version of 'So Doggone Lonesome' in February.

GO, BOY, GO

There'd never again be a time when so much classic rockabilly material was selling like this, and much of what missed out on the big time was equally worthy of note. If the trick was to sound like Presley's Sun material, then a prize should certainly have been awarded to Phil Gray and His Go Boys, who put out 'Bluest Boy In Town'/'Pepper Hot Baby' on the tiny Rhythm

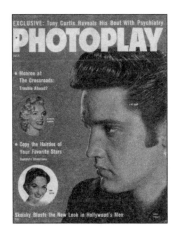

'Marlon Brando with a voice' –
Elvis wows the film fans

label in either 1956 or '57 (dating it more accurately is difficult, since it seems to have been completely ignored in the trade papers), whose label confidently states, 'Introducing Mr Go Boy'. 'Bluest Boy In Town' in particular takes Presley's 'That's All Right' as its template, and both sides are extremely fine examples of the classic rockabilly style, yet it seems to have wound up selling, in Billy Lee Riley's immortal phrase, 'like yesterday's hot cakes'.

Many of the excellent rockabilly singles issued in 1956 probably never stood a hope in hell of imitating Elvis's success. Some, like Jimmy Murphy's frantic 'Grandpaw's A Cat'/'Baboon Boogie' (November 1956), had the backing of Columbia Records, and he himself was judged by *Billboard* to have 'a fine feeling for the idiom, which is strongly orientated to the rockabilly style'. Jimmy, however, was already thirty-one, with a string of releases on various labels dating back to 1951, and was therefore unlikely to be mistaken for Elvis by any passing teenagers, whose parents were probably also in their thirties. Just what it was about The Hillbilly Cat that made the young fans scream so much was a question posed by a journalist from the *Lubbock Avalanche-Journal* back in April '56, when

Elvis passed through town, 'turning Fair Park Coliseum into a bedlam before two screaming audiences totalling 10,000 persons':

> 'What's he got? He's got everything. He's Marlon Brando with a voice.' That was one of the thousands of teenagers who pushed close to the platform where Presley was raising the dust with one of his western renditions. Another said, 'Man, he looks and acts just like one of us crazy mixed-up kids. Only when he gets up steam, he blows it off.' 'Don't he look cool. Man, don't he look cool.' 'Why do we like him? Man are you crazy? Why did we have James Dean? Why do we like Marlon Brando?'

This was the problem in a nutshell. All the companies were looking for another Presley, but that was about as futile as – in other decades – looking for another Hendrix, another James Brown or another Sinatra. With Elvis, it was the whole package: the way he sang, the way he looked, the way he moved. Most surviving rockabilly performers of those days will tell you that they've never witnessed anything like him, before or since. Sure, he was good looking, but that'll only get you part of the way, and in the very late 1950s the industry tried swamping the charts with identikit 'rock'n'roll' singers who'd have been better off working as male models, and most of what *they* served up was inconsequential fluff for the pre-teen market. It's no surprise that those fans in Lubbock equated Elvis not with other singers, but alongside Dean and Brando, two actors with a solid air of danger about them, who could never be mistaken for run-of-the-mill matinee idols. Significantly, Buddy Holly, who supported Elvis in Lubbock back in the Sun era – and cut a string of first-class rockabilly tracks before 'That'll Be The Day' changed his fortunes for ever – broke through on the strength of his songwriting talent and his guitar playing, proving that you could look like the ordinary guy next door and still sell a million.

Carl Perkins also had the songwriting talent, the lead-guitar skills and a hell of a voice, but, even without his car crash, he was still probably way too downhome, too Southern to sell to the mass market in the way that Elvis had. Carl's lyrics in songs like 'That's Right' and 'Dixie Fried' tell of wild, adult nights in the west Memphis honky-tonks. Furthermore, he was already married, in an era when that alone could hinder the record company's ability to market you to a target audience that was largely female and in their early teens.

SOME PEOPLE CALL ME A TEENAGE IDOL

A much more likely bet was young Ricky Nelson, who was not only closer in age to that of his target audience, but also had the benefit of film-star good looks, and a national TV show on which to promote his latest releases. Ricky's musical parents starred in their own family show, *The Adventures of Ozzie & Harriet*, which had been running on the ABC network since 1952, in which they and their sons appeared as a fictionalised version of themselves. The teenage Ricky was blown away by

the sounds he'd been hearing on various Sun singles, particularly those of Carl Perkins, as he told Trevor Cajiao in 1985: 'Well, you know, at that time I was listening to all those Sun records, y' know. I used to go down and buy as many of those as I could 'cause I liked that sound … I was a real fan, and still am, of those early Sun records.'

Understandably, Ricky then jumped at the chance to sing a song (a version of Fats Domino's 'I'm Walkin'') on the *Ozzie & Harriet* show's 10 April 1957 episode, as part of that week's storyline. Audience response was so favourable that a record deal with Imperial soon followed, and by that September he was flexing his muscles in the studio, covering two recent Carl Perkins songs, 'Your True Love' and 'Boppin' The Blues'. The following month he tried a version of another Sun hit, 'Whole Lotta Shakin', and hit his stride on 8 November, on his first date with guitar sensation James Burton, cutting 'Stood Up' and 'Waitin' In School'. Finally, on 17 February 1958, he really nailed it with the storming rockabilly classic 'Believe What You Say', which features a blistering, superbly judged Burton guitar solo. Sure, Ricky had the good looks and the teen-idol marketing, not to mention the ballads aimed directly at the swooners, but he could rock with the best of them when he put his mind to it.

Still, by 1958, if you didn't fit the correct mould, it had become extremely difficult to break through the Presley-shaped hole which had been kicked in the music industry's defences. They'd figured things out, found a way to tame it and then sell it right back to you, and if you wanted to compete, then like Johnny Burnette, Buddy Holly and many other former rockabillies who kept on selling, your material generally had to be a lot less wild than it had been back in 1956. The industry and the media were soon eagerly trying to bury rock'n'roll, regarded as just a passing fad. David Hammond, the regular music correpondent for British magazine *Picturegoer,* confidently informed readers of his 'Disc Parade' section as early as March 1957 that rock was on the way out, and calypso might well conquer all:

Music publishers forecast an early end to rock'n roll. There will be a need to replace it with a new craze and the indication from America is that calypso is the answer … Make no mistake, the calypso trend has already begun. Almost every major record company has scrambled to release a disc of 'The Banana Boat Song', current favourite.

A month later, the same magazine decided that this was all nonsense, and 'you can bet a pair of battered bongoes to a conga drum that this is one music revolution that won't set the world of music aflame'. Who was it that now had no faith in calypso? David Hammond. Still, in September of the same year, all was well, and he could inform his readers that since rock had 'been knocked practically cold', there was perhaps something new on the horizon: 'Hawaiian music could have a fling … though there is no great evidence that those grass skirts will start a prairie fire.' Wise words indeed.

THROWN OUT OF THE SCHOOL CHOIR

Despite such distractions, for a brief while the field had been wide open, and some remarkable maverick rockabilly talent was given national exposure. But just as Elvis had moved from rockabilly to more mainstream sounds as Parker attempted to reposition him as an all-round 'family entertainer', inevitably the industry followed, and soon after '56 things were cleaned up, sanitised, and a lot of good songs were swamped in redundant, sub-Jordanaires vocal backing. The impulse on the part of record companies to go for looks over musical ability is illustrated by the words of Bob Marcucci, head of Chancellor Records, interviewed by *Picturegoer* magazine in 1959 about how he first discovered teen singing sensation Fabian out in the street:

I chatted to him for a while … I had the feeling that

127

he had IT – that he could make the big time. I had the same feeling about another of my boys, Frankie Avalon. Another thing in Fabian's favour was that he looked kinda like Elvis Presley and Ricky Nelson. So, without hearing his voice, I said to him: 'Kid, I'm gonna make you into a singing star'.

Fabian's initial response to all this? 'I should warn you – I was thrown out of the school choir.'

By the end of 1958, when *Life* magazine decided to revisit the rock phenomenon in a lengthy illustrated feature entitled 'Rock'n'Roll Rolls On'n'On' – informing its adult readers that against all odds the rock cult was showing no signs of lying down and dying – the accompanying pictures mostly showed unthreatening, clean-scrubbed idols like Sal Mineo, Frankie Avalon and Johnny Mathis. The anonymous writer even bemoaned the fact that technology had advanced to the point where access to recording equipment had become much easier in recent years:

> The rock'n'roll business is crazy. Anyone – *anyone* – can record and press 5,000 records for $1,200. So there now are more than 1,500 little pop record companies who press almost any song or sound that comes along and hope the lightning will strike. It rarely does. Said a disgruntled recording executive, 'Anyone who thinks he can pick what the kids'll want next, his orientation is in Cloudsville.'

Elsewhere in the feature, *Life* magazine used the word 'rockabilly' when describing the Everly Brothers, and also ran a wonderful selection of action photos of a new performer called Tony Conn rolling around on the floor, clutching a guitar. He was promoting his debut single, 'Like Wow'/'Dangerous Doll', and someone either in Tony's management or at his record label, Decca, clearly had some clout in order to get him such a prime piece of exposure, but the piece concentrated less on Tony and more on those who were pulling the strings:

> ...the lesser rock'n'roll artist has come to depend greatly on 'props' – well-arranged hair, trademark costume, distinctive gestures or gyrations and sly eye-rolls. These are important because his voice is often inaudible above the audience's interruptive shrieks. So he quickly acquires props. Tony Conn, 23, whose first record will be released this month by Decca, took hours of patient instruction from his tutor-managers. He selected as his costume a leopard-skin jacket with sequinned lapels and orange pants. He also devoted weeks to his musical education which includes daily workouts in a gymnasium where he practises splits and bends. 'He had a tendency to be over-wild,' say his managers. 'We've toned him down.

Four short years on from Elvis's first instinctive, electrifying appearances on stages around Memphis and the South, the whole thing had already been formularised, smoothed over and marketed. The prevailing trend was all there in that one sentence – 'We've toned him down'. Little did Tony Conn's managers suspect that their protégé would wind up cutting songs in the 1970s for Ronnie Weiser's cult rockabilly Rollin' Rock label, and starring alongside porn stud John Holmes in Johnny Legend's rockabilly flesh film *Young Hot 'n Nasty Teenage Cruisers* (1977), with a soundtrack featuring the likes of Mac Curtis, Charlie Feathers, Alvis Wayne, Ray Campi and Jackie Lee Cochran. Somehow, though, the film failed to set US box offices alight, presumably leaving the way clear for disco-dancing Travolta and Newton-John in *Grease* the following year. The viewing public can be fickle at times.

As even 'Colonel' Tom Parker discovered with Tommy Sands, you could search all you like, you weren't going to find another Presley. But a *female* Elvis? Well, as the publicity for Janis Martin quoted earlier shows, a lot of people were looking...

9 QUEENS OF ROCKABILLY

HOT BOPPIN' GALS AND HILLBILLY FILLIES

In terms of record sales, you can count the number of successful female rockabillies on the fingers of one badly mutilated hand. Outside of Wanda Jackson or Janis Martin, most didn't get the breaks. The labels were basically looking for another guy like Elvis, so being a woman was a disadvantage, and there were many hurdles to be faced. The recording industry's natural inclination was to aim any talented women singers squarely at the country market, following in the footprints of solo acts such as Kitty Wells, or the more frequently encountered sister or family acts such as the Carters or the Davis Sisters. Furthermore, if the much-discussed onstage 'gyrations' of Elvis were considered lewd and shocking by many at the time, how much more difficult was it for a woman in those days to get up on stage and rock? In a frequently conservative society where religion still held a powerful influence, such movements were controversial, to say the least.

Many of the women who recorded rockabilly tracks in the 1950s, and a fair few of the men, started out as country singers, and eventually returned to that genre. Wanda Jackson

Wanda
Jackson

exemplifies this; having cut some of the wildest female rockers
of the 1950s, she has also pursued a long and distinguished
country career, as well as recording extensively in the gospel
field. Wanda was, and remains, a force of nature. While still
a teenager, she wrote and sang her own songs, played guitar,
toured the South with a racially mixed backing band, and was
even dating Elvis for a while, but before she met The Hillbilly
Cat she'd been recording straight country on Decca for a couple
of years. By 1956 she had a new label, Capitol, and had been
playing shows with Elvis, who advised her to try recording
rock'n'roll, as she explained to me:

Let me say this before we move on. Elvis, he had a sense

about things. I don't know what you'd call it. Maybe business – you know his motto, 'Taking Care of Business' – but I think he was smarter than people gave him credit for. He told me, in the very beginning, about Johnny Cash, 'This guy is going to be the biggest thing to ever hit country music.' I said 'You're crazy', you know [laughs], but he felt that. And he explained to me that we no longer had to do songs aimed at an adult audience, which we always had had to do, that the young people were buying records, so if I wanted to sell records, and get airplay, I should be doing this kind of stuff. My daddy picked up on that too, he said, 'Elvis is right, we've gotta try it.' And the rest was history, but I didn't have a hit with it until 1960, but I kept recording it. We'd put a country song on one side of a single, or an album, and rock things on the other...

Of course, if you're going to rock, you need some songs to sing, and, as Wanda points out, 'nobody was writing songs for girls, of that type of stuff'. Her father, who managed her career up until her husband Wendell Goodman took over in the 1960s, gave her the encouragement she needed:

So that's when Daddy said, 'Start writing your own,' and he helped me, he'd say, 'You've gotta keep to simple titles.' We didn't want more than three words in our titles – 'Mean Mean Man', 'Right Or Wrong', 'Rock Your Baby'... So he'd give me some ideas, and I'd write 'em.

As Wanda says, she didn't have a proper hit with the rockin' songs until 1960, when a track she'd cut in April 1958, the throat-shredding classic 'Let's Have A Party', began to be played obsessively by a deejay in Des Moines. He'd taken it from her first album, and the resulting fuss prompted Capitol to release it as a single, whereupon it stormed the charts, as *Billboard* noted on 3 October 1960, under the headline 'Country Thrush Scores Pop Hit':

> Capitol Records has hit the pop hit parade with another in a continuing stream of country artists who manage to cross the barrier between the two fields. Latest example is Cap's Wanda Jackson, for some time recognized as a top country thrush, who has now made the Hot 100 for the first time in her career with 'Let's Have A Party'.

As far as the trade papers were concerned, she'd always been a country singer – a news item about her move from Decca to Capitol in 1956 described her as 'country singer Wanda Jackson' – but on occasion they had also used the 'rockabilly' word when reviewing some of her singles, such as 'Rock Your Baby'.

COLDER THAN A GAMBLER'S HEART

Wanda went so far as to tour Alaska in 1956 – then quite outside the normal gig circuit – as did another female performer who started out in the country field but certainly gave the rockers a run for their money: Charline Arthur. Born in 1929, in Henrietta, Texas, Charline had started recording back in 1950, and went on to record for labels such as Bullet, Imperial, RCA and others. She cut the magnificently titled 'He Fiddled While I Burned' early in 1954, and the following year covered a song by The Cues called 'Burn That Candle' at the same time as Bill Haley's hit version: 'From the r.&b. field, Miss Arthur has picked up a tune well suited to her style. She gives it a fast, expertly-turned reading accompanied by a big beat backing.'

By 1955, Charline certainly had the opportunity to see

Charline
Arthur

which way the wind was blowing, having appeared on a bill at the Fair Park Coliseum in Lubbock on 13 February, supporting Elvis (a night when the opening act was Buddy Holly with Bob Montgomery, which Crickets guitarist Sonny Curtis credits with turning Buddy firmly in the direction of rockabilly). It's probably fair to assume that she enjoyed this gig a little more than her 1956 tour of the Yukon and all points north. Whatever the locals may have made of it, Charline doesn't seem to have been impressed, as she told *Billboard*:

> Of her recent trip to Alaska, Charline Arthur, of 'Big D Jamboree,' Dallas, says the weather was colder than a gambler's heart, ham and eggs were a buck and a half, and cokes in the niteries went for six bits. She reports that she blew two tires on the Alcan highway and all her dates

135

didn't materialize. 'Don't think we'll book any more up there,' comments J.F. Dolan, 'Big D' tub-thumper…

Charline may have done a show with Presley, but she doesn't seem to have been actively promoted by her record company as 'The Female Elvis', which is perhaps fortunate, since that title was already being used in several other quarters. As previously mentioned, when the King's new label, RCA Victor, signed the sixteen-year-old Janis Martin in 1956, they actively publicised her as his female equivalent. Indeed, A&R man Steve Sholes, the man who signed both Elvis and Janis, described her to the press in March 1956 as 'a female Presley'.

Born in Southerlin, Virginia, in 1940, Janis already had a showbusiness pedigree going back several years in talent shows and on radio, having been a regular on the syndicated *Old Dominion Barn Dance* on WRVA, out of Richmond, Virginia, at the age of thirteen. Her debut RCA single appeared in March 1956. She'd written the song 'Drugstore Rock'n'Roll' herself, and it rocked a lot harder than the A-side it was paired with, 'Will You Willyum'. The song's subject matter came naturally to her, as she later recalled when interviewed by *Rocktober* magazine: 'I wrote "Drugstore Rock'n'Roll" in about ten minutes. Everything in that song is actually the scene that was happening for us. The drug store was the only place we had to go and hang out after school.'

In addition to recording a song called 'My Boy Elvis', she was further linked to Presley with the release by RCA in South Africa of the now ultra-rare 10-inch album *Janis and Elvis*, which reportedly upset Tom Parker owing to the order of the billing. Despite the backing of a major label, a string of high-profile television appearances and tours in 1956, a series of events that would eventually curtail her career had already been set in motion before she even signed to RCA:

I had married in January 1956. I was only fifteen years old, but kept it secret when I signed to RCA. I went overseas on a tour of US bases in 1957 and my husband was stationed over there as a paratrooper. He got a 30-day leave and my son was the result of that. RCA did not know I was married until my husband wanted to travel with us. I had my son when I was seventeen. I stayed on the road after he was born, but I needed to be a mother. I retired when I was twenty-one.

WARM ATTRACTIVE THRUSHING ON AN EFFECTIVE WEEPER

As it turned out, Janis Martin wasn't the only 'Female Elvis' that RCA would find themselves marketing around this time. The King's former home, Sun Records, had been recording a new singer, Jean Chapel, whose contract RCA swiftly acquired, and marketed her under that tag in October 1956. Until the mid-1950s, Sam Phillips at Sun had moved from R&B and blues into hillbilly and then rockabilly, having released only one single by a female artist. In fact, when he followed the December 1955 single 'Daydreams Come True'/'How Long' by Maggie Sue Wimberly with 'There's No Right Way To Do Me Wrong'/'You Can Tell Me' by The Miller Sisters, the appearance of these very two fine country records was considered worth a news item in *Billboard*:

> For the first time, Sun Records has just released two platters cut by fem performers. One has Maggie Sue Wimberly, popular in the Tri-Cities sector of Alabama, featuring 'How Long?', and the other has the Miller Sisters, of Tupelo, Miss., stressing 'You Can Tell Me.'

Fourteen-year-old Maggie Sue's 'How Long' remains one of

the most perfect country heartbreakers ever released on Sun, and she later achieved fame during the 1970s in that field under the name Sue Richards, but no one would have claimed that this was rockabilly. The Miller Sisters – who were actually sisters-in-law, known as Elsie Jo Miller and Mildred Wages to their friends – were also dealing in classic country harmonies, as the reviewers noted, praising the 'warm, attractive thrushing on an effective weeper'. In fact, they'd already had a record issued six months earlier on Sam Phillips' short-lived subsidiary label, Flip, which was also in the straight country vein, but then in August 1956 they had their one shot at rockabilly, with the song 'Ten Cats Down', on which they got to chant 'rock, cats, rock' along to an insistent double-bass figure.

Still, Sam seems to have resisted marketing them as the female Presley sisters, and when he issued Jean Chapel's uptempo single 'Welcome To The Club'/'I Won't Be Rockin' Tonight' in June 1956, he then sold her contract to RCA, who promptly reissued it on their own label. According to what Jean herself told Randy McNutt, it was they who started calling her 'The Female Elvis':

> Sam then put a record out on me, but I don't think it got much distribution. Not long after that he sold my contract to RCA Victor, just like he did with Elvis. Steve Sholes, the RCA executive, labelled me his 'female Elvis Presley,' and I could never get over that.

By this time, the former Opal Jean Amburgey from Neon, Kentucky, was already thirty-one years old, and a veteran of the long-running radio show the *Renfro Valley Barn Dance*. As it happened, RCA had issued a version of 'Welcome To The Club' at the same time as Jean appeared on Sun, by their own long-time rockin' gal, Charline Arthur. Aside from a cover of Mamie Van Doren's 'Oo-Ba-La Baby' the following year, that was pretty much it as far as Jean's rockin' record career went, but she eventually became a significant figure in the songwriting world during the 1960s and '70s.

THE BACK SHACK SOUND, FEMALE STYLE

A woman who stayed far longer on the Sun label, and on its subsidiary, Phillips International, was Barbara Pittman, probably the most flat-out rock'n'roller of the female artists recorded by Sam Phillips. A Memphis native, her family had known the Presleys since she was a child – she even went to the same school as Elvis – and she'd been knocking on Sam's door asking for an audition even before she was a teenager. Having spent a year on the road with whip-cracking western performer Lash LaRue, Barbara finally got her break at Sun in 1956, cutting her hugely confident debut single, 'I Need A Man' on 15 April. Unusually for Sun, it waited almost half a year to be released, but *Billboard*'s reviewers were impressed when they heard it: 'Here's the back shack sound, female style … A good side that merits plenty of plays.'

After such a confident beginning, you might think there'd have been a swift follow-up in the established style, but when Barbara's next disc appeared, it was over a year later, and Sam was partly pitching her at a different market. 'I'm Getting Better All The Time' was a rocker, but 'Two Young Fools In Love' was a sparse, beautifully judged ballad with teen-flavoured lyrics. Rocking material like 'Sentimental Fool' was recorded but left unissued until many years later, and Barbara had to wait until the middle of 1958 for the release of her third single, 'Everlasting Love'/'Cold, Cold Heart', which deserved to sell much better than it did. It's tempting to think that if she'd had more frequent single releases when it counted, and been cut loose with more of the wilder material to which she was definitely suited, Barbara might have had far greater success. It's been said that Sam Phillips didn't really see his female artists as rock'n'rollers. He certainly left Patsy Holcomb's fine June 1957 rockabilly performance, 'I Wanta Rock', in the can, and it remained unissued until the 1970s.

Over at Decca (home of much rockabilly activity in 1955 and '56) was a woman who'd made the front page of *Billboard* when signing to the label back in 1954 as a country artist, Mimi Roman. Voted 'Queen of the Rodeo' in September '54 at Madison Square Garden in New York, she'd conveniently just signed a record deal as 'a country and western warbler'. The paper reported this under the title 'Wax Pact Snap For Gal With Right Talents', right next to a feature headlined 'Diskeries Discover Sales Pull of Female Form as Cover Art'. Following various C&W releases, she issued 'a lively country blues with good pace' in December 1955, and took a particularly active part in promoting it, allowing her home address to be printed in the paper:

> Mimi Roman plugged her new Decca release 'Wrap It Up And Save It' b/w 'My Tears Are Beginning To Show' on the Pee Wee King TV show from Chicago last Saturday (17). Disk jockeys may obtain a copy of the platter, together with a photo of Mimi, by writing to her at 417 Ocean Avenue, Brooklyn 26.

If you're looking for rockabilly, the point where Mimi finally hit it was midway through 1956, with the release of 'Little Lovin'/'I'm Ready If You're Willin' on Decca, with a solid backing that sounds very much like the same musicians who are on cuts by Roy Hall, Don Woody and other Decca rockers recorded around that time. This prompted the papers to reach for their handy stand-by comparison: 'Miss Roman gives a rock and roll tune the fem Elvis Presley treatment with listenable results, which should pay off in considerable play, both country and pop.'

A final candidate in the 'female Elvis' stakes was Alis Lesley, who cut just the one single, 'He Will Come Back To Me', in the spring of 1957 out in Hollywood for the Era label. Born in Chicago in 1938 as Alice Lesley, she seems to have changed this slightly to Alis in order that her whole name would sound similar to that of Elvis Presley. While her recording career may not have amounted to much, she certainly had some spectacular breaks. Following a debut show in September 1956 supporting Gene Vincent & the Blue Caps and the Coasters in Los Angeles, she then wound up as the opening act the following year on one of the greatest overseas rockabilly packages of them all: the legendary October 1957 Australian tour starring Little Richard, Gene Vincent and Eddie Cochran. On the cover of the special concert programme, Eddie, for example, is billed simply as 'Recording Star', and undeneath Alis's name is written, yes, 'The Female Elvis Presley'. She certainly looked the part, but although she shared the Era label with a roster of crack rockabilly talent like Glenn Glenn, Johnny Faire and Dorsey Burnette, her one single doesn't seem to have inspired them to issue a follow-up.

DOWN WITH THE KIDS

Also out in Hollywood were the Collins Kids, the brother-and-sister teenage singing combo who'd been regulars on the *Town Hall Party* TV show from 1954 onwards. They began cutting rockabilly in 1955 for Columbia with the 'Beetle Bug Bop', all the while remaining very popular in the country field. The Collins Kids could really belt out the songs, with thirteen-year-old Lorrie playing acoustic guitar and singing while eleven-year-old Larry picked a dazzling slew of notes on a double-necked electric and jumped all around the stage. They recorded a string of rockabilly classics over the next five years, including 'Hop, Skip and Jump' (1957) and 'Hoy Hoy' (1958), not to mention a fine rockin' version of Elvis's 'Party' (1957, aka 'Let's Have A Party'), which Wanda Jackson then picked up on, as she told me: 'They had it first, you know. Elvis [sang it] first in the movie, and I guess it was just available on the soundtrack, and then Lorrie and Larry is the one where I heard it. Then I got their record and learned it, and started singing it as an opening song.'

The women so far discussed were some of the successes, who at least had the benefit of established labels, and reasonable publicity and distribution behind them. Even so, in most cases the teenagers seemed to be less inclined to spend their money on female rockers, so there was little real encouragement from the record companies for women to sing flat-out wild material. Much easier to package them in the more conventional country mould, turning out what the trade papers referred to as 'weepers', and smiling sweetly on TV shows like *Ranch Party*.

Of course, there'd long been women in the hillbilly and country field who'd cut uptempo material: Rose Maddox did a fine job with 'Wild, Wild, Young Men' (1955, covered by Johnny Carroll the following year as 'Wild, Wild Women'); 'Rock-A-Bye Boogie' (1953) by the Davis Sisters moved along at a rocking pace, aided by some deft harmonies and superb, echo-drenched guitar work; while Ella Mae Morse swung the living daylights out of her duet with Tennessee Ernie Ford, 'False Hearted Girl' (1952), a hillbilly bop/western swing recording not a million miles away from what Elvis would do with 'That's All Right' two years later. Even Mother Maybelle Carter's daughter Anita, who had one of the purest country voices of them all, briefly

Cordell Jackson with George Reinecke and the Mud Bugs

Cordell Jackson

tried her hand at rockin' in 1957 with 'He's A Real Gone Guy', but it wasn't really her style, as the reviewers noted: 'Miss Carter goes rockabillie on the Nellie Lutcher oldie, but the effort doesn't come off too appealingly.'

Someone who walked the walk and talked the talk far more convincingly was Sparkle Moore, a blonde-haired, sharp-dressed multi-instrumentalist who wrote her own material, and was sometimes promoted as the 'Female James Dean'. Born Barbara Morgan in Omaha, Nebraska, in 1939, she later told Miriam Linna how she came to be nicknamed 'Sparkle': 'I had real long blonde hair at the time and all the girls back then had their hair cut short so folks would just call me Sparkle because of the character Sparkle Plenty in the Dick Tracy comic strip, who had long blonde hair clear down to her seat.'

Having written and sung her own tune into a primitive home-recording machine which her father had bought, she managed to interest a local deejay, who helped her get a record deal with the Fraternity label out of Cincinnati, Ohio, in 1956. The result was a double-sided, self-penned slab of rocking wax entitled 'Skull and Cross Bones'/'Rock-a-Bop' – which prompted

Billboard's reviewers to reach for the P-word once again: 'Gal pulls a fem Presley and belts out a catchy rock'n'roll ditty with style and drive.' This was no country performer trying to appeal to the kids, but a teenage rock fan who knew just the sound she was after, as Sparkle recalled: 'I wrote both sides, "Skull And Cross Bones" and "Rock-a-Bop", and they were both *my* style of music. I liked a lot of echo and I liked a lot of screaming. I wanted things to be exciting – wild.'

Sparkle gigged with the likes of Gene Vincent, the Wilburn Brothers and Ernest Tubb, released one more single in 1957 which she wasn't quite as happy with, and then gave up the business in order to have a baby.

ROCKIN' RECORD BOSSES – CORDELL JACKSON AND MIRA SMITH

Of course, another option as a female rocker was to start your own label and record the material exactly the way you wanted it. This was a radical move for the 1950s, but it didn't stop Cordell Jackson. She later rightly described herself as 'the first female to write, sing, arrange, accompany, record, engineer, produce, and distribute her own music'. Born Cordell Miller in Pontotoc, Mississippi in 1923, she learned several instruments under the influence of her fiddle-playing father. Aged twelve, she was told: 'Young girls don't play the guitar.' 'Well, I do,' she replied. Having moved to Memphis, in 1947 she became the first woman recording engineer in America, eventually starting her own label, Moon Records, in 1956. Their finest hour was probably the Cordell-penned 1958 rockabilly classic 'Dateless Night' by Allen Page & The Deltones.

Meanwhile, down in Shreveport, Louisiana, home of the *Hayride*, Mira Smith started her own label and studio, Ram Recording Co., in 1955, to take advantage of some of the talent appearing on the town's famous radio broadcasts. Mira sang, played guitar, engineered sessions and wrote songs, moving into the rockabilly market in 1956 with a single by James Wilson and the Jimmie-Cats. Local teenage guitar ace James Burton appeared on many of Mira's recordings, and she also released sides by several notable female rockers, such as Linda Brannon and Margaret Lewis. Brannon and Lewis co-wrote much of their own material with Mira, and it was also Margaret and Mira who came up with the classic 'Reconsider Me', Margaret's magnificent, haunting original demo of which only surfaced many years later.

Then of course there were the women who made just one or two excellent singles for small labels, and who, like many rockabilly performers, seem to have appeared almost out of nowhere and left behind little trace except their music. Fine examples of this are Coleen Frazier's 'Your Mama's Here' (1958), released on the Fable label, from Los Angeles; 'Glue Me Back, Jack' by Nancy Dawn with the Hi Fi Guys on Salem Records from Chicago, a nice, easy-rolling boogie-style rockabilly number; Joyce Allen's self-penned 'Baby Oh Baby' (1961), seemingly the one and only release on Reb records out of Denham Springs, Louisiana; or the Canadian singer Vanda King's 'Ooh, Watcha Do!', which appeared in 1958 on the Apex label, from Lachine, Quebec, and at least merited a favourable review: 'A cute rhythm piece with a blues structure, right in the teen lovin' groove. The thrush brings a fresh, breathless quality to the vocal.'

WILD WILD WOMEN

For one-off mayhem, there were records like the frantic 'Stop' by Little Rita Laraine, issued at some indeterminate date by the Bluebonnet label from Fort Worth, Texas, featuring the thirteen-year-old Rita Lorraine Rasmussen belting out the words at a hundred miles an hour. Aiming at a different kind of market was the double-entendre-strewn rocker 'Chili Dippin' Baby', recorded in 1957 by Joyce Poynter for the Goldenrod label, out of Scottsville, Kentucky. The previous year Joyce had co-written both sides of an excellent rockabilly single for the same label ('Rock and Roll Mister Moon'/'Baby Fan The Flame' by Harold Shultters and His Rocats), but on 'Chili Dippin' Baby' she was following in the footsteps of the salty female blues singers of the 1920s, with lyrics that used food as a thinly disguised metaphor for something else. There was also an adult theme behind Ann Castle's 'Go Get The Shotgun, Grand'pa' (1959) released on the tiny X-Power label, from Millville, Pennsylvania; an uptempo rocker which drew the following dry comment from a reviewer: 'This is all about a wedding in the traditional country style.'

The outright prize for the wildest female rockabilly recording of the 1950s must surely go to Joyce Green, from Bradford, Arkansas, who at the age of nineteen wrote and sang the remarkable revenge song 'Black Cadillac' – a full-on assault driven along by the searing guitars of Benny Kuykendall and Tommy Holder, where Joyce details all the ways in which she's going to celebrate once her no-good lover is safely buried six feet under. She cut the record one day in 1959 at the studio of radio station KLCN, Blytheville, Arkansas, for a local label called Vaden, owned by Arlen Varden, which also issued fine rockabilly singles by the likes of Larry Donn and Teddy Redell. Larry happened to be in the studio the day she made the record, and tracked her down three and a half decades later for *Now Dig This* magazine. He had been at KLCN recording his own killer rockabilly single, 'That's What I Call A Ball', and recalled his memories of meeting Joyce that day:

Joyce and a young man I later learned was her very protective brother had just arrived in the control room on the other side of the big double-paned window that separated the two rooms. They were talking to Arlen Vaden. Shortly, all three of them came into the studio and Vaden introduced her to us. Her brother must have been a nice guy because, although I shook Joyce's hand as we met, he let me live.

Exactly how Joyce Green managed to come up with such a remarkably fine song with its black-humoured, savage lyrics, about killing and burying her man, is hard to say. Asked about her musical background, she told Larry: 'I grew up singing in church, and with different family groups, then I sang with a trio of girls at schools, fairs, rodeos and about anywhere they'd let us sing.'

After this, and some time on local radio shows in 1958, she then turned in one of the wildest performances of them all – a record to put next to 'Love Me' by The Phantom as an absolute high point of the genre; both of them recorded near the tail-end of rockabilly's classic decade, at a time when the charts were full of neutered pretty boys. 'Black Cadillac' turned out to be Joyce's one and only record, but, quite honestly, how do you follow something like that?

10 I'M GONNA CUT ME SOME WAX

**THE ONE-OFFS, THE WILDMEN AND THE
ONE-HIT WONDERS**

Part of the joy of rockabilly is the thousands of one-time performances by people about whom virtually nothing is known, who somehow managed to find their way into a studio for one night of glory and howl their hearts out into a microphone. For every Elvis or Carl Perkins, there was a seemingly endless queue of talented singers who never quite got the breaks, but left behind vinyl which still jumps and moves like a juke joint on Saturday night. The well-documented history of the blues – in which some remarkable pre-war records are known to us only because of the survival of a handful of examples, or even, in cases such as Kingfish Bill Tomlin's 'Hot Box Is On My Mind' (1930), what seems to be a sole remaining copy – should have demonstrated by now that great music sometimes has no luck whatever finding an audience in its day.

In the museums and art galleries of the world, no one is trying to judge the artists of the past in terms of whether they sold many paintings during their lifetime, or commanded high prices, but the music industry has often used sales figures as

Not your
average
rockabilly
wildman –
Guy Mitchell

the sole method of determining a performer's importance, and sticks with that judgement long afterwards. By this standard, Pat Boone would be one of the most significant artists of the rock'n'roll era, with the likes of the Fontane Sisters, Perry Como and Guy Mitchell following on behind; Mitchell even made the Top Ten in the pop charts in 1957 with a song called 'Rock-a-Billy'. These people shifted huge numbers of records, and so did Elvis, but that was about all they had in common. Many genuine hepcats who dreamed of Presley-like success found that their one stab at glory was released on a tiny label with a pressing which numbered in the low hundreds. Right from the start, the dice were loaded against them, but half a century later their music remains, and often wipes the floor with many big-selling commercial products of the day.

Take the case of Jackie Morningstar, who fulfils just about all of the requirements for rockabilly immortality. He cut just the one great record, 'Rockin' In The Graveyard' (1959), replete with demonic howls and killer guitar. Right at the start, before

149

the song proper kicks in, Jackie namechecks a couple of other songs that had sold millions, before confidently stating that he's also got one that'll do the same.

'Rockin' In The Graveyard' was released on the Sandy label, Box 248, Mobile, Alabama. Morningstar also called himself Jackie Morrell, although his real name was Willie Morrell, Sr. It's been speculated that he may have picked his name because of some Native American ancestry, but there had also been a hit Natalie Wood film the previous year entitled *Marjorie Morningstar*, so it's possible that this may have provided the inspiration. In June 1959, Jackie's lone masterpiece even rated a mention in *Billboard* ('Ghoulish rocker is sung in sprightly rockabilly fashion'), but the writing was already on the wall, as a glance at that week's Hot Hundred confirms. Admittedly there were some tough rockers still in the charts: Freddie Cannon was belting out 'Tallahassie Lassie', Wilbert Harrison scoring big with 'Kansas City', and Chuck Berry was coming up strong with 'Back In The USA', but in the main it was the smooth boys who'd taken over. Teens all over America were apparently swooning to the wholesome sounds of Frankie Avalon ('A Boy Without A Girl'), Paul Anka ('Lonely Boy'), Ed Byrnes ('Kookie, Kookie, Lend Me Your Comb') and Fabian ('Tiger'), so what hope was there for an Alabama wildman singing about being belted over the head with a rock by a thing from beyond the grave?

On top of all this, the business was still reeling from the payola scandal, as it became clear to the wider public how much money had changed hands and how many freebies had been dispensed in order to hype certain records into the charts. *Billboard*'s editorial that week addressed this very question, calling for an end to 'the practice of giving away records by the bucketfull and lamely crawling out from under the returns', and observing that 'more and more dealers tell us "Do you know

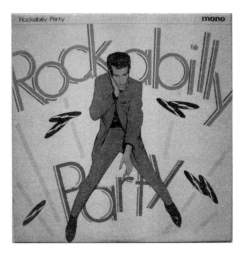

how many records sell absolutely nothing?'" In short, if you weren't playing with the big boys who could afford to give away promo copies in bulk, your record's chances could be slim, at best. Even at the height of the rockabilly boom, many fine singles which had the kudos of a release on the Sun label were pretty much lost in the shuffle because Sam Phillips really only had the clout to push one contender at once, and in rockabilly terms, artists on Sun were among the ones who'd made the big time.

As for Jackie Morningstar, that one review was more or less his career highlight. Three years later, he issued a non-rockabilly follow-up on his own label, Jay-Em, under the name Jackie Morrell and His Jazz Masters, and he apparently led an outfit in the 1970s called Willie Morrell and the Down South Band, but that's where the trail seems to halt. Yet around that time, 'Rockin' In The Graveyard' began showing up on rockabilly compilations, and has been reissued on numerous occasions over the years. If you add them all up, Jackie's track just may well have sold a million.

I DON'T KNOW WHEN

Of course, there are those who might say, 'Well, at least Jackie Morningstar's record was actually *released* in the fifties,' and they'd have a point. The remarkable thing about the rockabilly reissue boom of the 1970s was just how many great 1950s performances stayed in the can at the time, emerging only decades afterwards when their teenage performers were pushing middle age. Ask most rockabilly fans about Hal Harris, and probably the first recording that comes to mind would be the awesome 'Jitterbop Baby', a cast-iron classic of the genre which Hal laid down for the Starday label some time in 1957 at Bill Quin's Gold Star studio in Houston. Just for good measure, he also cut another killer, 'I Don't Know When', on the same day. Yet the session wasn't even his – Harris was actually using up time at the end of a recording date for George Jones, on which he'd played guitar. Hal's main claim to fame in those days was as one of the hottest rockabilly guitar players around, and his work can be heard on some of Starday's finest cuts, such as 'All The Time' by Sleepy LaBeef (1957) or 'Don't Be Gone Long' by Bob Doss (1956), both of which he also co-wrote. It wasn't until Ace Records in England issued their landmark *Rockabilly Party* 10-inch LP in 1978 that 'Jitterbop Baby' and 'I Don't Know When' finally surfaced, and it's astonishing that work of this quality remained unissued for so long.

Someone else who found lasting fame as a sideman on other people's records, but managed to show up briefly as a vocalist in their own right on a timeless rockabilly stormer, is Hargus 'Pig' Robbins, who for decades now has been one of Nashville's most sought-after piano players. His career stretches all the way from playing with Dylan on *Blonde On Blonde* (1966) to handling the keyboards on both sides of Arthur Alexander's sublime debut single 'The Girl That Radiates That Charm'/'Sally Sue Brown' (1960) – not to mention backing most country singers of the past forty years worth a damn – but in 1959 he stepped out a little on his own. Under the name Mel Robbins, he cut a tune which he'd co-written for Chess subsidiary Argo entitled 'Save It'; a deranged, heavy-breathing beast of a song which still refuses to lie down and stop writhing after half a century. Justifiably covered by the Cramps in 1981, it was a tale of barely restrained lust, superbly delivered by a man who in real life had been blind from an early age, but who once drove a car down a Nashville alley when stoned: 'I didn't hit any telephone poles or cars,' Robbins later recalled, 'so I guess I did alright.'

PLEASE GIVE ME SOMETHING

If we're talking of rockabilly hymns to the fevered pursuit of the opposite sex, then this is probably a good moment at which to mention 'Please Give Me Something' by Bill Allen & the Back Beats (1958), a primal howl of a song in which the narrator is looking for rather more than a peck on the cheek. Half a decade later a group from Liverpool were asking whether they could hold your hand, but that was kids' stuff next to this. Born Wilfred Allen Snively, Bill Allen had one previous rock'n'roll single in 1957 on the Eldorado label out of New York, but 'Please Give Me Something' was licensed to Imperial. Between these two records, Bill and his band from Akron, Ohio, had appeared on a month-long, memorable package tour alongside a stellar rockabilly line-up of Carl Perkins, Roy Orbison, Eddie Cochran and Gene Vincent, although the royalties from sales of the Imperial single were hardly likely to have bought them many Cadillacs. Bill later told his local newspaper, the *Akron Beacon Journal,* that he once received a cheque for a grand total of $1.98: 'We hardly got paid. The same happened to us that happened to many, many, many rock'n'roll groups. The people who promoted them made money, the managers made money, but the people who actually did the work had to hitchhike home usually.'

All things considered, though, in commercial terms Bill and the boys were a howling great success story compared to the likes of Jesse Stevens, who turned in a breathless, barnstorming piece of acoustic rockabilly called 'Mama, Mama' in June 1958. It was loosely modelled on Elvis's 'That's All Right', but taken at a far more frantic pace, as if all concerned had been plugged directly into the mains. By

rights, it might just have found a place in some chart or other, since there was no shortage of wild material selling that month: Link Wray had just broken through nationally with 'Rumble', Little Richard's 'Ooh! My Soul'/'True Fine Mama' was also doing well, as was Ricky Nelson's finest rocker, 'Believe What You Say'. Yet Jesse's self-penned single, released on his own Bluegrass label out of West Van Lear, Kentucky (in a package deal with the Starday label), came and went without troubling the mainstream music industry. Maybe it was the downhome lyrics (in which he describes having a girl in 'ole Kentucky' and another in Tennessee, and boasts that his gal loves him and 'loves that beer and wine'), but a more likely explanation was the limited pressing and poor-to-non-existent distribution.

Whatever the story, Jesse's record was one more example of fired-up rockabillies taking an Elvis Sun single as a blueprint and running wild with it. 'Mama, Mama' used 'That's All Right' as a template, as did 'Walking, Talking Babydoll' by The Three Ramblers (1958), 'Play It Cool' by Ray Campi (1957), and the decidedly back-to-basics 'Party' by Al Sims & the Alpine Two (1958). Elvis's version of 'Baby Let's Play House' directly inspired numerous rockabilly songs, among the best of which are the slap-bass tour de force 'Cool Off Baby' by Billy Barrix (1957), 'Stack-a-Records' by Tom Tall (1958) and

'You're So Dumb' by Mack Banks & His Drifting Troubadours (1956). Echoes of The Hillbilly Cat's final Sun single, 'Mystery Train', can be heard in 'How About Me Pretty Baby' by Jimmy Johnson (1956), 'Run Baby Run' by Claude King (1957), 'My Woman' by Burrie Manso & the Bonnivilles (date uncertain) and Conway Twitty's 'Long Black Train' (1960). Even Presley tracks like 'You're A Heartbreaker' inspired songs such as 'You're A Cheater' by Don Sessions (1959), while other singers simply chose to adopt the King's early style wholesale: for prime examples of this, try the wonderful 'Mama Don't You Think I Know' by Jackie Lee Cochran (1956) or 'Baby Fan The Flame' by Harold Shultters & His Rocats (1956). The interesting thing about all the above-named songs is that, while they wear their influences right out in the open, they all bring something genuinely individual to the mixture. The form is simple, but the varieties are endless.

THOSE CATS DOWN THERE REALLY PLAYED GUITAR

Of course, not everyone could be Elvis. It helped if you were handsome enough to make the girls scream, like Huelyn Duvall, whose toughest rockabilly side was probably 'Three Months To Kill' (1958), a storming rocker written for him by the very talented Danny Wolfe. Good looks weren't everything, though, as was proved when Danny wrote another song called 'The Will Of Love' (1958), released on a Texas label called Twinkle, which Wolfe co-owned with multiple-label entrepreneur Major Bill Smith. Brilliantly performed by Tooter Boatman & the Chaparrals, with Danny himself on piano, 'The Will Of Love' was a driving powerhouse of a tune backed by some of the finest rockabilly drumming of the era. Major Bill later summed up the difference between Tooter and Huelyn, speaking to Bill Millar, Ray Topping and Adam Komorowski:

[of Duvall] There's very little to say about the guy, he was a pretty boy, very, very handsome... He played guitar and was the one the women would crave... but Tooter was more talented; he was a great rockabilly singer and he could make a guitar walk down the street ... Tooter was all Texan, heavy set and he had a finger missing but he could still play that guitar... Charlie O'Bannon who played lead – he'd been in a fire or something and his face had been burned and he had a little bitty ear left on one side – but a great, great, great guitar player, those cats down there really played guitar.

Tooter had only one other solo single (issued in 1962, with his name listed on the label as Tutor Boatman), but as a member of the Chaparrals he was involved in another cracking 1958 rockabilly record, 'Poor Gal', issued on the Rebel label out of South Pittsburgh, Tennessee. He died in a car crash in 1964, leaving behind a large number of impressive 1950s rockabilly recordings which have since surfaced on a variety of albums.

Several of the wilder singles of the late 1950s were recorded by people whose main success, like Danny Wolfe's, lay in songwriting rather than performing. When not turning out hits for Gene Vincent and others, Wolfe himself sang several of his own excellent rockabilly songs for the Dot label, such as 'Let's Flat Git It' (1957) and 'Pucker Paint' (1958), while Baker Knight – the man behind a string of Ricky Nelson's finest, including 'Lonesome Town' (1958) – turned in a killer performance of his own on 'Bring My Cadillac Back' (1956), under the name Baker Knight & the Knightmares. Nelson, of course, was also benefiting from the songwriting talents of another pair of rockabillies, Johnny and Dorsey Burnette, who would have seen an awful lot more cash from those activities than they ever did for their groundbreaking Rock'n'Roll Trio recordings. Then there's Ric Cartey, who made a handsome amount of money from co-writing the country ballad 'Young Love' for Sonny James (1956), but who also sang pure-bred rockabilly songs like 'Born To Love One Woman' (1957) and the frantic 'Scratching On My Screen' (1958).

However, songwriting didn't always pay off, no matter how good the material. Macy 'Skip' Skipper wrote and sang fine songs, and was in the right place at the right time – he even cut material for Sun Records in 1956 – but the money failed to roll in. His Sun material wasn't issued until decades later, which is a real shame, since it included his own hymn to amphetamine-fuelled dancing, 'Bop Pills', while Skipper's one great single, 'Quick Sand Love'/'Who Put The Squeeze On Eloise' (issued circa 1957 on what appears to be his own label) undeservedly failed to set the charts alight. When contacted by writer Randy McNutt in 1987, Skipper sounded heartily sick of the whole business:

> Now I am sixty-seven years old and all this sounds so trivial to me. Unless, of course, somebody wants to pay me for my trouble. I'm not going to work for nothing. That don't mean a thing to me… As far as I'm concerned, the music business is dead. Hear me? I'm not going to bother with it, either. I wouldn't send you a picture if I had it. You tell all those people to spin those records till they wear out, 'cause I don't care. It's a dumb business no doubt. I'd like to get paid for my trouble.

THE CALL OF THE WILD – TOM REEVES AND NERVOUS NORVUS

Some people, like Skipper, were writing perfectly good songs, but never saw the success their music deserved. Then there were others who didn't really fit neatly into any particular category, and are hard to place, even now. In October 1956, Tom Reeves unleashed a single on the Crest label, out of Hollywood, California, entitled 'Primitive Love'. Crest had issued Eddie Cochran's rockabilly classic

'Skinny Jim' a few months earlier, just before Eddie hit the big time, but 'Primitive Love' was really something else: jungle noises, caveman sounds, bleating goats – this one had it all. It may have been cut in Hollywood, but Reeves was from Alabama, and his vocal was as country as they come. Sure it was a novelty record, but it still exerts a weird power that takes it to another level completely. Crest were probably hoping to have a similar freak hit to that enjoyed in June of the same year by Nervous Norvus with his blood-happy dangerous-driving single, 'Transfusion', which, astonishingly, even merited a full-page article in *Life* magazine (an honour never granted to Gene Vincent, say, or Jerry Lee Lewis). 'Transfusion' was an unstoppable megahit which came completely out of nowhere:

> The newest example of gruesome song hits to be let loose across the land is 'Transfusion', which already has sold half a million records since its release two weeks ago. 'Transfusion' imparts a noisy moral about a reckless driver who crashes on the highway – the sounds of his smash-up play a big part in the song. The wounded driver yelps for a transfusion – *Slip the blood to me, bud ... Put a gallon in me, Allen* – then resolves to drive carefully ever after. The song was written by James Drake, an ex-truck driver who now calls himself Nervous Norvus because

he is so jumpy. Norvus, who is 44, began composing four years ago ('Ape Call', 'Noon Balloon from Rangoon'), says he gets ideas sitting in his California backyard, wearing dark glasses, going 'Ump, ump'.

It was the great American success story – if ol' Jimmy Drake could do it, so could you. There was even a swift cover version performed by The Four Jokers. Still, not everyone was exactly thrilled to see 'Transfusion' riding high in the Top Ten, nestling alongside 'Heartbreak Hotel'. While deejay Lou Barile of WKAL, Rome, New York, called the record 'a terrific plug for safe driving … aimed right at the age group the National Safety Council has been trying so desperately to reach', Frank Bleam, over at WAYB, Waynesboro, Virginia – a station which banned the record – said 'we consider the lyrics in poor taste'. Poor taste or not, it sold by the bucketload, and after that, the field for novelty rockers was wide open.

WORE TO A FRAZZEL

Finally there are many hundreds of performers, probably thousands, about whom pretty much nothing is known at all, yet whose music continues to fascinate rockabilly enthusiasts. Round about April 1958, a one-off single appeared on the Sunset label out of Tannersville, Virginia – the sole release by that imprint – both sides of which are so ridiculously good that it seems unthinkable that those responsible never did anything else in the music business. Perhaps they changed their names. Perhaps they died. Whatever the story, that lone 45, 'Wore To A Frazzel'/'Sunset Blues', by Tony and Jackie Lamie with the Swing Kings, beats the output of many well-rewarded 1950s chart artists absolutely hollow. Lyrically and musically it's got what the trade papers called that 'back shack' sound, and the band rattle along like an express train running on hill-country hooch. We know that Tony Lamie sings the vocal, and one or other of the Lamies wrote the songs, because it says so right there on the label. Starday issued it as part of a custom deal, but that's about all that can be said, except that it sounds like the work of people who knew *exactly* what they were doing, and had a hell of a fine time in the studio doing it.

Much the same is also true of Dale Vaughn, who cut the exuberantly savage 'How Can You Be Mean To Me' at some indeterminate date, and seems to have come out of nowhere and then swiftly disappeared, leaving behind a world-class slice of rockabilly brilliance. Vaughn's band kick up a barely controlled guitar storm over which his vocal rides like a professional surfer, and the savage sound of the record is one which anticipates the likes of the Stooges by over a decade. His sole 45, credited to Dale Vaughn and the Starnotes, seems to have been the one and only release on the Von label, which was apparently based in Memphis. The flipside, 'High Steppin'', was also pretty good, and Dale himself wrote both songs. As far as solid information goes, that's about it. So who was Dale Vaughn? Well, he doesn't appear to be connected to Dell Vaughn (aka Dell Vaugh), who, confusingly, cut a song for a Detroit label in 1964 under the name Dale Vaughan. Outside of that, like the Lamies, he seems to have left no trace.

This is the remarkable thing about those times, when even in the late 1950s, as the music industry was fending off public scandals, it was estimated at the time that somewhere between fifteen to twenty new labels were starting up each week. Someone, somewhere reckoned they could make money issuing all sorts of music, giving rise to an explosion of talent in which people like Dale Vaughn at least had their shot at making a record.

As late as the mid-1990s you could still turn a profit on an album or a single which might only sell a couple of thousand copies. These days the same record would shift only a tiny fraction of that, owing largely to illegal downloading, and so the small labels which used to bankroll these discs, and the independent distributors that marketed them, have largely gone out of business and the records aren't even being made. It costs money to be a musician. Last time I looked, recording studios were still charging fees, and so were rehearsal rooms, and guitar shops, and gig venues. It's only the bands who are apparently supposed to give their work away for free. If this situation was transposed to the 1950s, we'd still have Pat Boone. He wouldn't have starved, and his records would still have been made. But we wouldn't have Tony and Jackie Lamie, and we wouldn't have Dale Vaughan. There'd have been no percentage in it.

11 ALL ABOARD THE BANDWAGON

TREND JUMPERS, HILLBILLY CONVERTS AND THE
OLDEST TEENAGERS IN TOWN

Rockabilly had deep roots in hillbilly and country music. Of course, these strains were mixed up into a wild stew with R&B, boogie-woogie and blues, but then the hillbilly and western swing boys had also been drawing on those influences for decades. Yet it's often said that Nashville and the country music establishment initially viewed the rise of rockabilly and rock'n'roll with something like the same enthusiasm as the citizens of London greeted the bubonic plague in 1665.

There is a fair amount of truth in this, but it's not the whole story. In 1958, country deejay Carl Shook, of WGRC, Louisville, told *Billboard* that he'd lately interviewed Walter D. Kilpatrick, chairman of the *Grand Ole Opry*, about the state of country in this new era of rock'n'roll:

> It was an extremely interesting chat, with the meat of the thing being that real c&w music will always be the prime product of *Grand Ole Opry*. Trends like rockabilly will be tolerated but genuine country material and

artists have been, and will continue to be, the lifeblood of the *Opry*.

In other words, keep calm, and with luck it might just go away. Even today, the current edition of Bill C. Malone's landmark study, *Country Music USA*, when speaking of the late 1950s, repeatedly talks in terms of the 'threat' of rock'n'roll. At the time, however, many people in the country business soon noticed how much money was being made, and a fair few mainstream entertainers who were way too old to know better began attempting to get down with the kids. Some even recorded under assumed names, just in case it might hurt their careers or drive away their regular family audience. This often said more about the mood of the times than their ability to deliver the goods. Certainly there were those who turned in half-hearted or unconvincing shots at the rockin' sound, but a surprising number delivered very satisfying performances, even if a few of them looked like they'd have more in common with the chairman of Western Union than the King of Western Bop.

CARSON ROBISON – THE SINGING DIRT FARMER

If Elvis at Sun was a nineteen-year-old 'Brando with a voice', then you might think that a veteran hillbilly singer-songwriter born in 1890 would be rather unlikely to follow in his hepcat footsteps, but Carson Robison – last encountered in Chapter 1 writing hit material for Vernon Dalhart in the 1920s – gamely weighed in with a double-sided rockabilly single in 1956, 'Rockin' and Rollin' With Grandmaw (On Saturday Night)'/'Hand Me Down My Walkin' Cane'. Old enough at that stage to qualify for his pension, Robison had been successfully recording and writing a huge variety of material for the hillbilly market during the intervening years, testing out his songs on all manner of country dwellers, as this 1945 *Billboard* profile shows:

> Carson J. (Robbie) Robison, who has written more than 1,000 songs, is a successful dirt farmer. He has a 200-acre farm at Pleasant Valley, N. Y., where he puts in most of his time. Robbie tries out his effusions on the cattle, pigs and chickens, then on the neighbors. If everything seems to be all right he bundles up the tunes and takes them to New York to the offices of Bob Miller, Inc., his publishers, talks about plantings, crops, etc., gets a free meal from his publisher, then goes back to the farm to write more songs. He has just recorded four of his latest compositions for Bluebird.

'Rockin' and Rollin' With Grandmaw' was pretty much Carson's swansong: he was born seven years before Jimmie Rodgers and had outlived him by more than two decades, but died in 1957, having at sixty-six been probably the oldest first-generation singer of rockabilly. Robison, however, was by no means the only hit-maker from the previous decades to attempt the new style. Take the case of Bill Nettles, a comparative youngster born in 1901, who had long been pounding out hillbilly boogie records in a career stretching back to the 1930s. In 1954, when he was a deejay on KNOE, Monroe, Louisiana, he signed a three-year record deal with the Starday label, cutting a fine slab of rockin' wax called 'Wine-O-Boogie'. This was probably an attempt to revisit the success of his 1947 hit 'Hadacol Boogie', a song about a then-popular alcohol-filled 'health tonic' drink, and his new record continued the theme with enthusiasm. Nettles may have been in his fifties at the time of recording, but when it was picked up and reissued on the 1980 Ace Records LP *Kings Of Rockabilly Volume One*, it fitted right in without any trouble at all.

Starday provided a home for a fair few hillbillies-turned-rockers around that time, such as western swing veteran Link Davis. Born in 1914, he'd helped pioneer the styles that would lead to rockabilly, and had taken lead vocals on the Crystal Springs Ramblers' 'Fort Worth Stomp' (1937). In the mid-1950s, Davis wound up as a staff musician at Starday, went on to play sax on 'Chantilly Lace' by the Big Bopper (1958), and also recorded a selection of rockabilly tracks of his own for a variety of labels from 1955 onwards. One of them, 'Trucker From Tennessee' (1956), used a lyrical device which became quite popular with those from the country field who were attempting rockabilly – if in doubt, write a song about Elvis.

CHASIN' THAT HOUND DAWG

The King and his song titles showed up in all sorts of records, but the great honky-tonk singer Onie Wheeler (born 1921) managed to write a whole song about The Hillbilly Cat without once mentioning him by name. It was called 'Onie's Bop' (1956), in which Wheeler explains by means of a series of pin-sharp vocal impersonations that he can sing just like the established roster of hillbilly heroes such as Hank Williams, Ernest Tubb and Lefty Frizzell, but that his attempts to sound like the year's new singing sensation end in disaster. The irony is that it's a nice gently rocking record in its own right, and that Onie then moved to Elvis's old

home, Sun Records, the following year, where he turned in a number of deeply satisfying rockabilly performances such as 'Walkin' Shoes' and 'Tell 'Em Off'.

It wasn't just the well-known hillbilly singers who tried to score a hit by associating themselves with the King. There are a fair few one-off singles referencing him by obscure outfits like Jimmy Woodall & His Tarpins, one of several who used the drafting of The Hillbilly Cat into the army as an excuse for a song. Jimmy's record was titled 'Uncle Sam's Call' (1958), and repeatedly refers to Elvis as a 'high-geared daddy' – a double-entendre phrase taken from the title of a Jimmie Davis hillbilly recording from 1937, meaning that he was a wild one for the women, fired up like a hot-rod motor – but now, predicted Woodall, Uncle Sam was going to change that. Other people took the simple route of mentioning one or more of Presley's hit songs prominently in their lyrics, or coming up with a superficially similar title. The excellent downhome rocker 'Pink Bow Tie' (1956), by Jerry Dove & His String Busters, attempts to make the title phrase as much of a slogan as 'Blue Suede Shoes' – a song which is also name-checked repeatedly in the lyrics – and while the band's vocalist Bill Massey does a sterling job, he still sounds as if he's been around the block in the hillbilly business many times before discovering his inner teenager.

Then again, rather than singing about Elvis, you could always just copy one of his songs. Much of the King's Sun material consisted of cover versions, but he'd made them completely his own, and when *Grand Ole Opry* regular Marty Robbins decided to bring out a version of 'That's All Right', six months after The Hillbilly Cat, it was clear that he'd patterned it on the Sun cut rather than Arthur Crudup's 1946 original. Marty and his band closely follow the blueprint laid down by Elvis, Scotty & Bill, except that there's a fiddle solo in place of the guitar break, and the vocal is less personal, lacking the driving passion which Presley brought to the song. Robbins hadn't been the first to cover Elvis, however – that honour seems to have gone to western swing veteran Cliffie Stone (born 1917), who tried his own revved-up version of 'Blue Moon Of Kentucky' for Capitol in September 1954, just a month or two after Elvis's disc started causing a fuss. Phil Gulley then cut a similarly urgent rendition for Decca in October.

Other country singers commented more generally on rock'n'roll: Jack Turner (who covered 'Hound Dog' back in the pre-Elvis days of 1953 when it was an R&B hit), wrote and sang 'Everybody's Rockin' but Me' (1956), a bemused cry for help from someone confused by hipster talk of 'alligators' and 'crocodiles'. Jack's tune was in turn covered by another country artist, Bobby Lord, who himself cut some excellent rockabilly records for Decca that year, such as 'Beautiful Baby'.

You could go even farther, announcing your change of direction by spelling out the word 'rockabilly' in the title of your song. Some unexpected people turned in reasonably creditable efforts, as was the case with Guy Mitchell's mainstream 1957 pop hit 'Rock-a-Billy' (something of a surprise, given that this was the man who'd given the world 'Feet Up (Pat Him On The Po-Po)' in 1952, a song about the joys of changing a nappy). Far less convincing was a witless nursery rhyme of a tune called 'Ding Dong Rockabilly Wedding', cut in New York for the jazz label Savoy in 1957 by Libby Dean with the Ray Charles Singers, and covered by Marion Ryan in the UK, where its toe-curling chorus of 'hey dilly dilly, we'll play rockabilly' sounded more likely to provoke an outbreak of Morris dancing than frenzied hepcat bopping.

Better by far was 'Let's Go Rockabilly' (1957), recorded for Decca by the ever-laconic Tex Williams. Tex, a regular star of the *Town Hall Party* TV show out in Los Angeles, was forty years old at the time, and had made it big in the 1940s with great records such as 'Smoke, Smoke, Smoke (That Cigarette)' (1947) – Capitol's first ever million-seller – and 'Life Gets Tee-Jus, Don't It' (1948). On 'Let's Go Rockabilly' he keeps his cool, and manages to get away with youth-flavoured lyrics about a bebop baby and a teenage crush, and if only someone could have persuaded the Anita Kerr Singers to have taken the day off it would have been an outright winner. Tex's single 'You Rocked When You Shoulda Rolled' (1958) was greeted with less enthusiam in *Billboard* ('Tex Williams sings this rock and rolled effort nicely, but it's rather weak for the market'), but even so, he seems to reinforce the notion that not all of the old guard hated the new trend.

THE HAYRIDE DOES THE BOOGIE

In truth, the hillbilly fraternity had been getting accustomed to hopped-up, R&B-influenced country songs for some years before the rise of Elvis, so the hostility shown by some factions probably had much more to do with the overt sexuality of his performances and the wild crowd reaction he provoked than the musical content itself. The ease with which country star Webb Pierce was able to rework his 1951 hit 'Hayride Boogie' into the 1956 rockabilly release 'Teenage Boogie' shows how little distance there was between the new music and what the mainstream audience would accept. Similarly, Bill Carlisle was able to re-record his 1933 risqué song 'Rattlesnake Daddy' as something close enough to rockabilly in 1954, and find an appreciative audience. The fans, after all, had already heard songs like Fairley Holden's 'Papa's Gettin' Old' (1950) – near as damn a rockabilly song half a decade before the term was even invented – or Jack Guthrie's superb 'Oakie Boogie', which could easily have been cut by a rocker in the mid-1950s, but was in fact from 1947. Then there was megastar Eddy Arnold, who came out with a song called 'Hep Cat Baby' the very month that Elvis's Sun debut was released, in which he jokingly complains that he can't understand a word his young girlfriend is saying, because she's continually using hipster phrases like 'solid, Jack', 'dig this' and 'real gone'.

In 1953, a year before Eddy Arnold discovered the joys of jive talk, thirty-nine-year-old country deejay Arlie Duff ('The Singing School Teacher', from Jack's Branch, near Warren, Texas) had one of the smash hits of the season with the rousing hillbilly song 'Y'All Come', which was promptly covered by Bing Crosby on Decca and Johnnie Hicks on Columbia, among several others. Duff became a regular on the *Ozark Jubilee* show, and issued spirited follow-up singles such as 'Let Me Be Your Salty Dog' (1954). If you're looking to judge just how much a part of the mainstream country scene he was

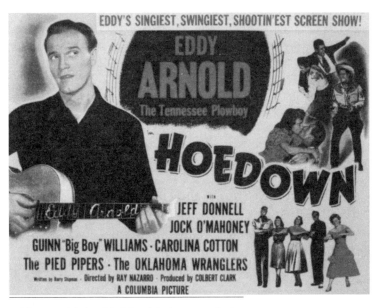

EDDY'S SINGIEST, SWINGIEST, SHOOTIN'EST SCREEN SHOW!

EDDY ARNOLD
The Tennessee Plowboy

HOEDOWN

with JEFF DONNELL
JOCK O'MAHONEY
GUINN "Big Boy" WILLIAMS · CAROLINA COTTON
The PIED PIPERS · The OKLAHOMA WRANGLERS
Written by Barry Shipman · Directed by RAY NAZARRO · Produced by COLBERT CLARK
A COLUMBIA PICTURE

Eddy Arnold, lookin' for his hep cat baby

at this point, when he married that same year, his best man was Red Foley, and the ushers included Porter Wagoner and Hawkshaw Hawkins. Then, after Elvis had made his mark, Arlie tried his hand at a rockabilly-flavoured record which poked gentle fun at the new terminology, 'Alligator Come Across' (1956), in which his gal is called Alligator because she 'creeps around'. It may have been satirising the genre, but it's also an enjoyable rocker in its own right. As it happens, Arlie's erstwhile best man also tried to join the rock'n'roll party in 1956, though with limited success. Born in 1910, Red Foley had started his career on the *National Barn Dance* radio show in 1930, and he'd notched up his fair share of million-sellers along the way, but his 1956 Decca release, 'Rock'n Reelin'', has too much of the square dance about it, and he sounds less than convinced about the lyrics he's delivering, despite their talk of 'country hipsters' and words like 'cool', 'crazy' and 'swingin''.

HONKY-TONK MEN – JOHNNY HORTON AND GEORGE JONES

As we've seen, many of the people trying rockabilly had well-established hillbilly credentials. Johnny Horton, however, not only gigged with Hank Williams in the early 1950s, but actually married Hank's widow three-quarters of a year after the great man passed away, and, to borrow a phrase from David Allan Coe, 'if *that* ain't country, I'll kiss your ass'. A veteran of the *Louisiana Hayride*, in 1956 Johnny made the switch to rockabilly like he was born to it. His opening gambit, 'Honky Tonk Man', was a damn-near flawless recording, showcasing Grady Martin's low-down, single-note guitar licks and a moonlighting Bill Black on rock-solid slap-bass. Johnny had driven to Memphis specially to ask Elvis whether he could borrow Bill for the recording session, because his own bass player/manager Tillman Franks was worried he wouldn't be able to achieve the required sound, as Franks later recalled: 'I could slap the bass, but I couldn't play it like Bill. Elvis said we could take Bill, but if anyone asked who was playing bass, we should say it was me.'

In that one evening session at Owen Bradley's studio in Nashville, Horton and his crew delivered three songs which were first-class rockabilly, and Johnny went on to borrow Bill Black for one further recording that year, the flat-out classic 'I'm Coming Home', a driving, powerful song of deceptive simplicity which sustains the tension by using just the one chord the whole way through.

The new husband of Hank Williams's widow may have taken to rockabilly like a natural, but Leon Payne, who wrote one of Hank's greatest songs, 'Lovesick Blues', seemed less comfortable with the genre. The well-respected hillbilly songwriter (who'd written the standard 'I Love You Because', and would later pen the magnificent 'Psycho'), was approaching his fortieth birthday when he dipped a toe in the rockabilly waters with his June 1956 Starday single, 'That Ain't It'/'Little Rock Rock', which he issued under the name Rock Rogers. Although the label's backing musicians handled the job with their usual expertise, Leon's voice sounds decidedly less suited to the genre than another country artist on the same label who opted for some kind of anonymity that year, George Jones. Admittedly, George was hardly likely to fool many people with his choice of pseudonym, Thumper Jones, particularly since the songwriting credits list one 'Geo. Jones' as the writer of both sides of that May 1956 single, 'How Come It'/'Rock It'.

Jones, who'd been singing country for the label since 1954, had already tried his hand at covers of 'Blue Suede Shoes', 'My

Baby Left Me' and 'Heartbreak Hotel' so far that year – the latter issued under the name Hank Smith & the Nashville Playboys – but he really got up a proper head of steam once he started writing his own rockabilly material. Nevertheless, just three months after this rockin' release, Starday were taking out large adverts in the trade press celebrating the success of his more Hank Williams-flavoured material such as 'Why Baby Why', and thanking deejays for voting him 'Up And Coming Country Vocalist' in a recent poll. They list the 'five hits in a row' he's just enjoyed, but make no mention of his lone rockabilly single. Even so, perhaps his finest rocking moment was still ahead of him, recorded right at the end of the decade, when a song written by the Big Bopper, 'White Lightning', took him to the top of the country charts. They may have called it country in Nashville, but it sure sounds like rockabilly to me, and it's no surprise that Eddie Cochran and Gene Vincent chose to cover this particular song on British TV in 1960.

It may seem by this point that just about everyone and his dog at the *Grand Ole Opry* and all points south moonlighted as a rockabilly singer some time around 1956, but of course there were many who didn't. Some people in the business absolutely despised rock in all its forms, not least powerful Columbia Records A&R man Mitch Miller, who famously dismissed it as 'pimple music' (which didn't stop him from negotiating with Tom Parker about buying Elvis's contract from Sun, or from producing Guy Mitchell's 'Rock-A-Billy' single). Others simply wanted to carry on the hillbilly tradition just as it was, and felt little need to don the requisite cat clothes. One such was Jimmy Ringo, who used to gig at a club called the Playhouse in Hollywood, run by Fred Maddox, former bass player with the Maddox Brothers & Rose (who'd made their own fine hillbilly/rockabilly recordings in the mid-

1950s, including a berserk 1956 parody of Elvis's version of 'I Got A Woman' which they titled 'The Death Of Rock'n'Roll'). Fred wrote a song called 'I Like This Kind Of Music', which Jimmy Ringo then sang on a single for Dot Records in 1958. It was a banjo-and-fiddle-propelled defence of old-style hillbilly music, with lyrics that took issue with anyone who criticised the genre, and said flat out that the singer didn't like rock'n'roll. Yet it's a fine piece of country rock, and its guitar solo is very close to those played by Scotty Moore on the early Elvis sides. The dividing lines between the two types of music were definitely blurred, then as now, which is why in 1956 Lattie Moore was able to re-record his own earlier hillbilly hit 'Juke Joint Johnnie' in response to the rise of rock as 'Juke Box Johnnie', adding a slightly heavier beat and tweaking the words just a little.

NUTHIN' YOU CAN TELL ME I DON'T ALREADY KNOW – JIMMIE LOGSDON

It would be wrong to leave a chapter about country singers who embraced rockabilly without mentioning one of the best of them all: Jimmie Logsdon, sometime hillbilly singer, songwriter and radio deejay from Panther, Kentucky, born in 1922. Jimmie had gigged with Hank Williams back in the day,

Jimmie Logsdon, a.k.a. Jimmy Lloyd

173

and had cut singles in the early 1950s for labels like Harvest and Coral. Unlike Mitch Miller, however, Jimmie was blown away by rockabilly when it came along, as he later told Colin Escott:

> I was really hung up on rock'n'roll like the kid in the street. I idolized Elvis. I had him on a remote in late 1955, just after he'd signed with Victor. I told him I'd been playing 'Good Rockin' Tonight' on the radio, at home, all over. I said to him, 'One day you're gonna be as big as Hank Williams.'

Jimmie cut a stripped-down single for Starday in his fiddle player's bedroom in 1957, 'No Longer'/'Can't Make Up My Mind', which showed off the pure hillbilly side of his voice to excellent effect, but when he moved to the Roulette label later that year, he really made an impact. His name changed from Jimmie Logsdon to Jimmy Lloyd, and although the company advertised him prominently as a country artist, his self-penned debut on the label, 'Where The Rio De Rosa Flows' (1957), was a prime example of easy-rolling 'back shack' rockabilly style, rocking enough to be covered by Carl Perkins a few months later. It was on the 1958 follow-up, however, that Jimmie really nailed it for all time. One side was a pounding rocker called 'You're Gone Baby', featuring superb guitar work from Grady Martin and Hank Garland and a totally convincing vocal from Lloyd. If there was ever any doubt about hillbilly boys making the transition to rockabilly, this would remove it, but the other side of the record was even better. It was a song which Jimmie and his agent Vic McAlpin wrote on the way home from an appearance at the *Louisiana Hayride*. If this had been the only recording of his entire career, Jimmie would still be up there with the best of them. He claims it was just meant as a novelty lyric, and sidesteps the double meaning which generations of listeners have found in the title, saying 'I don't know if it's dirty – it's in the mind of the beholder'.

Whatever the motivation, the song delivers all the way down the line. A rockabilly hymn to the joys of unbridled lust, it was a song to soundtrack every late drunken night down at the local juke joint, with stinging guitar runs, barrelhouse piano and a lyric sung by someone whose 'fuse is lit'. The song's title? 'I Got A Rocket In My Pocket'.

12 JUKE JOINT JOHNNIES

THE LIVE SHOWS, THE CLUBS, AND BUILDING AN AUDIENCE IN THE GIN JOINTS

It's 1955. Let's say you've just caught an Elvis show in somewhere like Texas or Louisiana as he, Scotty and Bill came swinging through your town on a series of one-nighters aimed at selling a few publicity photos and promoting those Sun 78s which had been causing such a stir. You're eighteen, you see the crowd go crazy, particularly the girls, and you tell yourself that looks like a damn fine way to make a living. Want to be a rockabilly singer? Better find yourself somewhere to play.

This was the first step on the ladder, and it could be a mighty rough one. Carl Perkins recalled playing joints where the chairs and bottles flew every Saturday night, and the whole band packed weapons just in order to defend themselves onstage when things turned nasty. Other singers played school auditoriums, flatbed trucks outside used-car dealerships or anywhere they could be heard. Amplification was generally one amp for the whole combo – including vocals. Stages were minimal or non-existent, so it was down to the performer to put the music across in as wild a fashion as possible. Some dressed up in masks, others walked out along the bar-top, using 50-foot mic leads – anything to get noticed. The sixties generation has always liked to spread the word that the fifties just consisted of 'How Much Is That Doggie In The Window' and a lot of 'moon/June' sappiness, but many of their acts would barely have lasted five minutes in a Louisiana roadhouse on a Saturday night. If you wanted to play, boy, you'd sure as hell better put on a show.

When Johnny Cash first saw The Hillbilly Cat perform, there wasn't even a stage involved. It was 9 September 1954, less than two months after Elvis started gigging, when he and his band the Blue Moon Boys hadn't yet played a show outside the Memphis area. That particular day found them appearing out in a car park, promoting the opening of a new shopping centre at the junction of Lamar and Airways, as Johnny recalled in his autobiograhy: 'The first time I saw Elvis, singing from a flatbed truck at a Katz drugstore opening on Lamar Avenue, two or three hundred people, mostly teenage girls, had come out to see him. With just one single to his credit, he sang those two songs over and over.'

Local paper the *Memphis Press-Scimitar* ran an article publicising the event on the day, promising music from the Choctaw Ramblers

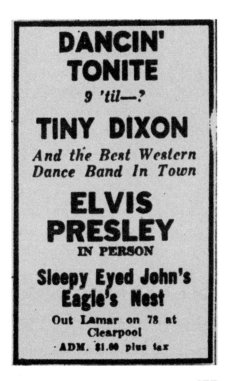

('the only Indian hillbilly band'), and explaining that the crowning architectural feature of the new shopping complex, a 28-foot-high model of an American Indian, 'can be seen from all approaches'. Katz employees would be wandering through the crowd 'dressed as black cats', handing out trinkets, and, as if all this were not enough, The Hillbilly Cat would be there too: 'Sleepy-Eyed John, the Eagle's Nest band and Elvis Pressley [sic], new recording artist, will finish off the first day.'

At this stage the newspaper obviously felt that its readers would be more likely to have heard of Sleepy-Eyed John Lepley, a local deejay on station WHHM, or the Eagle's Nest club, off Lamar Avenue, than the nineteen-year-old local boy whose name they hadn't yet figured out how to spell. Elvis had played a couple of shows at the Eagle's Nest in August, and would be back there twelve times before the year's end: tickets a dollar, ladies 50 cents, bring a fifth of booze in one of your pockets and buy youself a mixer at the bar.

If the *Memphis Press-Scimitar* mangled his name, Elvis would have looked in vain to find any mention of himself among the Katz attractions previewed in rival paper the *Commercial Appeal*. They did promise, however, that 'major prizes' would be handed out, including 'an original $1,000 oil painting' and 'a pedigreed pet puppy', not to mention 'jugglers, clowns, magicians and other entertainment' – the latter presumably including Elvis, playing second fiddle to a hound dawg for perhaps the last time in his career (although, come to think of it, the straights did force him to sing to a basset hound on the Steve Allen TV show in 1956).

Another teenage rockabilly who started out playing in parking lots and at store openings was Buddy Holly. Growing up in Lubbock, Texas, while still at school he had played at many of these kinds of promotional events from 1953 onwards, sometimes for free, in a hillbilly duo with his friend Bob

Montgomery, as the latter remembered: 'We played anywhere we could get to a microphone.'

All the wild clubs in Lubbock were carefully placed just outside the city limits, because, as a local resident remarked to Holly's biographer, John Goldrosen, 'This isn't just the Bible Belt, it's the *buckle* of the Bible Belt.' Strong religious sensibilities kept the prohibition on alcohol sales in town on the statute books until 1972, meaning that anyone looking for action headed for the honky-tonks just outside. In Lubbock in 1955, Elvis, Scotty & Bill came through town several times as part of a package tour playing at a substantial venue, the Fair Park Coliseum, but after the show, they usually headed out down Highway 84 to play another gig at a swinging joint called the Cotton Club, where white and black patrons could mix, and school-age musicians like Sonny Curtis could not only gain access to the building to watch the show but sometimes also get up onstage and play. Lubbock's Cotton Club had a moment of national fame of sorts when the January 1957 issue of scandal magazine *Confidential* ran a cover feature on the alleged womanising exploits of the nation's new rock sensation, under the headline: 'GIRLS! BEWARE OF ELVIS PRESLEY'S DOLL-POINT PEN'.

Other articles in the same issue of the magazine informed the discerning readership that 'Picasso Is An Opium Addict!' and gave them the lowdown on 'Joan Crawford's Back Street Romance With A Bartender', while in those same measured tones, *Confidential* explained how The Hillbilly Cat was supposed to be spending his time after hours at places like the Cotton Club:

> Directors of the Parent-Teachers Association would have fainted at the sight. It's a little past one in the morning inside a huge, barn-like nightclub on the Slaton Highway, just outside the usually quiet, sleepy town of Lubbock, Texas ... Elvis 'The Pelvis' Presley has just finished an undulating show that still has a lot of kids wriggling ... 'Oh, Elvis,' he hears, 'wait for me!' Turning, he watches as a pretty young girl rushes towards him. 'Would you please autograph me?' she shrieks. And with that she pulls a sheer blouse off her shoulders, revealing a low-cut bra. Older and wiser entertainers might have hesitated at having a three-quarters-bare bosom thrust at them for a signature. But not Elvis. With a flourish, he hauled out his doll-pointed pen and signed just above the dotted swiss line. Elvis on the righty. Presley on the lefty.

SONNY BURGESS – THE ARKANSAS WILDMAN

Future Sun rockabilly artist Sonny Burgess first saw Elvis, Scotty & Bill at an Arkansas club, the legendary Porky's Rooftop, in Newport, on 2 March 1955. (The club played host in the next few years to a stunning selection of Sun rockabilly heavyweights like Billy Lee Riley, Warren Smith, Carl Perkins, Jerry Lee Lewis, Roy Orbison and Charlie Feathers, as well as others such as the athletic Bobby Lee Trammell, who climbed

Sonny
Burgess &
the Pacers

up into the rafters while singing.) The next time Elvis came
through town, on 21 July, to play the Silver Moon Club out
on Highway 67, Sonny's band were the support act. They were
called The Moonlighters at that time, and had been gigging
regularly at another local club on 67 which played a key role
in the careers of many rockabilly musicians – Bob King's B & I
Club. It was King who'd given The Moonlighters their start in
the business, as Sonny told me:

> He was the first guy we started playing for back in '55, '54.
> Bob hired us back then to play, gave us ten dollars apiece,
> Friday nights. Oh, that was great money – I was working
> for forty dollars a week at the factory. So we'd make out
> well there, and we'd play right on up the road at Mike's
> 67 Club, which was a different type crowd than Bob's.
> Bob's was more farmers, more rednecks, and Mike's was
> more town people. We played 'em both, one on Friday,
> one on Saturday, got the same kind of money – so that's
> twenty dollars we made there for eight hours on two
> nights, and had all kinds of fun. Boy, just wonderful.

Sonny's many nights playing the honkytonks in Newport,

Arkansas inspired his best-known song, the joyous rockabilly smash 'We Wanna Boogie' (1956), his debut on Sun: 'Always liked that "We Wanna Boogie". I wrote that about downtown Front Street, Newport, Arkansas and goin' out to clubs out here on Highway 67.'

Bob King, from Battle Axe, Arkansas, opened his B & I Club in 1951, and ran it right up until his death in 2008 at the age of eighty-three. A one-storey brick building, it went on to host rockabilly shows by many of the original Sun label roster, including Harold Jenkins (before he changed his name to Conway Twitty) and Jerry Lee Lewis, who according to Bob always gave the club's piano such a pounding that the strings would need replacing. Things could get rough when the farming crowd came out to drink and let off steam, but Bob could handle himself.

Being the regular band at Bob's club had advantages for Sonny and his outfit (who soon changed their name to the Pacers), such as the night of 9 December 1955, when Elvis had played a show earlier in the evening at the local high school in Swifton, Arkansas, and then headed down to the B & I Club to wail a little more, for the princely sum of $450. Sonny's band had opened for Elvis earlier in the year when he'd played the Silver Moon Club, but this time they actually played along with him, as Sonny recalls: 'We did a jam session with him, at Bob King's, December '55, when he came up there.' This was also the night when Bob gave another new Sun signing, Johnny Cash, $20 to get up and sing a couple of songs. According to Sonny, that evening was a turning point for the Pacers, because of a conversation he had with Elvis's manager:

> Bob Neal was his manager, and he suggested we go to Sun, so we went over there and seen Sam, and Sam said, 'Well, go back and add some more to your band,' or

something like that. We picked up Jack [Nance], and Joe [Lewis], who was still going to high school. That made us a six-piece band. Went back over and recorded in '56.

Booking agent Bob Neal had been deejaying on the radio in Memphis since 1942, but it was when he switched to broadcasting an all-country show on WMPS in 1948, *The Bob Neal Farm Program*, that things really took off. This eventually led him to combining his radio activities with a parallel career as a concert booker, as he told *Rockville International* in 1973:

> The reaction to the programme was very good and I started occasionally doing some little shows within a hundred or a hundred and fifty miles' range of Memphis. I would take some local people, and every now and then some Nashville musicians like Johnny & Jack, Kitty Wells or Bill Carlisle, and I set up arrangements for them to play at a high school auditorium, a gymnasium or a ballpark or something. I would plug the shows on my radio programme, and I'd go out and be the host and MC and so on.

Neal also helped the career of another teenage singer, who was already under contract as a country artist, but changed to rockabilly after being booked by him on a succession of shows in July 1955 with Elvis. As Wanda Jackson told me, her father had been looking for an agent for her, and found Bob's name in the paper:

> He got a *Billboard* and thumbed through it and he found Bob Neal, in Memphis, so he called him. Bob said, 'I'd like to have a girl on the show with this young man that I'm booking that's getting very popular, very fast, and I

could use a girl on there.' So that's how it came about. I met Elvis, and I didn't know him, I'd never heard of him. I had cousins that lived in Odessa, Texas, and I just happened to write them and said, 'I'm getting ready to do my first tour with this guy named Elvis Presley, I never heard of him, blah, blah, blah.' They fired a letter back – you know, we didn't call much in those days – and they were *so* excited, because they knew him, you know.'

T FOR TEXAS

Elvis, Scotty & Bill had been criss-crossing Texas for the past nine months, and had gigged in Odessa four times already that year, so it's not surprising that Wanda's cousins were hip to his music. By this stage, Presley's ever-growing popularity meant that he was starting to move out of the clubs and into bigger venues, as Wanda says: 'Wherever we were with Elvis it was full. We did schoolhouses, like auditoriums in the schools, municipal auditoriums in the towns. I don't remember ever doing a fair with Elvis. The one club is all I remember, the rest were auditoriums of some sort.'

The speed of Elvis's rise from playing tiny clubs to much larger venues had been commented on by local paper the *Memphis Press-Scimitar* back in February 1955, when he'd been gigging for little more than half a year:

In the past three months he has traveled more than 25,000 miles on personal appearances, played to crowds of 3000. He travels by car with his instrumental teammates – Scotty Moore, hot guitarist, and Bill Black, bass, both Memphians. Their schedule for one week – New Orleans, Friday; Shreveport, Saturday; Ellis Auditorium in Memphis, Sunday; Ripley, Miss., Monday; Alpine, Texas,

Thursday; Carlsbad, N.M., next Friday and Saturday. Elvis will be 20 this month, and things are moving fast.

You might find yourself playing in the open air – at a store opening in a parking lot, as Elvis had done – or maybe in a tent at a larger agricultural fair. John Peel, who moved to America in 1960 and broke into the deejay business while in Dallas, told me he'd seen Roy Orbison performing at such an event around that time, just as the Wink Westerner was completing his transition from Texas rockabilly to superlative ballad singer:

I saw him on the midway at the Texas State Fair, doing one of those shows where you'd come out with a drummer and a bass player, on a little platform outside a tent – do a couple of numbers, and then somebody'd come out and say, 'If you wanna see the rest of the show, come on in', which is like something from the thirties, you think it only happens in the films...

Local municipal halls, capable of holding a fair-sized crowd, were put to all sorts of uses. If you were a teenage musician just starting out, even if you couldn't make it to the main stage, then maybe they'd let you play in the lobby. Other rockers found inspiration hanging out by the back doors of hardcore juke joints, like the legendary club on Fourth Street in Ferriday, Louisiana, called Haney's Big House, a black establishment that stayed open twenty-four hours a day. Inside were poker tables and high-stakes gambling, bouncers sporting brass knuckles, and live music from the likes of B. B. King and *Good Rockin' Tonight* star Roy Brown. Unsurprisingly, young Ferriday native Jerry Lee Lewis spent his formative years loitering with intent around Haney's, trying to sneak inside. Over in West Memphis – the wilder district across the bridge from Memphis itself – Jim Dickinson would do the same thing at a seriously rockin' black juke joint called the Plantation Inn as he explained to the writer Robert Gordon: 'The Plantation Inn was like a roadhouse out of a movie. The bouncer's name was Raymond Vega, big ol' nasty guy. Wore a cast on his arm but his arm wasn't broken. It was for hitting people. Sometimes he'd have a cane, and I remember thinking, what's this crippled guy going to do?'

The Plantation Inn was where the black artists played, but young rockabilly musicians cutting their teeth gigging at the other two legendary West Memphis nightspots, the Cotton Club and Danny's Club, found that these too were rough-and-ready joints with a beer-drinking, hell-raising clientele. The former venue fended off would-be stage invaders with an electrified wire which ran across the foot of the bandstand, while the latter opted for the less technological approach of having the artists play behind chicken wire, protecting them from flying bottles and other missiles. Rockabilly artists like Eddie Bond gigged at Danny's Club, while Carl Perkins and his band, who'd come up the hard way through many nights playing West Memphis clubs, commemorated those times in the song 'Dixie Fried' (1956) – a hymn to the rough-cut, stone-drunk, honkytonk life which tells the story of a reveller who uses his razor for something other than shaving.

Of course, not every gig involved dodging the bottles and knives. Package tours and one-off big shows, headlined by a major star but also featuring a long list of smaller names, were a good starting point for new artists looking for exposure. Elvis's first big gig was an appearance low down on the bill at a Slim Whitman show promoted by Bob Neal on 28 July 1954, a mere eleven days after the release of 'That's All Right'. Although he was fighting for space alongside country performers such as Sugarfoot Collins, Sonny Harvelle, Tinker Fry and Curley Harris, the fuss that had already been stirred up around The Hillbilly Cat on local radio by Dewey Phillips and Sleepy-Eyed John meant that he was singled out for a small preview of his own in the *Commercial Appeal*:

MEMPHIAN ON FROLIC. Feature Of Folk Music Show At Shell Tonight. Elvis Presely, the Memphis youth whose locally-recorded 'Blue Moon of Kentucky' and 'That's All Right, Mama' are getting attention all over the record industry, will be featured on the folk music frolic at 8 tonight at the Overton Park Shell. So will Slim Whitman of the Louisiana Hayride and Billy Walker, the Tall Texan, sponsor Bob Neal said yesterday.

One dollar got you an advance ticket to the show, kids paid seventy-five cents.

Of course, if your records hit the big time, then the crowds and the halls became larger, and so did the money. Bill Haley, who for a year or so was as big as just about anybody in the rock'n'roll field, was regularly playing for anything from 10,000 to 20,000 people across the US and Canada during 1956, and his cut of the ticket receipts was generally somewhere in the region of $1,500 a night. But that was for the select few who had already made it. For the moment, the club circuit was the best way to hone your live show and your repertoire, and it really didn't hurt if you could also get yourself a regular slot on the radio.

13 HOWDY, FRIENDS AND NEIGHBOURS

RADIO EXPOSURE – *GRAND OLE OPRY, LOUISIANA HAYRIDE* AND EVERYTHING ROCKIN' ON YOUR RADIO DIAL

In the England of the 1950s, there were no local radio stations. It was national or nothing, and the BBC had the monopoly, spoon-feeding those troublesome teenagers with a solid diet of real-gone hepcats like Dickie Valentine, Max Bygraves and Ruby Murray. If you weren't already a star with some solid industry muscle behind you, then your chances of getting on the radio were slim. In America, however, things had always been very different. With hundreds of local stations, there were numerous opportunities for all kinds of artists to be heard. These days you first make a record, then hope to wind up on the radio, but in 1950s America it was the other way round: local radio exposure was often the stepping stone to a recording career.

Many people who later became part of the first wave of rockabilly singers started out doing fifteen-minute guest spots on local US radio, often in the most informal situations, and at remarkably young ages. Children of eight or nine who

Max Décharné

could hold a tune or strum a guitar were able to gain access to some sort of listening public, usually by the simple process of turning up at the station one day and asking to be given a chance. In small communities the public were quick to ring up the broadcaster and let them know whether they approved or disapproved of a performer, and anyone able to cut the mustard was likely to be rewarded with the offer of a regular weekly, or even daily, radio slot.

Key rockabilly cities like Memphis or Dallas may have had populations little short of a half-million in the mid-1950s, but many other communities in which the new breed of rockers grew up were towns of just a couple of thousand people, or fewer. In such places, it could seem as if pretty much everyone knew everyone else, and access to homegrown radio was distinctly within the bounds of possibility, even for a teenager. Years before the Everly Brothers rose to national fame, they were cutting their teeth as schoolboy guests on the regular local shows in Iowa, hosted by their musical parents, Ike and Margaret, as Phil Everly told Robert K. Oermann:

> My brother started in radio before I did. He had a little show in a town called Shenandoah, Iowa, on a station called KMA – *The Little Donny Show*. He was in the third grade. On Saturday we'd go down there, and he would sing for fifteen minutes. And all the third grade little girls just thought he was swell. And I was smart enough to notice that. So it wasn't that much longer that I joined him.

Present-day Shenadoah has a population of five and a half thousand, so it would hardly have been a bustling metropolis in the early 1950s, but that was still a good deal larger than Wink, Texas, where Roy Orbison was growing up, which still has

190

The Everly
Brothers

fewer than a thousand inhabitants. Roy and his family moved
there in 1946, when he was ten years old, from his much larger
birthplace, Vernon, Texas (currently home to 11,660 people),
where he had already been presenting his own regular radio
show on station KVWC since the age of eight. If you had the
talent, your age didn't necessarily matter: when eleven-year-
old recording artist Brenda Lee was belting out the rockabilly
song 'Bigelow 6-200' (1956), Decca's labels on the single even
exaggerated her youth, billing her as 'Little Brenda Lee (9 Years
Old)'. A veteran at eleven, she'd already been a regular radio
performer for five years.

I'LL HAVE TO ASK MY MOTHER

It was a network TV show – the *Ozark Jubilee*, out of Springfield,
Missouri – that was eventually credited with giving Brenda

Lee her big break, which is also where she met another young perfomer who'd been working in radio for several years, Wanda Jackson. As Wanda reminded me, with a smile: 'I was there *first*, just to keep the record straight…' Radio played a decisive role in bringing Wanda to the attention of the music business, when a major country bandleader passing through her home town of Oklahoma City heard her singing on her own regular show in 1953. Hank Thompson, riding high in the wake of his huge hit of the previous year, 'Wild Side Of Life', was knocked out by the sound of Wanda's voice, but was surprised to learn how young its owner was:

> I remember him ringing up and saying, 'I'm in town, can you come and play this ballroom, could you sing with my band, Saturday night?' And he's my favourite singer, my all-time favourite, and I nearly fainted. He remembers it, and me too: I said 'Mister Thompson, I would *love* to, but I'll have to ask my mother'; and he said he thought, 'Well, how old is this chick?' He'd just heard me on my own programme, and I was only fourteen, going on fifteen – I don't remember what time of year it was – but I worked with him when he was in town, 'cause I was still in school, and he helped me get my first recording contract with Decca. That's something, to go to a major, with your first recording contract, but that's how he helped me. And I was with him two years, and then I went to Capitol, which was his label.

For a flavour of those informal, local radio broadcasts being made by numerous teenage performers all over the US in the days before rigid adherence to Top Forty playlists strangled the life out of the whole system, look no farther than a remarkable set of recordings which first surfaced as an LP on the Rockstar label in 1986 under the appropriate title *Radio Rockabillies*. While a number of authentic 1950s broadcasts have somehow survived from that era when most shows were live to air and never recorded – most notably several of Elvis, Scotty & Bill's appearances on the *Louisiana Hayride* – in general the audio quality is much less satisfying than the studio sound that labels like Starday or King were capturing. This makes it all the more remarkable that the pretty much unknown band featured on *Radio Rockabillies* managed to capture the full-blooded essence of their music on just a portable tape recorder. Based in Malden, Missouri (current population under 5,000), and led by Jerry Mercer and future Sun rockabilly Narvel Felts, they cut these fine performances in a room at their bass player's house, at Richardson's Music Store in Dexter, Missouri, and the Zanzi Club in nearby Hayti, on various occasions in late 1956. No engineers, no producer, no announcer – just the band themselves running through whichever songs might be in their regular live set at the time, interspersed with laconic introductions from Mercer, and the odd word about upcoming shows.

These performances were recorded for their regular Saturday afternoon slot on KTCB Malden, the songs played in a relaxed, good-natured way by teenagers who were gigging most nights of the week and were eager to cover the very latest Sun releases such as 'Go Go Go' (Roy Orbison, May 1956), 'All Mama's Children' (Carl Perkins, May 1956) or 'Dixie Fried' (Carl Perkins, August 1956). Their spirited version of this latter celebration of the knock-down, drag-out honky-tonks, played by a young band whose life revolved around performing at just such venues, is probably as close as you'll get to the sound of what the entertainment in local clubs would have been like. As well as an abiding admiration for Elvis – it's fascinating to hear someone cover 'Heartbreak Hotel' and 'Mystery Train' this close to the date of the originals – there's also a solid dose of black boogie and R&B. Their joyous cover of Big Joe Turner's 1955 barnstormer 'Boogie-Woogie Country Girl' turns the song into one of the best slap-bass rockabilly movers of the time, yet it remained unissued for thirty years, and its singer, Jerry Mercer, gave up music soon after, and never cut a record in his career.

'Boogie-Woogie Country Girl' was a perfect choice of cover: an uptempo black boogie tune orginally recorded by one of the giants of a genre that had inspired rock'n'roll – custom-written for that artist in response to the new music by white songwriter Doc Pomus with his pianist Reginald Ashby – about a hepcat farm girl who still dresses in solid hillbilly fashion (red check shirts and dungarees), but who 'don't dig squares 'cause Daddy taught her how'. It perfectly sums up the cultural and musical blend that produced rockabilly.

BORDER RADIO

Those informal recordings of Felts and Mercer, sometimes made with a handful of friends and fans present in the room, were tailored for a local audience, yet the approach was very similar to that employed by the Carter Family at the end of the 1930s on station XERA, when playing for millions of listeners. Located just over the border from Del Rio, Texas (on Mexican territory, to avoid US government restrictions), XERA had a massive 500,000-watt transmitter, powerful enough to be heard all the way up to Canada, but the Carter Family – its star performers – simply played and sang with no showbusiness trappings as if sitting in the corner of their own front room. This was in marked contrast to other established hillbilly shows of the time, such as the *National Barn Dance*, from WLS in Chicago (established 1924), or the *Grand Ole Opry* on WSM out of Nashville (1925). Both had originated in the radio boom years, when hillbilly programming was proving a solid financial success, and they had each gradually developed a format in which the studio audience was a key element. These shows were performed live in front of a large crowd, featuring a trusted team of regular presenters and stars, and broadcast from venerable theatres. The *Opry* had several homes in its first years, but from 1943 onwards it had been based at the Ryman Auditorium in Nashville, a late-nineteenth-century church building where the audience would sit on time-worn wooden pews listening to the giant stars of the country field such as Hank Williams, Roy Acuff and Little Jimmy Dickens.

As Elvis discovered, the *Opry* wasn't necessarily the right home for an upcoming rockabilly hepcat. After all, this was the show that had eventually tired of Hank Williams and his drink-and-pills-fuelled ways. The message seemed to be that it was all right to get up at the Ryman and sing about the honky-tonks, but anyone living too much on the wild side of life eventually found themselves being shown the door. With the coming of the rock'n'roll era, the *Opry* opened its doors to the likes of the Everly Brothers and Johnny Cash, but even the Man in Black was eventually asked not to bother coming back one night in 1965, after he smashed every one of the footlights at the front of the Ryman's stage with the base of his microphone stand.

PIPING HOT IN SHREVEPORT

If the dice were mostly loaded against a rockabilly artist making it onto the *Opry*, then its great rival, the *Louisiana Hayride*, was a different matter entirely. Indeed, the show produced in Shreveport, Louisiana, by the powerful 50,000-watt clear-channel station KWKH, had already played host in the early fifties to several musicians who would go on to make fine rockabilly recordings, such as guitarist James Burton and piano player Roy Hall. So many performers moved away from the *Hayride* and on to greater things that the show began billing itself as the 'Cradle of the Stars' – although Hank Williams went from there to the *Opry* and then back again, after the powers that be at the Ryman decided he was too

much trouble. Although it had difficulty holding on to its major stars, the *Hayride* quickly became a Southern institution, even celebrated in song by one of its upcoming singers, Webb Pierce. He cut the 'Hayride Boogie' at the start of his career in 1951, and went on to become the artist with the highest overall score in *Billboard*'s country charts in the whole of the 1950s, but that didn't stop him from successfully rewriting the song in 1956 for the rockabilly crowd and recording it as 'Teenage Boogie'.

The *Louisiana Hayride* began broadcasting every Saturday night from the Shreveport Municipal Auditorium in 1948, hosted by Horace 'Hoss' Logan, who'd broken into the radio business back in the early 1930s, passing an announcer's audition at KWKH by coming up with the phrase 'The delicate, volatile oils of Half Past Seven Coffee'. Two decades later, attempting to calm a *Hayride* crowd who'd been stirred up to distraction by The Hillbilly Cat, he coined the immortal words 'Elvis has left the building'.

It was the *Louisiana Hayride* which really set Elvis on the road to fame. He first appeared with Scotty and Bill on the show very early in his career, on 16 October 1954; just one of about twenty performers on that evening's show. He did well enough to be asked back the following week, when he was

ELVIS PRESLEY
Adults $1.00   Children 50c
Tickets on Sale At
THE COFFEE CUP
6TH AND AUSTIN

Elvis at the
Hayride, April
23, 1955

rewarded with a year's contract. Acts on the *Hayride* were supposed to have already had some sort of a record released, but they certainly didn't need to be on a major label, as Hoss Logan explained to Earl Porter in a 1976 interview: 'I didn't require an RCA or a Columbia. It could be the Po dunk label – a little small label – but we had to have something we could play and promote.'

Elvis was on Sun, which was hardly the big time in 1954, but KWKH had been plugging the two singles he'd released thus far, paving the way for his debut appearance. Logan had once turned away future star Johnny Horton, even though he was a friend, advising him to come back when he had a record contract. Once you got your break, it was all down to how you performed, how the audience responded, and whether Hoss Logan liked it:

197

Every week I would add one or two new acts and drop
one or so. If an act showed any promise – real promise –
I would keep them on the show for three months, or six
months, or nine months, or twelve months or longer …
The average audience for the *Hayride* for the ten years
that I ran it was 3,300 people each Saturday night … They
came mostly out of Texas, but they came out of Mississippi
and Arkansas and Georgia and Alabama and Oklahoma
and Arizona, New Mexico to see the *Hayride* because
KWKH covered a large area and because we were on the
network – on the CBS network for so long, we were known
throughout the country and in particular in the south, the
southwest. If we had to depend on the attendance from
the city of Shreveport, it would have died after the first
three or four weeks, and that's true of any show.

The list of Southern states given by Logan is matched by the
destinations of those endless one-nighters played by Elvis in 1954
and '55 when building his audience. He'd plug his Sun releases
on stage to a crowd that had likely as not been hearing them
regularly on the *Hayride* – a show he'd appear on upwards of
fifty times in the first two years of his career. Much of the nation
would theoretically have had the opportunity to chance upon
him on the radio, but the real fanbase was down South, among
those who'd also seen his astonishing live shows. Listeners who
tuned in to his 6 November 1954 broadcast also had the added
excitement of hearing the King of Western Bop laying down the
righteous word to the hepcats from a *Hayride* sponsor:

You can get'em piping hot after 4 pm
You can get'em piping hot
Southern Maid doughnuts hit the spot
You can get'em piping hot after 4 pm

The *Hayride* didn't just help give Elvis an audience, it also gave him a drummer, D. J. Fontana, who was one of the show's regular crew of musicians, as he told Randy McNutt:

In '54 I was playin' on the *Louisiana Hayride* as a staff drummer. I'm from Shreveport, you see, and I played in bands there from the time I was fifteen. After high school I played the strip shows, little clubs, anything I could find. On Saturday night, I played the *Hayride* ... I played with Elvis and his players, and I thought he had a unique sound, one that I shouldn't clutter up. I kept it simple.

D. J. Fontana wasn't the only local boy to use the *Hayride* as a stepping stone. Dale Hawkins, a teenager who was working at Stan's Record Store in Shreveport, cut a song with James Burton on guitar in 1957, late at night in the KWKH studio, after the radio station went off air for the evening (*Hayride* regular Hank Williams had done the same thing, using the down-time at KWKH after 1 a.m., several years before). Stan Lewis didn't just have a record store, he also had contacts, and the track wound up being released on the Checker label – a subsidiary of Chess in Chicago – and became a genuine rockabilly smash hit on the national pop charts. The song was called 'Suzie-Q', and it would help make Dale a household name and a regular on the *Hayride*. The roll call of rockers notched up by the Hayride's enlightened booking policy was impressive, including the likes of Werley Fairburn, Linda Brannon, Bob Luman, Endom Spires and the great Johnny Horton.

ROCKIN' THE SPORTATORIUM

If the *Hayride* was hep, so was its equivalent in Dallas, the *Big D Jamboree*. Since 1946, it had been kicking up a storm from a tin-roofed, 6,300-capacity local wrestling arena called the Sportatorium, on the corner of Cadiz and Industrial boulevards. An eight-sided structure, with a wrestling ring at the centre which doubled as a stage when bands played, it hosted the *Big D Jamboree* every Saturday night from 8.30 p.m. till midnight. The list of hardcore rockabilly artists who played there – not to mention all the country and hillbilly acts – is testament to the sheer good taste of its booking agents, and from 1953 onwards that meant one man, Ed Watt. The show was owned and run by Ed McLemore, and sponsored by local station KRLD, another powerful 50,000-watt operation like KWKH in Shreveport, with an equally long reach. Elvis first showed up there to play on 16 April 1955, a week or so before the release of his fourth Sun single, 'I'm Left, You're Right, She's Gone'/'Baby Let's Play House'; one of a number of appearances he'd make on the *Jamboree* that year. Given how many live gigs he'd already done in Texas since the previous summer, it's perhaps surprising it took him so long, but then he was still under contract to the *Hayride*. A whole sixty cents bought you a ticket to see Elvis, plus support acts including early female rocker Charline Arthur, and if you were feeling flush, you might want to lay out a further 10 cents on the official programme, which claimed it to be 'The Southwest's Biggest, Oldest, Boldest, and Best Country Music Attraction'.

On 14 January 1956 the *Big D Jamboree* hosted a show by none other than Bill Monroe & the Blue Grass Boys, supported by up-and-coming act Jimmy and Johnny. The latter had been releasing hillbilly records since 1954, but would shortly cut storming, fully fledged rockabilly singles such as 'Sweet Love On My Mind' (released October 1956) and 'Can't Find The Doorknob' (1958), featuring some of the best-recorded, most prominent slap-bass of the day. (Back in November 1954,

Sid King

they'd even headlined over Elvis at one of his early club gigs at the Eagle's Nest in Memphis.)

If you'd been in the right place at the right time, you could have seen at the *Big D* many rockabilly heavyweights, both national stars and cult successes, such as Carl Perkins, Gene Vincent, teenage sensation Ronnie Dawson (Mr 'Rockin' Bones' himself), Johnny Carroll & his Hot Rocks, Wanda Jackson, Sid King & the Five Strings, Johnny Cash, Groovey Joe Poovey, Rose Maddox, Johnny Dollar or Buck Owens.

There were many such radio progammes spread out across the South. WWVA's *Wheeling Jamboree*, from Wheeling, West Virginia, featured performers such as early Sun rocker Hardrock Gunter and MGM rockabilly Bob Gallion, while Janis Martin was a regular on the *Old Dominion Barn Dance*, broadcast by WRVA, Richmond, Virginia. Then there was WCMS's *Dixieland Jamboree*, which started broadcasting from the Von Theatre in Boonville, Mississippi, in 1954, and featured Elvis on the show on 3 January 1956, shortly before all hell broke loose with the release of 'Heartbreak Hotel'. Booked by promoter Charles Bolton, it presented a magnificent array of rockabilly talent, as he told Jim Cole:

> We had artists from the area and Memphis like Eddie Bond, Johnny and Dorsey Burnette, Charlie Feathers, Warren Smith, Johnny Cash ... Now keep in mind Elvis Presley and Johnny Cash were country artists. They called them rockabillies, but all they had was the electric guitar and the bass. They didn't have the loud drums and all that back then.

One way or another, anyone with a half-decent band and a little ambition had the chance at playing live on a radio show of some kind. Then again, even if all the various *Hayrides* and *Jamborees* weren't queuing up to give you top billing, there was always the chance that your local deejay might take a shine to a record you'd just cut one crazed evening in someone's garage and start playing it back to back, plugging it relentlessly in between all the adverts for hog feed and patent nerve tonics. In those days, most deejays were a law unto themselves, and if they liked a song, they'd play it, whether the artist was famous or not – or, indeed, even if that particular song wasn't supposed to be the featured side of the single. Nationally famous deejays such as Alan Freed eventually ran into a storm of controversy about just how much influence they'd exterted over the hit-making process (and how much money they might have made in so doing), but if you were lucky, your local town might have someone who completely followed their own path, and played whatever they damn well pleased. In Memphis, of course, there was the prime exponent of such behaviour, the legendary Dewey Phillips, who mixed up an intoxicating stew of everything that was swirling around, and bent the heads of local teenagers nightly on his *Red Hot & Blue* show. As Jim Dickinson recalled: 'It was years before I figured out that this stuff I heard on Dewey Phillips's show wasn't popular music.'

And for a brief, glorious moment, they even gave wildman Dewey his own television show. But that's another story...

14 SAME TIME, SAME CHANNEL

FROM LOCAL TV TO *AMERICAN BANDSTAND*

As with radio, an appearance on US television in the 1950s could prove to be a stepping stone to a record contract, rather than just something reserved for established stars. There were numerous local TV shows, all of them with airtime to fill, who often gave space to teenage musicians. So long as you didn't outrage the station's home-town sponsors or frighten the horses, you might well land yourself a half-hour spot in which to strut your stuff and publicise your gigs.

In the spring of 1955, a full year before his first record release on the tiny Je-Wel label, young Texan rockabilly Roy Orbison and his band the Teen Kings were given their own regular thirty-minute show on a TV station broadcasting across the region from Odessa. The group landed this spot by winning a battle-of-the-bands competition, their regular on-screen appearances sponsored by a furniture company. Thus on one occasion when Elvis came through town – as he did regularly that year to play the local high school field house – Roy was able to invite the Hillbilly Cat onto his own show for a guest performance. Similarly, Orbison's first meeting with

Johnny Cash came about because they were both booked to appear on another local TV show in Texas towards the end of 1955. Although Roy's first single, 'Ooby Dooby'/'Tryin' To Get To You', would first appear on a one-off label based in Albuquerque, New Mexico, in April 1956, his on-air meetings with two of Sam Phillips' brightest stars the previous year would certainly have set him thinking about approaching Sun in Memphis for a shot at the big time.

Home-grown TV stations provided a showcase for upcoming small-town talent, and sometimes played host to larger-than-life characters who were way too scary for the major networks – probably none of them as inspirationally crazed as Memphis's own Dewey Phillips. He'd already been in at the very start of what was to become Sun Records, when he and Sam Phillips (no relation) collaborated briefly on setting up the Phillips label in the summer of 1950. Billed as 'The Hottest Thing In The Country', it managed one release (three hundred copies of 'Boogie In The Park' by bluesman Joe Hill Louis) before disappearing without trace. Dewey had been a fixture on the Memphis radio scene since 1948 – a free-wheeling, jive-talking motormouth with a habit of playing any kind of record that appealed to him, whether black, white or Martian, on a one-man mission to tighten the collective wigs of his listeners. He talked, and sometimes screamed, over the sound of the records he was playing, and when advertising programme sponsor Falstaff Beer was on his show, Dewey's mouth went places that other announcers' wouldn't: 'If you can't drink it, freeze it and eat it. If you can't do that, just open up a rib and pour it in.' It's really no surprise that he became the first deejay ever to play an Elvis record, but it's to Memphis's great credit that someone in late 1956 also felt the need to give him his own TV show.

Daddy-O Dewey was already a full-blown local legend with

his *Red Hot & Blue* radio programme when he was handed the controls of his very own TV show, *Phillips' Pop Shop*, broadcast every day from 3.30 p.m. to 4.30 p.m. by WHBQ simultaneously on television and radio – a prime after-school slot. Did he tone down his frantic presentation style for the new medium? In a word, no. Breaking most of the rules of the format, he spun records then flung them casually to one side, exchanged banter with technicians and interviewed passing celebrities while his oddly disturbing sidekick Harry Frizius prowled around wearing a gorilla mask, basketball players threw balls around the studio, and the camera and sound crew wandered in and out of view. The show consisted of pretty much anything Dewey felt like doing or saying at that particular moment.

AMERICAN BANDSTAND – BRING ON THOSE ROTATING PELVISES

In a town where rockabilly was being created nightly in bars and clubs, and at studios like Sun, Meteor, Moon or Fernwood, it's no surprise that a TV show like this briefly flourished during the music's finest era, and that rockabilly musicians like Billy Lee Riley were not only featured on the show but were also some of its biggest fans. But even Memphis eventually succumbed to the power of the newer national music television outlets, in particular a show out of Philadephia called *American Bandstand*, which in time swept all before it. It began in 1952 as just a local show called *Bandstand*, but in 1957 it picked up a new host, Dick Clark, and the added muscle of the ABC network, and started broadcasting nationally in the 3.30 p.m. afternoon slot on 5 August that year. Although Dewey's Memphis programme would occasionally take network feeds of clips from *American Bandstand*, which he would cut into his show almost at

Dick Clark

random, *Phillips' Pop Shop* was eventually pulled by WHBQ in January 1958 and replaced by *Bandstand*. Dewey's show moved briefly to a late-night spot, but was cancelled after four episodes. By contrast, Dick Clark's far more mainstream show would last all the way through until 1989. Although Clark's teenage record hop format eventually survived for over thirty years, its debut broadcast was roundly panned by *Billboard*'s reviewer Bob Bernstein, under the headline '"Bandstand" Sociology But Not Entertainment':

> As a sociological study of teenage behavior, the premiere was a mild success. As a relaxation and entertainment, it wasn't ... Dick Clark, a handsome and personable host who deserves a better network debut, chatted briefly with two guest acts before they mimed to their own platters. The bulk of the 90 minutes was devoted to colorless juveniles trudging thru early American

dances like the Lindy and the box step to recorded tunes of the day. If that's the wholesome answer to the 'horrors' of rock'n'roll, bring on those rotating pelvises. Technically, the opener was a shambles, reportedly due to an engineering strike at the show's point of origination, Philadelphia. A local smash, the series isn't going to help that city's reputation nationally as a quiet town. ABC-radio has just banned records. Why doesn't ABC-TV?

Even so, ABC was hardly going out on a limb launching a national rock programme in the second half of 1957. Over on rival network CBS, Ed Sullivan's long-running TV show, originally called *The Toast of the Town*, had picked up huge ratings among the country's teenagers when they'd first included Elvis in his line-up on 9 September 1956. Sullivan's was very much an old-school vaudeville show, however, rather than a rock'n'roll jamboree. Two weeks later he featured Edith Piaf, and during that year he'd already hosted the likes of Humphrey Bogart, Doris Day, Cab Calloway, Noël Coward, Johnny Weismuller, Gracie Fields, Alberto Zoppe's Midgets, the US Naval Academy Glee Club and a selection of performing bear and chimp acts. Mr Sullivan certainly believed in covering all the bases. Dick Clark's *American Bandstand*, by contrast, was aimed squarely at the teenage after-school crowd, with likely-looking couples dancing on-screen to the latest hits.

The decision to give national airtime on the *Sullivan* programme to the likes of Elvis and those who followed him was hardly surprising, since the viewing figures and the obvious hysteria surrounding each of The Hillbilly Cat's 1956 appearances on rival shows hosted by Steve Allen, the Dorsey Brothers and Milton Berle would have swept away any reservations that Ed Sullivan may have had: if this was a (Memphis) flash in the pan, it was certainly a big one.

ELVIS AND THE NETWORKS – SUGGESTIVE ANIMATION

The *Steve Allen Show* had been launched by NBC on 24 June that year as a direct competitor to CBS's Ed Sullivan, going head to head with him in the prime 8–9 p.m. Sunday evening slot. Talking to the press before his show's launch, Allen played down the rivalry, but even though he was a professed jazz-playing hater of rock'n'roll, he'd nevertheless lined up the King of Western Bop in his initial run of guests:

> Allen does not feel that he has to go all-out to knock off Ed Sullivan, his CBS-TV opposition. He maintains that he would program the same kind of show if he were working for the British Broadcasting Corporation ... Allen's initial show will feature Kim Novak, Wally Cox, Vincent Price and Dane Clark. The second show will have as guests Andy Griffiths, Imogene Coca and Elvis Presley.

Elvis was such a sensation at the time that pretty much all the big TV shows scooped him up. Some, like Allen, attempted to humiliate him by dressing him up in tails and making him sing to a dog, while Milton Berle was much more interested in The Hillbilly Cat's effect on women:

> **BERLE:** I don't know what you're screamin' about. The way they're flippin' their lids, these girls down here... I wanna tell you, that beat with your foot is absolutely sensational. I wanna ask you something, Elvis, if I did that thing, the same way you did it, do you think I could get all the girls?

PRESLEY: Well, it might not help you get the girls, but at your age, it'd keep your blood pressure regular...

BERLE: How can I get these girls to scream over me this way? I really mean that, how can I do that?

PRESLEY: Well, Mr Berle, I don't think you'd like it. Well, I mean, I don't like it, all these girls screaming, always tearing your clothes off, always tryin' to rip you apart, always tryin' to kiss ya. I don't like it...

BERLE: You don't? Someone must have stomped on his head with those blue suede shoes.

Elvis's appearance on *Milton Berle* – in particular his movements while singing – stirred up a storm of controversy in the media. Jack O'Brien in the *Journal-American* wrote that 'Elvis Presley wiggled and wriggled with such abdominal gyrations that burlesque bombshell Georgia Sothern really deserves equal time to reply in gyrating kind ... He can't sing a lick, makes up for vocal shortcomings with the weirdest and plainly planned, suggestive animation short of an aborigine's mating dance,' while deejay Jerry Marshall on WNEW, New York, predicted on air that Elvis would 'have to drop the "hootchy kootchy" gyrations or end up as "Pelvis" Presley in circus sideshows and burlesque'. Despite all this, the show won the ratings war against its same-time-slot rival the *Phil Silvers Show* for the first time in months as a result of having booked Elvis.

The point to bear in mind is that all these top-rating network shows were variety – not rock music – programmes, designed to appeal to a general family audience, in homes where the choice of viewing was usually determined by middle-aged fathers who got a kick out of loudly questioning the singing ability and maybe the sexual orientation of any youthful entertainer served up in the firing line. The only thing that ensured repeat appearances was the undoubted pulling power and money-generating ability of these supposed one-hit wonders. As a *Billboard* headline put it, in the wake of the Elvis *Berle* appearance: 'Presley On Pan But Cash Keeps Rolling'.

The Hillbilly Cat rocked the *Milton Berle Show* on 5 June 1956, three whole months before Sullivan caved in and invited him onto his show (although Ed did find space for an outfit called the Hip Cat Hillbillies on 17 June). While it would be tempting to think that in 1956 Ed Sullivan had some kind of mystical conversion to all things hep and went from showcasing the likes of Victor Julian's Performing Poodles (1 May 1955) to presenting Mama Presley's rockabilly boy three times, this doesn't really square with the facts. More than a year prior to that first Elvis appearance, Sullivan had hosted the network TV debut of Bill Haley and His Comets, on 7 August 1955, where they had the pleasure of sharing a bill with pipe-smoking English crooner and children's favourite Max Bygraves, singer of 'Gilly Gilly Ossenfeffer' and 'You're A Pink Toothbrush'. Mind you, Bygraves was invited back the following week, whereas that would prove to be Haley's only *Sullivan* appearance. Bill and his Comets were riding high that year on the strength of 'Rock Around The Clock' being used as the theme song to the film *Blackboard Jungle*, so it's understandable that they'd have come to Ed Sullivan's attention, but it's far more intriguing that a couple of months later, on 20 November 1955, he gave programme space to Bo Diddley, alongside pioneering New York rock'n'roll deejay Tommy 'Dr Jive' Smalls. Diddley had only just broken through with his self-titled debut single on Chess records, and this was incredible mainstream exposure for him. Sadly, this would prove to be Diddley's sole network TV showcase in the whole of the 1950s, but it remains one of several precedents for Elvis's later *Sullivan* appearance.

To understand what all this meant in viewing figures, a report in the 13 October 1956 edition of *Billboard*, headlined 'Sullivan Chalks Up Top Viewer Count', spelt out the figures for the evening of the first Presley appearance on the *Ed Sullivan Show* (without once mentioning the salient point that Elvis had been a guest on that particular evening):

> Ed Sullivan's September 9 telecast reached the highest number of viewers of any regular show recorded by American Research Bureau. Its audience of 60,710,000 topped the previous ARB record of 58,900,000 for a September, 1955 telecast of 'The $64,000 Question'. Latest ARB results also give Sullivan the No. 1 rating figure of 57.1.

No wonder they asked Elvis back a week or so later. He sang four complete songs on the 28 October edition, sharing the bill with English comic actress Joyce Grenfell, and an outfit called The Little Gaelic Singers. If all this sounds like our man Ed had become an overnight convert to the joys of the Big Beat, the following week it was back to business as usual when they booked that well-known rockabilly, Nelson Eddy.

A REAL BIG SHOW

The coming year would prove to be the prime opportunity for rockin' acts wanting access to the *Sullivan* show and its huge national audience. Chart contenders such as the Del Vikings, the Everly Brothers, Bill Haley & His Comets, the Platters, Paul Anka, Tommy Sands, Billy Ward & the Dominoes and Frankie Lymon all appeared as Sullivan guests in 1957, and this also proved to be virtually the only year when the show presented genuine rockabilly artists. Charlie Gracie sang 'Butterfly' on the 10 March show (on which other guests included Henry Fonda); Texas rockabilly Buddy Knox and his partner in the Rhythm Orchids, Jimmy Bowen, performed 'Party Doll' and 'I'm Stickin' With You' on the 7 April show, alongside a line-up of talent which included the great hillbilly singer Ferlin Husky; Marvin Rainwater sang 'Gonna Find Me A Bluebird' on the 14 July edition (which also featured James Dean's old acting buddy, Sal Mineo, who'd just launched a pop career). The year closed with a couple of the finest rockers of them all. Gene Vincent and the Blue Caps tore up the 17 November show with a version of their current single, 'Dance To The Bop', and then 1 December 1957 saw Lubbock's own rockabilly sensations, Buddy Holly & the Crickets, break determinedly into the big time. They turned in gutsy versions of 'That'll Be The Day' and 'Peggy Sue' on a vintage *Sullivan* show which also featured former rockabilly Bobby Helms singing 'My Special Angel' and Sam Cooke performing his debut hit, 'You Send Me'.

As Charlie Gracie told the *New York Times* over four decades later, recalling how he wound up on the *Sullivan* show promoting his first single:

> It was pretty amazing for a poor kid from South Philly who didn't know anything to suddenly then have all of that, especially 'Ed Sullivan', which was such a big deal back then. It was really wonderful, and I thought I was ready for it. I was twenty, and had been studying my craft for ten years by then.

Following this remarkable stretch in which some genuinely exciting young rockabillies were presented on the nation's top-rated show alongside established showbusiness favourites, assorted ex-presidents and a veritable menagerie of performing animal acts, the *Ed Sullivan Show* seems to have then decided to become a little more cautious: no more bad-boy hellraisers like Gene Vincent, but the smoother tones of the Platters or the Everlys would be welcomed back time and again over the next couple of years.

By 1958, hepsters looking for rockabilly material on national TV would probably have been checking out *American Bandstand* instead. The show had begun its network debut by playing it pretty much safe. Guesting on that 5 August 1957 show were female vocal group the Chordettes, whom Sullivan had been featuring since 1954. A couple of weeks later, though, they turned up the heat with a 19 August show that included Jerry Lee Lewis and Jimmy Bowen. Interestingly, Jerry Lee didn't even have a new record to promote at that stage – this was five months after 'Whole Lotta Shakin'' and three months before the release of 'Great Balls Of Fire' – but any excuse to put the Killer on television was most certainly the right one, and he was back on the show on 10 October and 4 November. The reason for his initial booking would almost certainly have been Jerry Lee's sensational live appearance on the *Steve Allen Show* on 28 July, which had seen him rebooked for 11 August and a further slot in September. Allen may not have dug rock'n'roll, but he could certainly hear those cash registers ringing.

The Everly Brothers were firm favourites on *Bandstand*, just as they were on *Sullivan*. Yet the growing difference between the two shows is demonstrated by the 10 January 1958 *Bandstand* line-up, featuring Eddie Cochran and George Hamilton IV, who'd moved into smoother territory, but whose 'If You Don't

Know' (1956) was classic rockabilly. This kicked off a vintage year on *Bandstand*, which saw not only several repeat visits from Cochran, but also appearances by artists such as Jack Scott, Marvin Rainwater, Duane Eddy, Wanda Jackson and Ritchie Valens. By contrast, *Sullivan* saw out the rest of the fifties almost exclusively with a solid diet of less threatening light rock'n'roll fare like Bobby Darin and Fabian, although, to be fair, he did give airtime to Johnny Cash to sing 'Don't Take Your Guns To Town' on 8 February 1958.

Bandstand's presenter, Dick Clark, also had another influential ABC-TV programme, the *Dick Clark Saturday Night Beechnut Show*, which ran for 103 episodes from 15 February 1958 to 10 September 1960. Although it eventually finished up doling out glutinous weekly portions of Fabian, Bobby Rydell and Annette Funicello to the kids, in earlier episodes it found space for current or former rockabillies such as Conway Twitty, Jack Scott, Eddie Cochran, Link Wray, Bill Black's Combo, Dale Hawkins, Johnny Cash, Jerry Lee Lewis and Johnny Horton, alongside a prime roll-call of rock'n'roll and R&B performers. If you were looking for rockin' TV exposure in the late 1950s, Dick Clark was a handy man to know.

STRAIGHT OUTTA COMPTON – *TOWN HALL PARTY*

All the same, hardcore rockabilly music rarely made it onto national television, and its best chance of that kind of exposure was on country-oriented barn-dance TV shows such as ABC-TV's *Ozark Jubilee* (later renamed *Country Music Jubilee*), hosted by Red Foley from Springfield, Missouri, or Screen Gems' nationally syndicated *Town Hall Party* (sometimes known as *Ranch Party*), presented by Tex Ritter and broadcast by KTTV from Compton Town Hall, Los Angeles. It was on the *Ozark Jubilee* on 17 March 1956

Joe Maphis
lets Larry
Collins try
his guitar
backstage at
the Town Hall
Party, Los
Angeles

that Carl Perkins first unveiled rockabilly's all-time megahit 'Blue Suede Shoes' to an unsuspecting nation. He was due to promote it on the *Perry Como Show* the following week, but a near-fatal car crash put him and his band out of action, and Carl's one chance at perhaps overtaking Elvis was gone. Even so, as *Billboard* reported, the country music community was very proud of what their boy had achieved, not least the cast and crew of the *Ozark Jubilee*, who saw little difference between rockabilly and country:

> Altho rock and roll country and western style is stirring up considerable controversy nowadays in some c.&w. circles, ABC-TV's 'Ozark Jubilee' is all for it, according to that show's co-producer, Si Simon. Simon pointed out that 'Jubilee' has spotlighted rock and roll flavored

vocals by such guest artists as Pat Boone, Rusty Draper, Betty Johnson, Jim Lowe and Carl Perkins. In the case of Perkins, 'Jubilee' emcee-star Red Foley even advised the TV audience to catch the 'Blue Suede Shoes' man the following week on NBC-TV's Perry Como Show, which is telecast the same time as 'Jubilee'. Foley hastily added that he hoped folks would turn right back to 'Jubilee' after Perkins' performance (subsequently cancelled by his accident) but it was still a remarkable endorsement and indicative of the entire show's pride in the recognition currently accorded r.&r.-c.&w. in the pop field.

The *Jubilee* played host to regular rockin' names such as Wanda Jackson, Bobby Lord, Marvin Rainwater and Brenda Lee – although Crossroads TV productions, the company which made the programme, eventually filed suit against Brenda's mother in August 1957 in a dispute over her commitment to the show, prompting the newspaper headline 'Crossroads Sues Mother Of Moppet'. The show folded in 1960, but in its heyday it gave airtime to some fine rockabilly talent, including Skeets McDonald, Johnny Cash, Jimmy & Johnny, Roy Hall, Janis Martin, Glen Glenn, The Collins Kids, Onie Wheeler, Gene Vincent & the Blue Caps, Tom Tall, Charline Arthur, Rex Allen, Johnny Horton, Arlie Duff, Mimi Roman and Warner Mack – alongside a parade of country and hillbilly greats, not to mention the Lake Of The Ozark Tadpoles and the 1956 Cotton Bag Sewing Queen.

Some excellent footage survives of the *Ozark Jubilee*, as do many complete episodes of the *Town Hall Party*, the latter having been commercially released on DVD in recent years by the Bear Family label. They give a good flavour of these relaxed, informal live TV broadcasts of the late 1950s, in which Johnny

Cash felt comfortable not only playing his latest records, but also doing his 'impersonation of a rock singer'. This involved him combing his hair in a suitably dishevelled fashion all over his face, and then shaking his legs in prime Hillbilly Cat mode – a note-perfect, affectionate send-up of his former Sun label-mate Elvis. The format gave guests the chance to stretch out a little and play maybe six or seven songs – a big difference to just plugging your latest hit on *Sullivan*.

Wanda Jackson showed up on *Town Hall Party* for a superb performance in 1958, tearing through 'Mean, Mean Man' and 'Hard Headed Woman', as well as covering recent honky-tonk hit 'Pick Me Up On Your Way Down'. She appeared on the show in both its *Town Hall Party* and *Ranch Party* guises, as she explained to me: 'Well, those two shows, I have trouble separating them. They were the same thing. Local people, and a star, if they were coming through. *Ranch Party* had Tex Ritter kind of doing MC work, and then *Town Hall Party* had an announcer.'

It may have been a country show at heart, but Wanda never wanted to dress in western clothing, and on the show she wore a stunning fringed evening dress:

> I realised by the time I was about sixteen that I didn't like wearing those cowboy boots, and that old full skirt and cowboy hats. I said no, I wanted something sexier, 'cause I thought 'these cowboy clothes are covering up all my assets'. So we got our heads together, and we found that silky fringe that really shimmered, and spaghetti straps, with rhinestones. Not daringly low-cut, but lower than most young girls would wear.

Teenage rockabilly brother/sister duo The Collins Kids, who became lifelong friends of Wanda's, were regulars on *Town Hall*

Party, as was guitar ace Joe Maphis. Then there were the touring stars like Gene Vincent who would stop by, as did twenty-year-old local legend Eddie Cochran on 7 February 1959, having first appeared on the show in his pre-fame days as one half of the Cochran Brothers rockabilly/hillbilly duo. During his 1959 appearance, the now chart-topping Eddie was also interviewed on-screen by one of the show's regulars, Johnny Bond, the former vocalist for Bob Wills and his Texas Playboys, providing a solid link with rockabilly's hillbilly roots.

Bond, who begins by informing Eddie that 'We're visiting with some of our friends and neighbours at home on the television', eventually works around to a discussion of whether rock'n'roll will last, and where it all came from. Eddie reckons it'll certainly stay the course, but in a different form, while Johnny ventures that fifteen years earlier they were calling it boogie-woogie, and that even Jimmie Rodgers back in 1929 was occasionally making records that had a little rock'n'roll in them. For shows like the *Town Hall Party*, it was all a part of the history of country music, even if, as Bond points out, it 'used to be the bull fiddle was the backbone of the orchestra, now it's the drums'.

If the *Town Hall Party* was predominantly a country show with rock'n'roll leanings, there was another show on television which featured performers of all kinds, from jugglers to balloon acts, yet provided a crucial stepping stone for one of the

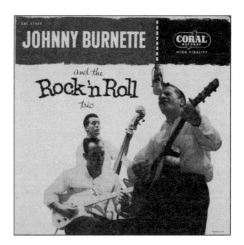

greatest rockabilly bands of them all. The *Ted Mack Amateur Hour*, a TV talent show, had been running in New York since 1948, and although it helped launch the careers of Pat Boone (on 18 July 1953) and a sixteen-year-old violinist called Louis Walcott (on 15 May 1949), who would later reinvent himself under the name Louis Farrakhan, the show bought itself a place in rockabilly history by giving a break to three Memphis musicians called the Rock'n'Roll Trio. Johnny Burnette, his brother Dorsey and Paul Burlison passed the auditions, and appeared during April and May 1956 for three weeks in a row on the show, broadcast nationally on the ABC network, which kicked up enough static for them to acquire a manager, Henry Jerome, and a record deal with Decca subsidiary Coral. A week or so earlier, they'd been scuffling. Within months, they'd be appearing in a Hollywood film...

15 HOLLYWOOD BE THY NAME

ROCKABILLIES ON FILM

Anyone growing up, as I did, in the 1960s and '70s could have
been forgiven for thinking that the motion picture camera
hadn't even been invented in the 1950s as far as music was
concerned, so much did the TV companies rely on 1960s music
footage and music feature films to fill their schedules. Of
course, there was always Bill Haley in *Rock Around the Clock*
(1956), which occasionally surfaced on British TV, yet how can
it be that even though 60 million people watched Elvis on *Ed
Sullivan*, there still isn't one decent colour film example of a
concert from his pre-army heyday? One, largely static, newsreel
camera caught several songs from his 16 September 1956 open-
air home-town show at the Tupelo Fairgrounds, with tinny
accompanying sound, but the best footage of all, where he's
swinging that leg and windmilling his arms while wearing
the gold suit from the cover of the *50,000,000 Elvis Fans Can't
Be Wrong* LP, not only lasts a matter of thirty seconds or so,
it's in black & white and it's *silent* (presumably having been
shot as everyday news footage). This, for one of the biggest-
selling singers of all time. Of course, he made feature films,

but they were so tightly controlled by a certain self-appointed colonel that the musical content was a mere shadow of what it might have been if they'd just rolled the cameras and turned him loose.

Compare this situation to the thousands of miles of cinema-quality, colour sound-film stock expended on the late sixties generation of artists, culminating in the three days of love, peace and inadequate toilet facilities which were stuffed and mounted for all time as the three-hour film *Woodstock* (1970). (There was even enough celluloid used at this event for the inclusion of a whole two extra hours of performance material in the 2009 edition.) Now imagine if the same attention to detail had been devoted to filming a certain outdoor concert at the Overton Park Shell in Memphis on 5 August 1955 – Bob Neal's 8th *Annual Country Music Jamboree* – which was advertised as follows:

in person
WEBB PIERCE
The Wondering Boys

ELVIS PRESLEY
Scotty and Bill
Wanda Jackson
Bud Deckelman
Johnny Cash
Sonny James
Red Sovine
Jim Wilson
Charlie Feathers
The Neal Boys

Me, I'd quite like a three-hour, CinemaScope version of *that* particular event, thank you, and yes, you can throw in another two extra hours of performance footage. All of which goes to show how skewed the filmed history of rock music is. We have a significant slice of the sixties on film – and more than we'll ever want of sorry reality-TV wannabes from our own MTV age – yet the electrifying performances of the rockabilly generation went largely unfilmed.

If you're wondering whether the technology existed to properly film and record an outdoor gig in the 1950s, check out Bern Stern's magnificent, lush-coloured feature-length film of the 1958 Newport Jazz Festival, released as *Jazz on a Summer's Day* in 1960. Effortlessly hip, superbly shot, it captures the likes of Thelonius Monk, Mahalia Jackson and Louis Armstrong playing live and loose, while also giving a real sense of the setting and the crowd at this coastal location, with sailing boats drifting past as the sun goes down. It even caught the young Chuck Berry performing 'Sweet Little Sixteen', backed

The adverts for the King's debut feature suggested there was plenty of rockin' on offer. Sadly, there wasn't

by a collection of jazz musicians, which wipes the floor with any of Chuck's appearances in conventional rock'n'roll films of the time like *Go, Johnny, Go* (1959), good as they are. If only someone with the skill of Bert Stern had captured one of the Sun rockabilly package tours with this kind of loving care.

ROCKIN' THE JOINT – BILL HALEY AND ALAN FREED

All that survives, apart from a proportion of the television appearances outlined in the previous chapter, are the mostly low-budget B-features turned out in a desperate hurry, aimed at the teenage drive-in trade, with fingers crossed that the rock'n'roll craze would still have some mileage left by the end of their two-week shooting schedule. Ever since the March 1955 premiere of *Blackboard Jungle*, a picture which used Bill Haley's 'Rock Around The Clock' over its opening titles, a significant percentage of film producers had assumed that the mere inclusion of such music or the prominent use of the word 'rock' in a film title would set the cash registers ringing. This was an era when practically anything could turn a profit on the Southern drive-in circuit, as long as it had a catchy exploitation title and a lurid trailer. Watching some of these low-budget rock'n'roll films today, it's mostly just the musical interludes which hold the interest, yet these were often shot separately and pasted into the storyline almost at random.

The prototype of the genre, *Rock Around the Clock*, was filmed over two weeks in January 1956, put together by producer Sam Katzman when he saw the fuss that had been created by the use of Haley's music in *Blackboard Jungle* the previous year. He hired Haley, named his film after the song that had caused all the commotion, and roped in top rock'n'roll deejay Alan Freed to front the film on-screen. Freed was paid a $20,000 advance and 10 per cent of the profits, which proved to be far greater than anyone dreamed. *Don't Knock the Rock* and *Rock, Rock, Rock* followed in quick succession; like *Rock Around the Clock*, all released in 1956 and all with Freed appearing as himself and introducing a cheaply filmed selection of acts.

Freed's best excursion into the genre was probably *Rock, Rock, Rock*. Fronting films like this went hand in hand with his top-rated radio show on WINS and the all-star stage bills he was promoting, as trade magazine *Billboard* commented in February 1957 when discussing the situation that existed in New York:

Rock and roll rules Broadway this month with two big stageshows and three r.&r. movies scheduled to open on the Main Stem. Deejay Alan Freed, WINS, will emcee the N.Y. Paramount Theater's first rock and roll stageshow, in conjunction with the screening of his movie, *Don't Knock The Rock*, starting February 22. Jocko Henderson, local WOV deejay, will head up another r.&r. stageshow – also a first – at Broadway's Loew's State Theater, starting February 19. Meanwhile, Jockey Tommy (Dr Jive) Smalls, WWRL, is taking another rhythm and blues stage unit into the Apollo Theater in Harlem, beginning February 22. Film-wise, rock and roll kicked off to an early start last week when the new Jayne Mansfield pic, *The Girl Can't Help It*, opened at the Roxy Theater here. The picture – first big-budget rock and roll movie – features a flock of r.&r. artists, including Little Richard, the Platters, Fats Domino, and Gene Vincent. Money-wise, rock and roll artists 'never had it so good'.

Alan Freed wasn't exactly a rockabilly boy, but even so, he managed to give a prime slot in *Rock, Rock, Rock* to one of the toughest outfits of them all, Johnny Burnette's Rock'n'Roll Trio. Fresh from their weekly triumphs on the *Ted Mack Amateur*

Hour, the three Memphis rockabillies found themselves catapulted into the big league, singing 'Lonesome Train' in a film that also featured chart-topping acts such as Frankie Lymon & the Teenagers (performing 'I'm Not A Juvenile Delinquent' and 'Baby Baby'), The Moonglows ('I Knew From The Start' and 'Over And Over Again') and a fine duckwalking performance from Chuck Berry ('You Can't Catch Me'). There were, of course, drawbacks. The plot was a joke from start to finish, and hardcore rockers in the audience would have also cringed at being forced, as usual, to sit through several squeaky-clean performances by one or other of the supposed romantic leads, and quite what anyone made of singing toddler Ivy 'Baby' Schulman warbling her way through something wretched entitled 'Baby Likes To Rock' can only be imagined. Even so, the good very much outweighed the bad.

Although Freed had already appeared in two films for Columbia, this was the first one in which he was allowed a free hand in selecting the music acts, and the Rock'n'Roll Trio probably owed their inclusion to the fact that they were on the same label that released Freed's own recordings with his Rock and Roll Orchestra, Coral Records. *Billboard* called *Rock, Rock, Rock* 'a low budget film of no great dramatic pretension', but praised the music generally, and noted that 'Johnny Burnette is on hand to inject a touch of rockabilly in "Lonesome Train"'.

The following year Freed slowed the pace, presenting a thinly veiled autobiography of his radio career under the modest title *Mister Rock'n'Roll* (filmed in October 1957 but released in '58). The definition of the title was loose enough to stand him shoe-horning long-established big-band jazz leader Lionel Hampton into the story, alongside some of his favourite contemporary acts including Chuck Berry, Little Richard, Frankie Lymon & the Teenagers, LaVern Baker, The Moonglows and Clyde McPhatter. There was nothing in the line-up comparable to the Johnny Burnette Trio, but when Freed appears on-screen introducing country star Ferlin Husky, he says: 'And now here's a guy who's already had a number 1 record in this country of ours, a wonderful rockabilly singer, Ferlin Husky, and "This Moment Of Love"...'

Well, the song certainly has a double bass, but the backing vocal chorus is pure Nashville country, which shows how loosely the word 'rockabilly' was being bandied around by the autumn of 1957.

Alan Freed fronted only one more film before being engulfed in the payola scandal which terminated his career, but, in terms of musical guest appearances, it was a good one. *Go, Johnny, Go* (filmed in January 1959 and released in June) was very much a showcase for Chuck Berry, who not only sang 'Little Queenie', 'Memphis Tennessee' and 'Johnny B Goode', but also had a significant speaking role in the film. Alongside him, the line-up included Jackie Wilson, Jimmy Clanton, Jo-Ann Campbell, The Cadillacs, The Flamingos, Harvey Fuqua and Jimmy Cavallo & the House Rockers. From a rockabilly point of view, the picture was notable for the inclusion of Eddie Cochran singing 'Teenage Heaven', and also for the sole filmed performance by seventeen-year-old Ritchie Valens, miming to his blistering guitar rocker 'Ooh My Head' – the kind of gutsy, primitive sound which was heading right out of fashion in that year of clean-cut, bloodless teen idols. Just a few weeks after filming his piece, Ritchie was killed alongside Buddy Holly, the Big Bopper and their pilot when they crashed shortly after a show in Iowa.

JACKIE WAS A LONGHAIR, BUT ROCK'N'ROLL GOT IN HER BLOOD

The big film money may have been mostly riding on Alan Freed, but he wasn't the only name in the game. What's odd is

that no one thought to make a film called *Blue Suede Shoes* in those days, given the sheer quantity of records that tune sold, and the fact that it was name-checked in dozens of other hit songs of the era. As for using the word 'rockabilly' in the title of a film, well, Twentieth Century Fox did actually get around to that, but the resulting picture, *Rockabilly Baby* (released October 1957), has about as much actual rockabilly content as the average episode of *I Love Lucy*. The come-on lines used in the trailer are perhaps encouraging: 'This is a different kind of teenage movie. Bright, full of bop, the kind that makes the whole world know how wonderful it feels to be young and in love … Jackie was a longhair, but rock'n'roll got in her blood … Baby it's HOT outside when this Rockabilly Ball gets Rolling!'

The accompanying visuals, however, of well-scrubbed teens gathering around the piano for a Sunday-school-type singalong, should have sounded a warning. Then there's the fact that the sole musical outfit employed is Les Brown and His

Band of Renown – a mainstream big band who'd been around since the mid-1930s, and whose leader was aged forty-five at the time of filming. This, indeed, was the orchestra who'd backed Doris Day on her breakthrough hit, 'Sentimental Journey', back in 1945 – one of the best bands in their own field, but rockabilly they weren't, and they wouldn't have claimed to be. (The film's director, William F. Claxton, later directed one of the great unintentionally hilarious horror movies of all time, *Night of the Lepus* (1972), in which a distinguished cast including Janet Leigh and DeForest Kelley are terrorised by giant mutant killer rabbits.)

A LOT OF WHAT THEY CALL THE MOST – *THE GIRL CAN'T HELP IT*

Twentieth Century Fox may have misled unwitting hepcats by calling a film *Rockabilly Baby*, but they can be forgiven, because they were also responsible for the undisputed classic of the genre; that all-star, all-colour slice of celluloid perfection known as *The Girl Can't Help It* (1956), which, if it had only restrained itself from interrupting Gene Vincent & the Blue Caps in full flow, would be just about perfect. Right from the start, as Jayne Mansfield walks down the street to the sound of Little Richard singing Bobby Troup's specially written title song, this is a class act all the way.

Filmed in the late summer of 1956 and released on 1 December, *The Girl Can't Help It* caught performers like Richard, Eddie Cochran and Gene Vincent just as they were breaking through into the big time. The story goes that the producers had wanted Elvis for Eddie's slot, but Parker asked too much money, so Cochran got his big break instead. They may have missed out on the King, but the line-up of talent which Twentieth Century Fox put together for this film is outstanding. In addition to having Gene & the Blue Caps perfoming their international smash, 'Be Bop A Lula', and Little Richard wearing the mother of all drape suits hammering away at 'Ready Teddy' and 'She's Got It', they also found space for The Treniers to belt out 'Rockin' Is Our Bizness', Fats Domino singing 'Blue Monday', Eddie Fontaine in the Jungle Room treating the world to 'Cool It Baby', and the otherworldly Julie London slinking her way through 'Cry Me A River'. The Platters appeared – as they seemed to in just about every rock picture of the late fifties – but, unlike other films, this one was mercifully short on sweating, middle-aged ten-piece combos playing endless instrumentals while desperately shouting the word 'rock!' every few bars.

With high production values and a couple of honest-to-goodness rockabilly wildmen like Vincent and Cochran, Frank Tashlin's *The Girl Can't Help It* set an impossibly high standard for filmed rock'n'roll, and for the most part, it was downhill all the way after that. Consider what 'Colonel' Parker saddled Elvis with that year. *Love Me Tender*, The Hillbilly Cat's debut feature, released just a month earlier than Tashlin's film, was not only in black & white, it also took the most incendiary live perfomer on the planet and stuck him in a historical setting and forced him to sing mostly indifferent, decidedly un-rock'n'roll songs. Imagine if they'd allowed him to sing 'Mystery Train', in his own hepcat threads, in full colour? As missed opportunities go, this was an artistic disaster. Elvis finally got the chance to show what he could do in *Jailhouse Rock* (1957) and *King Creole* (1958), but Parker was dead set on turning him into 'family entertainment', a sorry road that would lead Elvis all the way through to *Stay Away Joe* (1968), forced to serenade a farmyard animal with a song he despised, 'Dominic The Impotent Bull'.

Nineteen fifty-six had been a good year for cinema-going rock'n'roll fans, and they'd also have been queuing up in '57 for a film called *Jamboree* (aka *Disk Jockey Jamboree*). The rockabilly-friendly line-up featured Jerry Lee Lewis, Carl Perkins, Charlie Gracie and Buddy Knox, alongside the great Fats Domino. Jerry was hotter than a pistol that year, performing his second smash hit 'Great Balls Of Fire', although the mimed footage here pales in comparison with the phenomenal live version he put down on *American Bandstand* in 1958. Carl and his band, still recovering from their 1956 car smash, turned in a spirited reading of their current single, 'Glad All Over', with the man himself doing a little dance as he picks out the tune on his solid-body gold-top Les Paul, but again, if you want to see how great a live band they were in those days, the storming version of 'Your True Love' that they nailed on the *Ranch Party* TV show is probably a better bet. The makers of *Jamboree* simply took this selection of rockabilly acts and stuck them in an almost bare studio with no audience present and asked them to mime, so it's hardly surprising that live TV appearances in front of hundreds of teenage fans generally have the edge.

In 1958, kingpin manager Tom Parker mistakenly thought

A hefty dose of religion – *Sing, Boy, Sing*

he'd found another Elvis in Tommy Sands, and lined him up a starring role in the Twentieth Century Fox film *Sing, Boy, Sing*. Sands appeared as a preacher's son, singing watered-down rock'n'roll while attempting to replicate Elvis's life story, his voice and his moves in this whitewashed, sexless teen-idol yarn featuring a hefty dose of religion. There may perhaps have been some kids out there waiting desperately for a cod-rock'n'roll treatment of Martha Carson's 'I'm Gonna Walk And Talk With My Lord', but the cluttered big-band arrangements and wall-to-wall backing vocals made it all a long, long way from rockabilly.

In terms of the major studios, if Fox strayed away from the hard-rockin' trail blazed by *The Girl Can't Help It* and took a few wrong turnings with *Rockabilly Baby* and *Sing, Boy, Sing*, Warner Brothers made a better stab at it in *Untamed Youth* (released 18 May 1957), which not only featured Mamie Van Doren singing in her underwear – for purely artistic reasons, no doubt – but also had Eddie Cochran in the second of his three official film appearances, playing a character called Bong. Here, as in the other pictures, Eddie is shown without a band – in fact, in *Untamed Youth* he's not even allowed instruments, miming the virtually a cappella song 'Cotton Picker', as part of a work gang out in the fields.

BOPPIN' AT THE HIGH SCHOOL HOP

The only other major studio that got around to properly showcasing a rockabilly performer in a youth-oriented 1950s film was Metro-Goldwyn-Mayer, whose superb dope-dealing-hot-rodding-juvenile-delinquent exposé *High School Confidential* (1958) is one of the most thoroughly enjoyable exploitation titles of the era. This singer appears only during the opening titles, but when the artist in question happens to be Jerry Lee Lewis, belting out the title song from the back of a flatbed truck in glorious widescreen black & white, you know you're in for a treat.

In the weeks leading up to the film's premiere, Jerry Lee was riding high. In the 19 May 1958 issue of *Billboard*, several key record distributors listed Jerry's new Sun single 'High School Confidential'/'Fools Like Me' as their 'strongest new disk', and it was reviewed favourably in the same issue: 'Lewis belts "Confidential", a crazy, swingin' rocker, in his usual frantic style. It's the title tune from a forthcoming flick in which he does a guest stint ... Strong stuff for all markets.'

By 9 June – when his career was about to go into freefall, with the collapse of his English tour in the wake of revelations in the UK press that he'd married his thirteen-year-old cousin Myra, and bigamously at that – *Billboard* carried not only a favourable review of the film, but also a full-page advert titled 'An open letter to the industry from Jerry Lee Lewis', which began: 'Dear friends, I have in recent weeks been the apparent center of a fantastic amount of publicity and of which none has been good...'

It was all in vain, and Jerry would gradually rebuild his career in the early 1960s with lengthy tours of the very country where the trouble had started, England. But that was in the future.

GENE VINCENT & THE BLUE CAPS – THAT OLD GANG OF MINE

As it happened, 1958 also saw the release of a fine black & white slice of film starring another of the very wildest rockers who'd also spend the 1960s touring England playing to a fiercely loyal audience long after the US had lost interest. The picture was a low-budget item called *Hot Rod Gang*, which

wasn't likely to win many prizes for acting or set design, but had the huge advantage of starring the 1958 line-up of Gene Vincent & the Blue Caps in all their glory. As usual, the story wasn't up to much, but not only do the filmed musical inserts give a mesmerising glimpse of Gene's stage show at the time – swinging his leg over the microphone stand, flanked by his 'clapper boys' Tommy Facenda and Paul Peek – there's also an unbilled Eddie Cochran lurking in there as well. Eddie had been in the recording studio with Gene & the Caps at the Capitol Tower on North Vine Street in Hollywood from 25–29 March, joining in on songs like 'Five Feet Of Lovin'' and 'Git It', and came along the next day when they headed across town and shot the musical sections of *Hot Rod Gang*.

The male lead in the film is John Ashley (who cut some rockabilly for the Dot label, then spent the 1960s in beach party and horror films and the '80s narrating *The A-Team*). He also sings a couple of tunes, with Cochran on guitar. Gene & the Caps deliver 'Dance In The Street', looking like the baddest street gang in town, and also 'Baby Blue', at a staged concert where the front row for some reason consists of grinning grannies, self-consciously wigging out to the beat. The film was directed by prolific veteran Lew Landers, no stranger to these kinds of musical productions – back in 1944 he'd been responsible for a picture called *Cowboy Canteen*, with Roy Acuff & His Smokey Mountain Boys and Tex Ritter. There had always been money to be made showing the record buyers what their favourite musicians looked like on a big screen.

SELLING THE BIG TOMCAT BEAT

Such a philosophy lay behind two of low-budget king Roger Corman's earliest ventures into the film business. When not concerned with showing assorted Viking women grappling with sea serpents, or nameless *things* trying to conquer the world, he became involved in the new rock film boom when his backers, American International Pictures, latched on to one of the new star attractions, as he later told Ed Naha:

> AIP made a quick deal with the Platters to appear in a rock and roll movie. AIP said to me, 'If you can come up with something very quickly, we can use the Platters. They're leaving for a tour in two weeks so make it fast.' … Things got a bit crazy when it turned out that the Platters were only available for one day of shooting and that one day didn't fall into my schedule…

The resulting film was released in April 1957 as *Rock All Night*, and the Platters just appear in the first ten minutes of it, but the rockabilly fraternity would have been much more interested in the only other act featured, The Blockbusters, who sing the title song, and whose performance of 'Rock'n'Roll Guitar' in a little club (with seemingly no audience) is definitely worth checking out. They also show up in Corman's other zero-budget venture into rock'n'roll territory, *Carnival Rock*, which has a great deal to interest rockabilly fans. The poster may have been surprisingly lame for such an exploitation film – no musicians at all, just a poorly painted image of a couple in a clinch with the tagline 'No! Don't touch me' – but the lobby cards spelt out the real story: prime rockabilly movers Bob Luman and David Houston, both of them backed by an outfit named the Shadows, featuring phenomenal teenage guitarist James Burton. If you want to know what small-combo rockabilly looked like in the clubs in 1957, this is a good place to start. The lack of frills probably helped, since little else was done except to set the band up on a typical small stage in a dance hall and let them rip. Luman sings 'This Is The Night' and 'All Night Long' – both fine slices of rockabilly with James Burton well to the fore – and future country star Houston rocks along to a seriously slapping bass with a cracking version of 'One And Only'.

Similar budget restrictions also resulted in one of the wilder Texas rockabillies being captured at the top of his game in the film *Rock, Baby, Rock It* – an almost documentary-style snapshot of the Dallas scene, shot in 1956, released in '57. Johnny Carroll and His Hot Rocks had been cutting no-holds-barred rockabilly tracks for the Decca label that year, and were blessed with an ambitious manager who went by the name of J. C. Tiger. It was Tiger who came up with the ideal promotional gimmick for his charges – to star them in a film of their own.

Johnny sings four superb songs, doing his best Elvis moves, with his hair flying all over the place, in front of an audience who for some reason mostly look like they've been recently embalmed. 'Wild Wild Women' and 'Crazy, Crazy Lovin'' are different versions from the ones released as singles, but equally good, and the band also act as backing musicians for Kay Wheeler, 'National President of the Elvis Presley Fan Clubs', dancing the 'Rock'n'Bop', with Johnny singing from the sidelines. The trailer promised 'The Upbeatingest Of Downbeat Rhythms' in which 'Easy Livin' Guys and Easy-to-Love Chicks Move In On The Make For An Easy Buck'. Maybe the film delivered, maybe it didn't, but it sure as hell featured the finest footage of Sun R&B singer Rosco Gordon rocking out on a white piano with a live white chicken sitting on top of it you're ever likely to find, and for this and the Johnny Carroll scenes, it should be clear that *Rock, Baby, Rock It* deserves to be a cornerstone of any discerning DVD library.

As far as the 1950s go, that was mostly it. In 1960, sometime rockabilly star Conway Twitty showed up in no less than three films for maverick producer Albert Zugsmith (the man behind *High School Confidential*): these were *Platinum High School*, *College Confidential* and the decidedly weird *Sex Kittens Go to College,* starring everyone from Mamie Van Doren to Charles Chaplin Jr – not to mention the robot or the chimp dressed as a beatnik – in which our man Conway is featured onstage in a club, 'Selling the Big Tomcat Beat', as the trailer puts it. Twitty was already well on the way to his very successful country career by then, but even so, 1960 was also the year he cut his finest slice of flat-out rockabilly, 'Long Black Train'.

Another 1960 release was the film *High School Caesar,* with a title song sung by Reggie Perkins, and an appearance from Dallas rockabilly Johnny Faire (who also recorded as Dick Bush, Johnny Jordan and Donny Brooks), but if you

Johnny Carroll

wanted to survive in the sixties, maybe you had to diversify, like Ron Haydock. He'd started recording Gene Vincent-style rockabilly for the Cha Cha label in Chicago, most famously '99 Chicks'/'Be-Bop-A-Jean', as Ron Haydock & the Boppers, but branched out in several directions at once when he hooked up with low-budget auteur Ray Dennis Steckler. As a sideline, Ron was also holding down a career penning under-the-counter softcore novels, including the immortal *Ape Rape*, and he now brought his literary skills to bear, writing the script for Steckler of a unique celluloid artefact entitled *Rat Pfink A Boo Boo* (1966). Under the stage name Vin Saxon, Ron starred as the character Rat Pfink, uttering dramatic lines ('Ape! Drop that girl!'), and singing songs like 'You Is A Rat Fink'.

It's a long way from here to *The Girl Can't Help It*, but where else could you see a bona fide 1950s rockabilly singer sharing the screen with a bloke answering to the name of Kogar dressed in a gorilla suit? Like the man said, hooray for Hollywood.

16 OFF THE EDGE OF THE MAP

THOSE THAT JOURNEYED OVERSEAS, SPREADING THE
ROCKIN' WORD TO THE WIDER WORLD

Most rockabilly was confined to the American South, although there were outbursts of activity in places like Chicago or San Francisco, and yet, incredible as it may seem, some of the genuine article even made it over to Europe in the 1950s. Marvin Rainwater, a man who liked to stress his 25 per cent Native American heritage by dressing up in full Indian chief gear, toured Britain in the late fifties and even cut some tracks at EMI's Abbey Road studio while he was there. Perhaps more surprising is the fact that a good-quality 1957 English live recording exists of Philadelphia rockabilly Charlie Gracie playing at the Stockton Globe. Yet, for all that, these were relatively isolated visits, and even mainstream rock'n'roll stars didn't really begin touring the rest of the world in any great numbers until the early sixties. The diehard European enthusiast had a much better chance of seeing the first wave of genuine rockabillies live during the 1980s, when most of them made their first visits across the Atlantic.

Some hillbilly heroes had appeared in Europe during

the 1940s and early '50s, but these were shows organised specifically for the US armed forces, out of bounds to civilians. The object was generally to give homesick troops a chance to see some of the stars of the hugely popular *Grand Ole Opry* in person, to remind them a little of back home. In an era awash with slick dance orchestras and sobbing crooners, the top-rated show on Armed Forces Radio in Germany was the much more downhome *Hillbilly Gasthaus*, so it was no surprise that in November 1949 an all-star package of *Opry* regulars made the transatlantic trip for a two-week tour of German bases. The line-up included Roy Acuff, Little Jimmy Dickens, Red Foley, Minnie Pearl and even the *Opry*'s famous master of ceremonies, Grant Turner. Also along for the ride was a man who'd been causing an absolute sensation at the *Opry* that year, and who would inspire a generation of rockabilly artists, Hank Williams. All of which was wonderful news for members of the US military, but not much use for the locals, who couldn't gain access to the shows. The same could be said of April 1957, when a party of RCA artists including 'Female Elvis' Janis Martin and Jim Reeves came over to play shows exclusively for the US troops in Germany.

VOODOO RHYTHM HITS BRITAIN

In the UK, because of Musicians Union restrictions, there was precious little chance of any American artist being able to come over and play a show unless the booking agent could arrange for a comparable exchange visit whereby British performers went over to play in America. Until the beat boom of the 1960s, when the American public developed a thirst for groups from places like Liverpool, Newcastle and London, there were few UK rockers who were in demand across the Atlantic, which meant that many plans hatched by London promoters in the

Haley's film debut hits London,
August 1956

early years of rock'n'roll came to nothing, such as the attempt to bring Bill Haley & His Comets over for a string of shows in February 1956. In the event, Haley would make it over exactly a year later, for a tour that was met with huge crowds and fevered torrents of publicity: 'Haley is a dynamic worker. He beats fingers red'n'raw as the Comets lash out the voodoo rhythm of "Shake, Rattle & Roll".'

Often unfairly airbrushed out of modern accounts of the rise of beat music, Haley and the Comets certainly win the prize for being the first to take rock'n'roll overseas and tour the world, paving the way for everyone that followed. Not content with coming to Europe, where they were met with full-blown riots in Berlin and Essen, they also visited Australia and even South America. Yet in '56, the year rockabilly was at its height, not one single US rocker made the journey across to Britain, the country that would eventually give many of those artists a lengthy second career, long after some had assumed that their performing days were over.

That February 1957 UK tour from Haley & His Comets ushered in a much-improved year for British rock'n'roll fans, with gigs by Frankie Lymon & the Teenagers, the Platters and also Freddie Bell & the Bell Boys, who'd been seen to good effect in the film *Rock Around the Clock* (1956), and were supported on this tour by home-grown rocker Tommy Steele with the Steelemen. Bell and his combo fitted the rock'n'roll tag, but visits from genuine rockabilly artists were even rarer in 1950s Britain. Nevertheless, 1957 saw a full tour and national TV appearances by Charlie Gracie, the first one to blaze a trail that would eventually be followed in later decades by many of his rockin' contemporaries.

At the time of his tour, Charlie Gracie had already scored a couple of hits in Britain; 'Butterfly', which reached number 12 in April 1957, and 'Fabulous', which spent sixteen weeks in the charts from June onwards, and climbed even higher than its predecessor, to number 8. Small wonder that promoters were making moves to bring him over as they watched that second single on its way up to the Top Ten. An article in the *Daily Mirror* on 20 June introduced their readers to the new star: '[Charlie] began in showbusiness years ago as a child performer: is coached in singing and guitar by his dad. A good-looking kid. He's going to appear in a film soon – and is talking about coming to Britain.'

The *Mirror*'s showbusiness writer was obviously well informed about negotiations already taking place, because just a few months later Charlie arrived by sea on the SS *Mauritania*, kicking off with a show at Southampton Gaumont on 4 August. The tour ran continuously through to the end of September, and in some cities, such as London and Coventry, he was booked in for a string of

dates in the same venue. It was at one such residency, at the Stockton Globe, that someone had the good idea of hanging a microphone from the top of the proscenium arch, directly above the stage, and recording Charlie's performance on the night of 26 August, which was eventually issued as an LP in 1983 by Rollercoaster Records. In addition to his live gigs, there were also a couple of TV appearances on the shows *Six-Five Special* and *Meet the Stars*, which, in an era when Britain had only two channels, both of them national, made this a very high-profile visit.

Gracie's London shows were at the Hippodrome, and, as with all early rock tours in the UK, he was part of a typical middle-of-the-road variety bill. This was a great contrast to the situation in the US at that time. For example, the line-up for Alan Freed's July 1957 *Summer Festival Of Rock'n'Roll* package shows at the New York Paramount featured Chuck Berry, LaVern Baker, Clyde McPhatter, Frankie Lymon & the Teenagers, The Moonglows, Big Joe Turner, The Everly Brothers, Screamin' Jay Hawkins and six or seven other acts, all of them with a solid rock, R&B or doo-wop pedigree. By contrast, Charlie Gracie was co-billed at the Hippodrome with forty-two-year-old middle-of-the-road singer Dorothy Squires, whose appeal was much more to the older audience. TV reviewer Clifford Davis, writing in the *Daily Mirror* on 6 August, after the televising of one of the Hippodrome shows, gave his verdict on the contrast between Charlie and Dorothy, and also introduced tabloid readers to the word 'rockabilly':

America's Charlie Gracie, 21 – small and lean-jawed – spent twenty-five minutes before the microphone at the London Hippodrome last night belting out a quick succession of numbers that had every teenager clapping out the beat with him. Guitar-singing Charlie offered mostly beat ballads, rock'n'roll, and its express-paced successor, rock-a-billy. He worked hard, with his feet apart and his head thrown back. His lower jaw shook from side to side in the Johnnie Ray tradition. In fact, he turned out to be a more polished, versatile edition of our own Tommy Steele. *Does Charlie Gracie deserve to top the bill? Sorry, Dorothy Squires, but on last night's reception the answer is YES.*

Dorothy presumably came to the same conclusion, since she pulled out of the remaining shows. Gracie himself made enough of a hit with British audiences that he was brought back the following year for another two-month tour. When Charlie first showed up in England, he was hardly arriving in a land where teenagers had never heard of rock'n'roll. Bill Haley and Elvis had both enjoyed a string of hits, and Presley's image in particular was being used on the cover of all kinds of magazines looking to lure the youth vote (although one venerable music publication, *Melody Maker*, regarded rock'n'roll as a complete abomination, and took great pleasure in saying so, week after week). Similarly, while many rockabilly singles were unavailable in the UK, there were notable exceptions, such as the superb four-track EP of Roy Orbison's Sun material featuring 'Ooby Dooby', 'You're My Baby', 'Go! Go! Go!' and 'Rock House' which was released in 1957 on the London label under the title *Hillbilly Rock*. Of course, the obvious question is why no promoter was able to take advantage in 1956 of Presley's incredible popularity in the UK and bring him over for what would have been astonishingly well-attended and lucrative shows. Many stories over the years have alleged that Andreas van Kujik – the Dutch-born ex-carnival hustler known as 'Colonel' Tom Parker – was not only an illegal immigrant but had sinister reasons for not wanting to leave the US and faced possible arrest if he travelled to Europe.

Even in the 1970s, Parker was regularly turning down offers of many millions of dollars for overseas Elvis shows.

LEE GORDON – A PERFECT VIEW FROM EVERY SEAT

Late-1950s England was slowly becoming a place where you could finally see American rockers play live, but in 1957 the Australians were even more fortunate, because of a forward-thinking local promoter called Lee Gordon, who hailed originally from the US. Gordon began bringing over entire American rock'n'roll package tours, which was a major step up from the British 1950s model of one genuine US rocker supported by a dispiriting homegrown cast of jugglers, dog acts and end-of-the-pier comedians. Having already experienced considerable success promoting Australian shows for major stars such as Frank Sinatra and Johnnie Ray, Gordon then unleashed his groundbreaking January 1957 line-up of Bill Haley & His Comets, LaVern Baker, The Platters, Big Joe Turner and Freddie Bell & the Bell Boys – the kind of bill that cinema-goers had been used to seeing on-screen in Alan Freed's productions. The shows were met with wild enthusiasm, and, during the course of that one three-week tour, Haley and the others played to 330,000 people.

If the latter package sounds like a hard act to follow, in October the same year Gordon then pulled off the most stellar overseas rock'n'roll tour of the 1950s, with a phenomenal cast featuring Eddie Cochran, Little Richard, Gene Vincent & the Blue Caps, Alis Lesley and Australia's own rock'n'roll sensation, Johnny O'Keefe, who wrote and recorded the classic 'Wild One' (1958, aka 'Real Wild Child'). In Cochran, Vincent and Lesley, the crowds were seeing genuine US rockabilly performers in the prime of their careers, while the tour was also notable as the occasion on which Little Richard decided to forsake the Devil's music in favour of the Church, flinging his diamond rings over the side of a ferry into the Hunter River on 11 October as a statement of his intent.

Within months, Gordon brought over two more rockabilly giants, Buddy Holly and Jerry Lee Lewis, for a January/February 1958 Australian tour headlined by Paul Anka, which also featured Jodie Sands and Johnny O'Keefe. For Lewis and Holly, who'd both been scuffling around playing local gigs down South barely a year before, to find themselves halfway around the world performing to thousands of baying teenagers must have been a surreal experience. It was a mighty long way from playing in parking lots and at store openings in West Texas to stepping out onto the 10,000-capacity Sydney Stadium's 'New Electric Revolving Stage – A Perfect View From Every Seat', the centrepiece of what was by far the largest indoor arena in town.

Buddy Holly and the Crickets then went straight from the heat of the Australian summer to the bitter cold of Britain in March, where they had been a regular fixture in the UK Top Ten since September 1957, when 'That'll Be The Day' topped the charts. Following a strategy cooked up by his record company, some of Holly's records were appearing under his own name,

and others under his original band name, the Crickets (even though the same musicians played on all the releases), which enabled the label to issue several singles by the same artist at once. Hence, Buddy's initial hit record had been followed in quick succession by 'Oh Boy', 'Peggy Sue' and 'Maybe Baby' – all released in the four months up to the end of 1957 – so that when he and the Crickets began their tour in March 1958 at the Trocadero, Elephant & Castle, they were already a very big deal indeed. Arriving fresh from the enthusiastic crowds in Australia, they previewed their act on the ITV show *Cool for Cats*, and then, on 2 March, opened the prestigious live TV show, *Sunday Night at the London Palladium*, sharing a bill with comedian Bob Hope and ballet dancer Alicia Markova. The *Daily Mirror*'s reviewer, for one, was less than impressed, commenting that 'Bob Hope was on sparkling form for the 100th edition of ITV's Palladium variety show last night', but that the programme 'started off tamely with an American act, Buddy Holly and the Crickets. *They offered nothing that has not been seen here every week in 'Six-Five Special' from British artists'.*

Responses to the Crickets' gigs themselves were generally very positive, and they inspired many future members of the most famous British 1960s bands, not least Keith Richards. The *New Musical Express*'s critic Keith Goodwin loved the show:

> They rocked their way through a tremendous, belting twenty-five minute act without letting up for one moment ... and the audience showed their approval in no uncertain terms, via handclaps, whistles, shouts, and long bursts of applause ... Take my word for it – this is rock'n'roll like we've never heard it before in Britain!

Buddy Holly's influence would be felt in the UK for many years to come – indeed, he scored an incredible seventeen posthumous chart hits in Britain between his death in 1959 and 1968. He helped establish the idea that rockers should write their own material, and popularised the basic group pattern of two guitars, bass and drums. Holly also introduced many budding UK musicians to the solid-bodied electric guitar in an era when such items were unobtainable in Britain, playing his Fender Stratocaster at his live shows and on various TV appearances. That same guitar also showed up in Buddy's hands on the cover of his 1957 LP *The Chirping Crickets*, one of the earliest rock'n'roll albums available over here, although Shadows guitarist Hank Marvin, who in 1959 became the first UK musician to obtain a Fender Strat, was apparently inspired to go looking for one by an urge to imitate another great rockabilly guitarist, James Burton.

BIG CHIEF RAINWATER

Hank rose to fame backing England's own 'answer to Elvis', Cliff Richard, and although he may have owed his choice of guitar to James Burton, the guitar player formerly known as Brian Robson Rankin is said to have taken his new surname from a visiting US rockabilly artist, Marvin Rainwater, who came to Britain for a tour in spring 1958, just after Buddy and the boys headed home. Tabloid readers and television audiences would have been hard put to miss Rainwater's arrival: he dressed up in full Hollywood Sitting Bull gear, and posed for photos at the airport holding multiple umbrellas to highlight his name and guard against the English weather:

> Big Chief Rainwater came to London yesterday in a huge flying bird from New York. He is America's thirty-two-year-old pop singer Marvin Rainwater whose record 'Whole Lotta Woman' is No 2 in Britain's Pop Twenty list. Rainwater claims Cherokee Indian ancestry. He is a big-built six-footer who is as American as Elvis Presley ... Rainwater carried a guitar and – as a gimmick – SIX umbrellas. He might need them. He is opening his British tour in Manchester. He was laying on the Indian

'Much prefer Indian clothes…' – Marvin Rainwater

stuff happily when we met. 'Much prefer Indian clothes… beaded head-dress, calves leather jacket, moccasins. I have squaw and two little showers,' he announced solemnly.

As the above *Daily Mirror* report shows, Marvin was hardly a teenager, but he'd cut a hypnotic slap-bass rockabilly classic in 1956 entitled 'Mr Blues', and on 15 April, two days before his tour opened, he took advantage of the facilities at EMI's Abbey Road studios to lay down two songs, 'I Dig You Baby' and 'Dance Me Daddy', the first of which became his next single. This was a rare instance of a US rocker recording on this side of the Atlantic during the 1950s, and, as it happened, Rainwater's support act for the tour was a group led by a transplanted Tennessean who'd sung for a while with Chris Barber's band at the dawn of the skiffle craze, but had then gone out on his own as Johnny Duncan & the Blue Grass Boys. Johnny's one big hit had been 'Last Train To San Fernando' (1957) – a song he hated – but the flip-side of that single had been his self-penned gem 'Rockabilly Baby', which stands along with Lonnie Donegan's 'Cumberland Gap' (1957) and Vince Taylor's 'Brand New Cadillac' (1959) as one of the very few authentic examples of the genre to be produced on this side of the pond. As he recounted in the March 1958 edition of *Country & Western Express*, Johnny had married an English woman on 4 July 1953, joking that 'it seemed suitable that the day the US gained its freedom should be the day I lost mine'.

All things considered, teenage rock fans in the UK were doing well in the early months of 1958. Like Buddy Holly, Marvin Rainwater was given a TV slot at the London Palladium, the footage of which survives, and he seems to have enjoyed a pleasant stay in the country, telling the press how 'warm-hearted and friendly' he found the audiences. The same reaction would probably not have been forthcoming from the next US rockabilly to hit town, whose tour was shot all to hell within days of his arrival.

JERRY LEE LEWIS – WILDEST ROCKABILLY OF THEM ALL

On the face of it, when Jerry Lee Lewis came calling, only one short week after Marvin had wrapped up his own tour, it should have been just another routine example of the new teenage craze; something for the middle-aged critics to be mildly sarcastic about, and that the BBC and ITV would happily feature on shows like *Off the Record* or *Saturday Spectacular*. A publication called the *Record Song Book*, which specialised in printing the words to the latest UK chart hits, paved the way for Lewis's arrival by printing a fetching shot of the man himself on their cover, and introduced this 'taciturn individual of rugged appeal' in glowing terms, just a week or so before the tour:

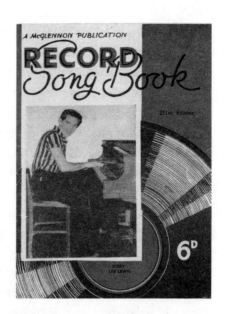

May 1958 – lookout
England, here comes the
Killer

A Louisiana boy with the fervour of music-with-the-modern beat is burning up the radio, television and film industries with an impact not felt since Frank Sinatra, Johnnie Ray or Elvis Presley became triple threats ... Jerry Lee, on the other hand, doesn't shake like Elvis. He doesn't have to. When he feels like it, he jumps up and kicks the piano stool across the stage and plays standing up. His legs get stiff, but his head shakes a bumper crop of blond hair down over his eyes. He has a beat and a rhythm like you've never felt ... He will be visiting here from May 24 onwards, appearing in 35 towns throughout the country, when we will have a chance to see this 'wildest rockabilly of them all'.

This wasn't the only mention of the word 'rockabilly' in that particular issue of the magazine, since they chose to print the words to that teeth-grinding abomination entitled 'Ding Dong Rock-A-Billy Weddin'', which, readers were warned, had been recently 'Televised and Recorded by Lorrae Desmond'. Still, anyone who shelled out the sixpence cover price would also have the words to Jerry Lee's 'Whole Lotta Shakin'', Ricky Nelson's 'Stood Up', Buddy Holly's 'Peggy Sue' and Marvin Rainwater's 'Baby Don't Go', so it wasn't all bad news.

In the event, far from 'appearing in 35 towns throughout the country', the Killer's tour ground to a halt after just three London shows – Edmonton Regal, Kilburn Gaumont State and Tooting Granada – at which point the tabloid press turned round and had him for breakfast. Headlines such as "BABY SNATCHER! CRIES GREET THE ROCK STAR WHO WED A GIRL OF 13' and 'WE HATE JERRY, SHOUT EX-FANS' were just a few of the examples of the media storm provoked by the revelation that Lewis' companion, Myra, was not only young but also his wife. Even the gentlemen of the House of Commons were roused out of their slumbers to utter a formulaic condemnation, in a question raised by Sir Frank Medlicott, MP:

Is my right hon. friend aware that great offence was caused to many people by the arrival of this man, with his 13-year-old bride, especially bearing in mind the difficulty that others have in obtaining permission to work here? Will he remember also that we have more than enough 'rock'n'roll' entertainers of our own without importing them from overseas.

The marriage itself lasted thirteen years – certainly a long time in the showbusiness world – and Myra herself said in a BBC interview decades later that marrying at that age was commonplace in the Southern states at that time, but when it came out this was already the *third* marriage for twenty-two-year-old Jerry, one of them bigamous, then the atmosphere turned decidedly hostile. 'CLEAR OUT THIS GANG', said the headlines, calling for action from the Home Secretary to 'issue an order expelling from this country the disgusting Jerry Lee Lewis and the shameless gang he has brought with him'. After just three shows, at one of which he responded to a heckler with the words 'somebody put a lid on that garbage can', Jerry flew back to the US, his career for the moment in ruins. Anyone still clinging to the old idea that all publicity is good publicity should try reading the national coverage which Jerry Lee received during those few days in May 1958; yet, in time, he would rebuild his reputation by means of return visits to the very country where those articles appeared. Beginning in April 1962, he came back repeatedly to England during that decade and played to packed houses, as did many of his fellow rockers such as Roy Orbison, Little Richard and Gene Vincent.

FUJIYAMA, MAMA...

Gene himself, minus the Blue Caps, who had finally split after numerous line-up changes, took the rockin' beat farther than most with his summer 1959 tour of Japan, where he and guitarist Jerry Merritt played to vast crowds over the course of three weeks, including 286,000 paid admissions in just one five-day engagement. Towards the end, Gene became homesick for his wife and young family and flew home early, after which the promoter suggested that Merritt impersonate Vincent, because no one would know the difference. This he duly did, and it apparently worked out fine.

Gene wasn't quite the first Western rocker to play in Japan, because in February and March 1959, Wanda Jackson had toured there. Wanda's song 'Fujiyama Mama' (1957) had been a huge hit over there, name-checking Hiroshima and Nagasaki in the lyrics and kicking up a storm. Just how big a sensation she would prove to be came as something of a surprise when she and her father landed in Tokyo, as she told me:

> When I got off the plane, the first time, it was a big to-do. My daddy and I, we saw out the window this red carpet and people up on the top of the airport with big signs. We couldn't read 'em, they were in Japanese. We said, 'Boy, we must have a movie star or some dignitary or something, keep your eyes open, see if you can see who it is.' We got out the door of the plane, and going down the steps and he tapped me on the shoulder, and he said 'Baby, I think you oughta start smilin', I think all this is for you.' And I couldn't believe it.
>
> I did my first press conference – I didn't even know what that was – and the interpreter said, 'Just say you don't mind at all, and I'll explain it when we're through, I don't have time now.' I said OK, and he said, 'Do you mind people throwing things at you when you're onstage?' Well, I nearly came unglued, you know. I said 'Oh no, I don't mind.' What am I getting into here? But that was their contact. They had little crepe ribbons of some sort, and they'd hold it in a spool and throw it, and it would come to you, and if it was within reaching distance you'd take 'em. I've got pictures of that stuff piled around my feet, I couldn't hardly walk, you know. And also, the kids could come up onstage, they could trust that because they're so mannerly, and quiet. Those little kids would come up onstage, bowing and hand me a little gift, a doll…

So, as the 1950s drew to a close, rockabilly was starting to reach out across the globe, and, fittingly, Gene Vincent made his first visit to England for a series of appearances on Jack

Good's *Boy Meets Girls* TV shows in December 1959. Tied in with his visit was one solitary gig, at Tooting Granada, where he delivered the goods to a hero's welcome, as the reporter from *Disc* magazine noted:

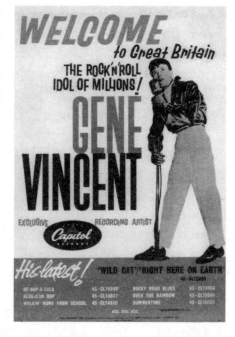

> Vincent is a man's man, a tough guy. He is rock'n'roll's James Cagney and it is for this reason that an unusally large proportion of his fan club consists of boys ... He spins, throws and catches the mike, and swings his leg over it in a single short burst of movement. Then, like a crouching tiger awaiting its prey, he will be stock still for minutes on end.

Within weeks, he was back playing a full string of UK shows, double-billed with Eddie Cochran, in a tour that ended in tragedy near Chippenham with Eddie's death and Gene's hospitalisation. Yet the hardcore rockers, Teds and bike boys who showed up to see Gene would return time and again to his UK shows throughout the rest of his short life – indeed, so much of his work was here that he lived in England for a fair slice of the 1960s. The history of that decade is often presented as the story of the all-conquering Beatles and their followers, but at the time they were very much regarded as something non-threatening for the twelve-year-old girls to scream at. A great many original US rockers whose audience back home all but dried up in the wake of Merseybeat's popularity found a profitable career touring Europe in general and the UK in particular. Some people grew their hair and changed their music to suit the times, but others simply dug in and kept on doing the thing they did best, regardless of fashion.

Rockabilly's chart hit-making days were largely gone with the 1950s, but the music itself would prove to have a life way beyond that particular decade.

17 THE SHOOTIN' WAR'S OVER BUT THERE'S STILL SOME RENEGADES OUT IN THE HILLS

THOSE WHO KEPT ON RECORDING LIKE IT WAS STILL 1955

Rock'n'roll music changed a great deal between 1955 and 1959. Many rough edges were smoothed away, and numerous identikit pretty boys were lined up by the major labels in an attempt to cash in on the huge teenage market while not offending the parents who controlled the pocket money. If you could smile nicely for the camera, shake Dick Clark's hand on TV and generally give the appearance of having spent more time and effort on your haircut than your music, then the world was your oyster. Or maybe not.

A stripped-down gutbucket rockabilly record like Carl Perkins' 'Blue Suede Shoes' could be a smash hit back in 1956, yet would probably have fared a lot less well three years later, but this doesn't mean that everyone out there cleaned up, knuckled down and tried to communicate with their inner Tommy Sands. Just as there are people these days who've been cutting pure 1977-style punk records solidly for the last two decades, regardless of shifts in popular taste, there were many rockabilly performers holding down regular gigs at their favourite neighbourhood bars who continued playing in the same way they'd always done. A few of them even managed to keep making records. Charlie Feathers is the classic example; a man whose back catalogue is almost impossible to navigate purely on audio evidence, since the stuff he was cutting in 1968 or '78 could easily have been made in 1955.

As long as you were prepared to settle for aiming at a local, rather than national, audience, there was no reason not to go on performing in your own personal style, regardless of changing trends. For years, some rockabilly reissue compilations would round up some of the huge torrent of obscure material from those days and list just the name of the song and the artist, without giving any clue as to the year of the performances. Diligent research work by rockin' magazine writers and sleeve-note specialists, and, in particular, the remarkable website *Rockin' Country Style*, heroically compiled by Terry E. Gordon, have now made it possible to date the vast majority of these performances. In the event, many records that sounded like authentic products of the mid-1950s are actually late 1950s or early 1960s recordings, produced by people who'd clearly taken The Hillbilly Cat as a blueprint and had precious little interest in becoming the new Bobby Rydell. Some looked back even farther. The beautifully judged 'Texas Woman' by Buck Wheat & the Wheatbinders harks back unashamedly to the classic late 1920s recordings of Jimmie Rodgers, yet was recorded right at the end of the 1950s, sneaking out on the Goldband label in August 1959. This appeared just a month or so after another record which flew the flag for old-style music,

'Hillbilly Rock' by Joe Kozack with The Frontiersmen & The Hale Sisters. This record came out of Canada on the Rodeo label, and blended traditional fiddles with rockabilly music, informing the listener that 'if you really wanna rock then do it country style'. Whether this was particularly what teenagers were looking to hear in a year of Fabian and Frankie Avalon is very much open to question, but the record swings like a demon, and clearly the singer and musicians were having a fine old time.

Such adherence to traditional styles was common in the blues, and has always been normal in the folk music world, so it shouldn't be surprising to also see this kind of continuity in rockabilly. Indeed, by 1960 most of the best music in the genre was being produced by marginalised artists who clearly didn't give much of a damn what the wider world thought, and just played their own music in the way that sounded good to them, which is probably why it holds up so well today.

AIN'T NO SIGN I WOULDN'T IF I COULD

Already, by 1958, rockabilly records were being issued that were probably way too downhome for any chance of real success: for example the excellent 'Shook Shake (Like A Big Mixed Cake)' by Ken Davis, issued on his own Badger label out of Racine, Wisconsin; the frantic 'I Got Me A Woman' by Buddy Miller & the Rockin' Ramblers, on the Security label from Mount Pleasant, Texas; and the remarkably assured 'If You Call That Love' by the Three Ramblers, a Starday package deal issued on the band's own Ozark label, from Sault Sainte Marie, Michigan. The following year, when number 1 chart hits included smooth sounds such as 'Lonely Boy' by Paul Anka, or former rockabilly Johnny Horton's historical story song 'The Battle Of New Orleans', there was no shortage of

Bill Browning hands out some rockin' household tips, 1957

authentic small-label material like the superb 'Don't Push, Don't Shove' by Bill Browning & the Echo Valley Boys, or the laconic, leanin'-on-the-old-front-porch brilliance of 'Ain't No Sign I Wouldn't If I Could' by Ford Nix & The Moonshiners on Clix Records, out of Troy, Michigan. This trend continued as the fifties gave way to the sixties, when authentic rockabilly music was still being produced in significant quantities, but was almost entirely confined to small labels and aimed at local audiences, with little thought that they could reach through to a national audience as Carl Perkins or Gene Vincent had done back in 1956.

Clearly, to some, the wild days of the early rockabilly explosion had never ended, and they made records that were magnificently primitive and bursting with life, just at a time when the music business seemed to believe that the recipe for success was to load a record down with syrupy strings, teeth-rottingly bland backing choruses and juvenile, non-threatening lyrics. One man who evidently had no thought of feeding the prevailing appctitc for slush was Larry Terry, who unleashed a howling monster of a record called 'Hep Cat' in June 1961. The days were long gone when major labels like Columbia would sign up wildmen from the hills, so it's no surprise that this, Larry's only single, appeared on an indie called Testa, based in Jennings, Missouri. When tracked down in the 1980s by Billy Miller and Miriam Linna from *Kicks* magazine, Larry told them he thought that this throat-shredding, savage-guitar screamer had 'a nice, fun Buddy Holly-type sound'. As Del Shannon used to say, hats off to Larry...

Equally wild, and equally out of its time, was the frantic 'Okie's In The Pokie' by Jimmy Patton (1960), which surfaced on the Hilligan label out of Phoenix, Arizona, and was then picked up a month or so later by the same city's Sims label. Patton himself, as his song title suggests, was born in Berwin, Oklahoma back in 1931, and threw himself head-first into this tale of a luckless native of his home state being banged up in the local slammer for outraging public decency with his girlfriend Jezebel. The musical backing tears along at the speed of a runaway horse, while Jimmy howls away in his country-boy accent, stretching the girlfriend's name out to 'Jez-e-*bay*-el' and generally heading flat out for the finish line. *Billboard* gave it a spin, and thought it so wild they said so twice: 'A wild rocker, in the wild rockabilly tradition is handed a frantic performance by the chanter here.'

Patton had surfaced before, in 1958, with the equally hopped-up 'Yah! I'm Movin'', on the Sage label, but he had another side to him that was forever Hank Williams, as is proved by the fine country ballad 'Lonely Nights', which wound up on the flip-side of 'Okie's In The Pokie'. His voice was flexible enough to handle both styles with ease, as the reviewer noted ('Patton sells this weeper with much heart over simple support'), but a glance at that week's Hot Hundred – which included one of the newly popular surf instrumentals, 'Walk Don't Run' by the Ventures, as well as the peerless uptown Latin-tinged harmonies of the Drifters with 'Save The Last Dance For Me', alongside horrors such as Bryan Hyland's 'Itsy Bitsy Teeny Weenie Yellow Polka Dot Bikini' – showed that the times had moved on, and the business had little use for anything in the 'wild rockabilly tradition'.

HANG UP MY ROCK'N'ROLL SHOES

The Hillbilly Cat himself was back from his stint in the army, and remained a regular feature of the charts, but his current material had long since moved away from the primal rockabilly of his early years. His current hit in the week that Jimmy Patton's song was reviewed was 'It's Now Or Never', which had its roots in Italy, rather than the blues or hillbilly, and took its melody from 'O Sole Mio'. Other former rockabillies also figured in that same chart, mostly having hits with tunes that were a long way from their rockin' beginnings: former Rock'n'Roll Trio screamer Johnny Burnette, who had been carving out a career as a teen idol, was there with his latest song 'Dreamin''; Johnny Horton was riding high with the decidedly non-rockabilly 'North To Alaska'; while Ricky Nelson had strayed a fair distance from his original desire to be Carl Perkins and had reached back to 1925 to cover Gus Kahn and Walter Donaldson's show tune, 'Yes Sir, That's My Baby'. Former Sun rocker Roy Orbison, at last achieving worldwide fame with a magnificent string of ballad hits, was climbing swiftly with his latest, 'Blue Angel', and Elvis's old bass-slapping compadre, Bill Black, was in there punching with a version of one of the boss's old tunes, 'Don't Be Cruel'. The only genuine rockabilly hit that week was a song that had been recorded back in 1958, but lately given a new lease of life after a radio deejay had begun playing it repeatedly, landing

The new family-friendly Elvis, sailing on a sea of Hollywood crud, 1964

Wanda Jackson the biggest hit of her career with 'Let's Have A Party'. Even so, by that stage she was well on the way to carving out a fine reputation in the country field, and would spend much of the sixties racking up hits in that area and becoming a featured attraction at Las Vegas in its glory years.

I FOUGHT THE FAB FOUR (AND THE FOUR WON)

As can be seen, many of the big rockabilly names who were still enjoying success achieved this by diversifying either into pop or country. Tone it down, tart it up and plaster an intrusive high-pitched backing chorus on to your music, together with some strings, and you might just blend in with the prevailing wind in the charts of the early 1960s. Or else do the twist, the madison, the frug, the swim, the hully-gully or the mashed potatoes (although the hunch somehow failed to sweep the nation, despite the sterling efforts of Hasil Adkins). Then, just as the new formula had been established, along came four mop-haired musicians from across the pond who'd based their line-up – and their name – on that of the Crickets, and suddenly it seemed as if the whole US music scene was falling over itself trying to fake a Liverpool accent. All of which meant that the rootsy Southern sounds of rockabilly were even more marginalised than before. John Peel, who'd come over from England and since 1960 had been in Dallas, home of the *Big D Jamboree* and of rockabilly wildmen like Ronnie Dawson, described the change to me:

It just went mad. I mean, I got mobbed in a department store in Dallas. I'd done a few programmes with a man called Russ Knight, 'The Weird Beard', and he'd been talking about Liverpool – talking bollocks, basically – and I'd phoned him up, 'cause I was the kind of bloke who had all the internal numbers, tried to correct him, and he said, 'Are you from Liverpool?', and I said, 'Well, yeah, near enough, you know.' So he put me on the air to talk about Liverpool, and then the following weekend asked me if I'd go down to a department store in Dallas where they were having a giveaway – some Beatles LPs. They'd imagined sort of fifty or sixty people would turn up, but in fact there were several thousand girls in there, and they just ripped the store to pieces…

If this was the way the wind was blowing in one of the great Texas rockabilly cities in early 1964, then one can only salute the likes of Sammy Masters, who that year released one of the very finest versions of the Sonny Curtis song 'I Fought The Law (And The Law Won)', or Glenn Mooney, whose wild 'Come Over Rover' sounds more like a session from 1955 than '64. Then there was 'Tennessee Rhythm' by Ted Newton, whose country-boy lyrics spoke proudly of shoeless hoedowns in a barn. In truth, the charts and the media may have gone Merseybeat crazy that year, but back in the juke joints and roadhouses, and on many local radio stations, there was still a solid market for good ol' boys who could pick and sing in the hepcat style. The main difference was that their chances of any kind of a record deal, or of making a living through their music, were severely diminished, and the incredible flood of rockin' releases which had been pouring out since the mid-1950s slowed considerably after 1964.

Even so, we find rockabillies like Eddie Bond turning in cracking performances like 'Here Comes The Train' (1965) on the aptly named Memphis label, on which was listed the familiar address 706 Union Avenue – Sam Phillips' original studio. Eddie co-wrote the song with former Sun musician Stan Kesler, and the Memphis label itself was jointly owned by Jody Chastain, who helped make rockabilly history back in '56 slapping bass with Charlie Feathers & His Musical Warriors. If you're looking for a rockin' pedigree, 'Here Comes The Train' has it in spades. Nevertheless, anyone trying for serious chart action in that particular year was up against the ultra-brite grins of Herman's Hermits singing 'Mrs Brown You've Got A Lovely Daughter' and 'I'm Henry VIII I Am', both of which were US number 1 records in 1965. Truly, someone had shifted the goalposts since the days when Dewey Phillips ruled the Memphis airwaves.

LIKE A HOG A-ROOTIN' UP UNDER A FENCE

Still, the rockabilly influence was there, even among a sea of Beatle haircuts and collarless jackets. Quite apart from joyous throwbacks like Hollis Champion's revved-up version of ol' Hank's 'Long Gone Lonesome Blues' (1965), or Link Wray knocking hell out of 'Good Rockin' Tonight' (1965), there was also the remarkable Bobby Fuller Four – who dressed like one of the new beat combos but had imbibed a solid dose of Buddy Holly's Texas rockabilly spirit. Bobby and his band supercharged the Crickets' 'I Fought The Law' so successfully in 1965 that this was the version which The Clash imitated virtually note for note in 1979. Equally satisfying was the Bobby Fuller Four's 1966 reworking of Holly's 'Love's Made A Fool Of You', which rocks even harder than the original. For the real underground rockabilly sound that year, however, you'd have to turn to the likes of Danny Darren & His Drifting Playboys, whose wonderful 'Fool About You' laid on the backwoods charm in fine style: 'I'm like a hog a-rootin' up under a fence, like a flop-eared mule that ain't got no sense.' Here is the hillbilly tradition stretching back in an unbroken line through Hank Williams to Jimmie Rodgers, regardless of what may have been happening in the charts that year.

The younger generation of music fans – who were enthusiastically growing their hair and would shortly be donning bells, tie-dyed clothing and Afghan coats – were about to welcome a new type of music that revolved around free-form psychedelic jams and half-hour guitar solos. This was a world away from most rockabilly songs, which kept it short and to the point and generally checked in at two minutes or less. With the rise of the hippy generation came a new type of music critic, for whom rock music began with the Beatles and the Stones, and the more distant past of the 1950s was indeed another country. When interviewed by *Rolling Stone*, however, many famous 1960s musicians themselves were happy to show some respect for those who'd blazed the trail. Otis Redding, speaking shortly before he died in 1967, was asked whether he'd ever liked country music. He replied: 'Oh yeah. Before I started singing, maybe ten years ago, I loved anything that Hank Williams recorded.' Similarly, Jimi Hendrix told the same magazine the following year that he was 'influenced by everything at the same time, that's why I can't get it together now. Like I used to like Buddy Holly and Eddie Cochran and Muddy Waters and Elvin James' [sic].

This was one more confirmation that back in those days musicians grew up listening to all kinds of music, black and white, on the radio, despite the segregation evident in society at that time.

Carl Perkins, who'd started out dirt poor in a sharecropping family, spent most of the 1960s playing guitar behind Johnny Cash, and he too was asked in 1968 by the same magazine to reflect on the old days at Sun: 'Sam is filthy rich and slowed down now, but then Sun was exciting. We heard about his little recording studio and tried to get in. We were playing this music that wasn't country and it wasn't pop and it wasn't rhythm and blues, but somewhere in between. Some called it rockabilly, but we called it country rock.'

Asked about the Beatles, who'd started out as fans of Carl's rockabilly material, and whom he'd met in England at the height of their early fame, he commented: 'They know all about me and idolised my songs. I was in the studio when they cut "Matchbox" and played guitar with George on one cut of it, but it's never been released. Their versions are okay, but the royalty checks were nicer.'

HIPPIE IN A RATHOLE, TIGHT FIT

Carl had his songs covered by the most famous band in the world, while other rockabillies like Hasil Adkins stayed holed up in the woods, knocking out tunes in glorious mono and hollering as if their lives depended on it, just the same way they'd always been doing. Others like Johnny Buckett stood back and took wry potshots at the hippy generation. Buckett – from Clarksdale, Tennessee, whose real name was Johnny Chisenhall – had already cut fine salacious rockers such as 'Griddle Greasin' Daddy' and 'Let Me Play With Your Poodle' as well as religious material like 'I'm Using My Bible For A Roadmap'. He responded to the new generation of flower children with the scathing 'Hippie in a Blunder', which concludes with the immortal words 'hippie in a rathole, tight fit'.

Not everyone was heading for San Francisco with flowers in their hair. The Hillbilly Cat himself broke away from the endless round of Hollywood slop that Tom Parker had been feeding him, taking a break from singing audio wallpaper like 'Yoga Is As Yoga Does' (1967) or 'Queenie Wahine's Papaya' (1966), and rediscovered his rockabilly roots in a TV showcase called *Elvis,* more commonly known as the *'68 Comeback Special.* Here, in the programme's most effective sequence, he hooked up again with Scotty Moore and D. J. Fontana, and kicked off with a stripped-down version of his debut single, 'That's All Right', going on to revisit a fair few other songs from the 1954–56 era, such as 'Heartbreak Hotel', 'Blue Suede Shoes' and 'When My

Blue Moon Turns To Gold Again'. It pulled the biggest audience for a TV special that year, and paved the way for Elvis to return at last to live appearances.

If the *'68 Special* was an event that drew headlines all around the world, there was another Memphis rockabilly return that year which few except the hardcore fans would have noticed, but still very significant in its own way. Breathless Dan Coffey, born in Ireland but living in Wales, had for some time been editing a rock'n'roll magazine called *Boppin' News,* and also importing large numbers of rare rockabilly singles into the UK. Then, in 1968, he contacted Charlie Feathers, who hadn't had a record out since 1962, with an offer to pay for him to cut a single. Coffey headed for Memphis and there, in the Select-O-Hit Studio run by Sam Phillips' brother Tom, Charlie Feathers laid down the double-sider monster 'Stutterin' Cindy'/'Tear It Up', co-produced by Dan and Tom. The label credits the performance to 'Charlie Feathers With Marcus Van Story's Old Sun Slappin' Bass', and it's probably true to say that this was the finest rockabilly bass sound anyone had achieved since the 1950s. The record may not have got within a hundred miles of any chart, but finding Charlie and cutting such a magnificent new example of the genre helped pave the way for the unprecedented wave of rockabilly activity which was to develop in the 1970s.

Comedy fifties pastiche group Sha Na Na had played at the hippy mudbath Woodstock, and there was talk in the media of a rock'n'roll 'revival', but something much more serious was bubbling under the surface, and artists who had started out on Sun and its competitors suddenly found themselves fielding requests for material they hadn't sung in over a decade, as Roy Orbison remembered in an interview quoted by Alan Clayson:

We didn't play our Sun records on stage for a long time – until about 1970, I think, when it became instant history, you know. All the information coalesced to the point where everybody thought that was a beginning – and so I took it more seriously myself because I had a few years to reflect – and Presley started singing 'That's All Right' and I started singing 'Ooby Dooby'.

A new audience was knocking at the door, from around the world, and they wanted the real deal.

18 BACK FROM THE DEAD, BIGGER THAN EVER

THE STRANGE RESURGENCE OF ROCKABILLY IN THE SEVENTIES

The US had given the world rockabilly, but Europe – in particular Britain, Germany, France and Holland – got hold of the patient when it had been left for dead and applied a serious jolt to its system, bringing it back from the brink of oblivion. If you were one of the original rockers who'd cut a handful of wild slices of wax back in the 1950s, the chances are that by 1970 you'd long since returned to your day job working at a gas station, driving a truck or selling insurance. Cult success doesn't pay the rent, and in terms of music, the times had changed so much, and so often, in the previous ten years that it was hard to think that the rock musicians of the new era were even in the same game as you had once been. Much safer and more familiar, if you'd stayed in the game at all, to have moved solidly into the country field, like former Sun rockers Jerry Lee Lewis, Conway Twitty and Charlie Rich, turned to gospel like Wanda Jackson or Hal Harris, to record production, like Jimmy Bowen or Roland Janes, to radio like Jimmie Logsdon

The face that launched a million impersonators – the King in Vegas

and Eddie Bond, or a mixture of music publishing, producing, distribution and promotion like Johnny Powers. The one thing that no one seems to have expected was that groups of record collectors in places like England would be diligently tracking down all those one-off slabs of vinyl these people had recorded as teenagers, and that reissue compilations of these

273

performances would find a fresh audience in a strange new world still reeling under the assault of Donny, Marie *and* Little Jimmy Osmond.

SUN GOES INTERNATIONAL AGAIN

It all started slowly, and one of the most important factors seems to have been the purchase from Sam Phillips of the Sun label by long-time record executive Shelby Singleton in 1969. By this point, Sam had long since lost interest in what had been pretty much the greatest record label in the world, and its final 45 rpm single to appear was a piece of inconsequential flotsam called 'Back In My Arms Again' (January 1968) credited to 'Load Of Mischief'. Having purchased the rights to the Sun name and all of the tapes (except for the Presley material, which had gone to RCA in 1955 as part of Sam's original deal), Shelby Singleton embarked on a huge reissue programme. Albums appeared under the new Sun International label, and in 1969 compilations were issued of Sun material by Jerry Lee Lewis, Charlie Rich, Johnny Cash and Carl Perkins. Even more significant than these big names was the release of a various-artists compilation entitled *Original Memphis Rock'n'Roll Volume 1*, which appeared on Sun in England in 1969, and on US Sun in 1970. This LP dug into the label's rockabilly heritage for the first time, showcasing the likes of Billy Riley's 'Red Hot', Warren Smith's 'Rock'n'Roll Ruby' and Roy Orbison's 'Ooby Dooby', although why, with the entire Sun catalogue and thousands of dynamite performances to choose from, the compilers found space on an eleven-track album for Carl McVoy's 'You Are My Sunshine' is anyone's guess.

On 24 February 1969, Johnny Cash played at San Quentin, with fellow Sun rocker Carl Perkins on guitar. Carl performed a few songs of his own before Johnny hit the stage, including

'Blue Suede Shoes'. The highlights of the show were issued as the number-one-selling album *Johnny Cash At San Quentin* (1969), and the famous documentary film of the event was shot by the English company Granada TV (who also filmed the previous year's Doors documentary, *The Doors Are Open*, and 1969's *The Stones in the Park*). Another high-profile outing for a couple of the original rockabilly generation came on 13 September 1969 when 20,000 people gathered in Canada at the University of Toronto's Varsity Stadium for the Toronto Rock'n'Roll Festival. Genuine rockers such as Gene Vincent, Jerry Lee Lewis, Bo Diddley and Little Richard were featured, alongside other acts like the Plastic Ono Band and Eric Clapton, whose connection to anything remotely rockin' was tenuous at best. Having said that, the sole image on the original flyers for the event depicted a typical long-haired musician of the time, with a guitar in one hand and a tambourine in the other, looking very much as if his dearest wish was to jam for several hours with the Grateful Dead, while other acts promised on the flyer were Alice Cooper, Junior Walker & the All Stars and the Chicago Transit Authority, so the promoter's definition of the phrase 'rock'n'roll' was clearly somewhat loose.

GARDEN PARTIES

In America, concert promoter Ralph Nader had concluded that there was an audience out there who'd want to see the original artists of the 1950s and early '60s, and hired Madison Square Garden's Felt Forum in October 1969 for the first of his long-running series of shows that were billed under the title Rock'n'Roll Revival. He later said that he'd done this 'because it was the music I grew up with and loved. I wanted to hear it and I wanted a place for those artists to play it'. As the line-up for one of his concerts on 12 June 1971 at the Felt Forum shows, he blended vocal groups with rock'n'rollers: on that particular evening it was Jerry Lee Lewis, Chuck Berry, Duane Eddy, Bo Diddley, The Shirelles, The Drifters, The Five Satins, Gary US Bonds and Freddy Cannon. In July 1972 *Billboard* reported that Nader had 'started at near-bankruptcy in 1969 and to date has produced 110 profitable "Rock'n'Roll revival" concerts throughout the US ... Nader puts in all his contracts that the acts must perform their original hits, not sing current material in a vain attempt to get contemporary again. "You can hear the booing roll in when a performer tries to sneak some new stuff into his act," he says.' This was probably a reference to former rockabilly Ricky Nelson's legendary appearance at one of Nader's shows on 15 October 1971, where he eventually walked offstage after the crowd booed his cover of a Rolling Stones song, an event which later gave Ricky a Top Ten hit, when he commemorated the evening in the song 'Garden Party' (1972).

VIVE LE ROCK

It's likely that the success of well-publicised events such as Nader's prompted a UK promoter called ARK to hire the massive Wembley Stadium in 1972 for the first rock show ever staged at that venue. Booking an outdoor football arena with a capacity of 85,000 was a supremely confident move, but Philip Davies, spokesman for the promoters, was in no doubt that a crowd would appear for the 5 August concert, telling the *NME* that they were expecting roughly 65,000 people. The line-up featured Chuck Berry, Jerry Lee Lewis, Little Richard, Bo Diddley, Bill Haley, The Coasters, The Drifters, The Platters and Screamin' Lord Such, not to mention the MC5 and Gary Glitter. Putting that bill together hadn't been easy, as Davies explained:

Bo Diddley? We flew to Mexico to get him. Jerry Lee Lewis came about because Ray Foulk flew to Memphis. Little Richard was a bit more difficult. We went along to one of his recording sessions and he made us hang around for a week until he'd finished recording.

Preparations for turning the huge stadium into a rock venue included the construction of a stage 150 feet wide, and building a sound system incorporating 150 speakers. Then, of course, there was the football playing surface to think of, as the promoters explained a week before the event: 'We are obliged to protect the Wembley turf by laying down coconut matting, but we are having difficulty obtaining sufficient. At present, a supply is on its way from India, and we only hope it arrives.'

Loitering with intent somewhere on all that coconut matting, hoping to sell their home-produced 'Vive Le Rock' T-shirts to the massed Teddy Boys and bikers from across the country, were a couple of stallholders taking time away from their shop at the seedier end of the King's Road – Malcolm McLaren and Vivienne Westwood – who'd been shifting clothes and ephemera to the fifties faithful for two years from a place they called 'Let It Rock'. Also present was the man who supplied rare original rockin' records to their shop, Ted Carroll, who went on to open the Rock On record store, and then jointly found the Chiswick and Ace record labels, which would be responsible for some of the most important rockabilly reissues of the following decades.

Nineteen seventy-two was a strange time in terms of musical tastes – on the one hand, the UK album charts at the time of the Wembley show included prog rockers Emerson, Lake & Palmer with *Trilogy*, not to mention Uriah Heep's *Demons & Wizards* and Jethro Tull's *Living In The Past*. Yet the glam artists who'd taken so much of their three-chord, foot-stomping energy from early rock'n'roll were up there too: lifelong Eddie Cochran fan Marc Bolan was at the height of his fame, with his T. Rex album *The Slider* heading up the charts, where it would sit next to Slade's *Slade Alive* and Bowie's *Ziggy Stardust*. Also in the Top Ten was the King of Western Bop himself, with his *Live At Madison Square Garden* LP. But who was apparently the nation's favourite, perched at the top of the singles charts? Donny Osmond, with the glutinous 'Puppy Love'. Then, as now, and in the days of the Beatles, it was usually the twelve-year-old girls who were calling the shots in terms of chart hits.

Still, if Donny and his pals didn't float your particular boat, there was a regular column in the back of the *NME* during '72 written by one Rockin' Henry, detailing all the upcoming gigs from UK rock'n'roll outfits like Crazy Cavan & The Rhythm Rockers, the Wild Angels, Screamin' Lord Sutch or Shakin' Stevens & the Sunsets. A network of rockin' venues had grown up to support these bands, such as the Railway Hotel at Wealdstone, the Bull at East Sheen and the Palace Bar at Southend, complete with specialist deejays such as Tongue Tied Danny and Jailhouse John Alexander of the Wild Wax Show. To help feed that audience, a few brave souls at the major labels had started looking back through the vaults and putting out something other than just greatest-hits packages of 1950s rockers. An early gem was the 1972 United Artists release *Eddie Cochran – On The Air,* which made available previously unissued recordings including those from the *Boy Meets Girls* TV show during his 1960 UK tour with Gene Vincent. The *NME*'s reviewer, Roy Carr, recognised the groundbreaking nature of this release: 'I can't stress the importance of this album [sic] and hope that in time it will motivate other companies to come to some arrangement with Thames Television to put out companion albums. For a start, how about some Gene Vincent tapes?'

PUT YOUR CAT CLOTHES ON

The Wembley show was a very public demonstration of the fact that upwards of 50,000 people in the UK would show up to hear the likes of Jerry Lee singing 'Whole Lotta Shakin'' and other 1950s material – as opposed to the country hits he'd been enjoying in recent years. Added to this, the quiet work which had been begun by Colin Escott and Martin Hawkins, of enquiring into the history of the Sun label and listening to endless hours of Sun out-takes, started to bear fruit in 1973 with the release of the landmark album they compiled, *Sun Rockabillys Volume One: Put Your Cat Clothes On*. Here at last were not only outright classics such as Jack Earls' 'Slow Down' (1956), Sonny Burgess & the Pacers' 'We Wanna Boogie' (1956) and Ray Harris's 'Come On Little Mama' (1956), but also previously unissued gems like Carl Perkins' blistering 1957 title track, Warren Smith's 'Red Cadillac & A Black Moustache' (1957) and Roy Orbison's ultra-suave 'Domino' (1956). This is sometimes said to be the first album to feature the word 'rockabilly' in the title, although Collector Records in Holland also issued a compilation entitled *Rare Rock-A-Billy* in 1973, so it was certainly an idea whose time had come. Collector had been putting out very interesting LPs since their *Ten Long Fingers* album in 1970, rounding up rare items from the likes of Curtis Hobeck and Groovey Joe Poovey.

Also over in Holland at the same time, the Redita label, run by Robert Loers, began issuing a string of very fine compilation albums such as *Sound Of Rockabilly* (1973), which included some of Johnny Carroll & his Hot Rock's classic Decca recordings, and *Memphis Rocks The Country* (1973), containing a slew of Sun cuts by the likes of Malcolm Yelvington, Hayden Thompson and Hardrock Gunter. Most intriguing of all was another 1973 Dutch album, on the Bopcat label, called *Good*

279

Rockin' Tonight, whose compilers clearly had access to unissued Elvis Sun material. With a line-up that included The Hillbilly Cat himself, alongside Jerry Lee Lewis, Billy Riley and Warren Smith, it must have sent the good folks at RCA into something of a spin, since they'd owned all the rights to the King's Sun material for years, although they'd never yet collected it all together. Finally, in 1975, Richard Weize started the Bear Family label in Germany with his partner, Hermann Knülle, and would go on to issue a remarkably high-quality series of country and rockabilly reissues over the years.

There was renewed action in 1973 from some of the original rockabillies: Charlie Feathers cut a single on the Pompadour Records label, 'Uh Huh Honey'/'Wedding Gown Of White', and Eddie Bond released a version of 'Rockin' Daddy' on Tab Records, out of Memphis, Tennessee, whose label proclaimed, 'The All-New Memphis Country Sound'. Jerry Lee Lewis, meanwhile, had been in England, making an LP at Advision Studios, backed by what appeared to be an entire London busful of celebrity Brit musicians such as Albert Lee, Peter Frampton and Maggie Bell. The *NME*'s John Pearce, who was at the sessions, reported that 'at one stage "the hillbilly rock'n'roller" even had a 60-year-old tea lady "bopping at the high school hop"', but in truth, the Killer needed all those extra musicians about as much as a hole in the head. Charlie Gillett, reviewing the resulting album, *The London Sessions*, in the same paper a month later concluded as much, under the headline 'A Case Of Too Many Cooks Spoil The Rock'.

Better, then, to rely on the stream of original 1950s rockabilly material being issued on compilation albums. *Sun Rockabillys Volume One: Put Your Cat Clothes On* was followed in 1974 by *Sun Rockabillys Volume Two: Carryin' On*, *Sun Rockabillys Volume Three* and the double LP *The Sun Story*.

Not everyone was impressed by the sounds of previous

decades: Andrew Tyler in the *NME* reacted to the release of some key fifties Dale Hawkins rockabilly cuts, many of which featured James Burton on guitar, with the following review:

> What we have here is a relatively obscure and often amusing catalogue of primaeval rockabilly – high school soda pop sentiments expressed with much zeal, and a demonstrable absence of finesse ... An apt and comic meander through the yellowing pages of yesteryear but let's not pretend they didn't make some lousy records in those days.

THE BOP THAT JUST WON'T STOP

Over the next five years the situation changed beyond all recognition, as hundreds of original rockabilly tracks were reissued, and a great deal more that had spent the previous two decades just sitting on a shelf were seeing the light of day for the first time. This helped prime the market for live appearances by an ever-increasing number of the original artists, and also led some of the younger members of the rockabilly audience to form their own bands and attempt to work in the classic Sun style.

In April 1977, at the Rainbow Theatre (where Carl Perkins and Chuck Berry had played back in 1964), the first major exclusively rockabilly event since the 1950s took place, when Warren Smith, Buddy Knox, Charlie Feathers and Jack Scott took to the London stage in front of thousands of fans. Such a specialist gathering of this size would have been impossible ten years before, but by this stage there was a younger generation coming through who'd been buying the reissues and were now keen to see the original performers play live. I wasn't living in London, and didn't even hear about the show until

Ray Smith

the following year, when the live album of the event appeared, but in '78 I did make the journey to the Rainbow, because I'd seen in the papers that Jerry Lee Lewis would be appearing there on 19 November. The support act was Duane Eddy, and the tickets cost £5, which was high for the time, in fact double the price that it had cost me to see the Ramones, Generation X and the Rezillos at the same venue the year before. Jerry Lee was apparently recovering from major stomach surgery at the time, so jumping on top of the piano was certainly not on the agenda. He put on a fine show, but the crowd got restless every time he tried some country songs, and when he finished and was clearly not returning for an encore, my chief memory is of the man in front of me, in full Ted gear, standing up in his seat, shaking his fist and shouting at the empty stage, 'Jerry Lee Lewis! I came here for some fucking rock'n'roll, and what have you given us? Fucking country and western!'

By then, of course, anyone looking for some rock'n'roll from the Hillbilly Cat himself would have been out of luck. When Elvis died in 1977, he sold more records in the following few months than in most of the rest of his career put together. The TV and the papers were full of pictures of him in his Vegas years, but the *NME* chose to put a classic mid-1950s black & white onstage picture of him in his rockabilly days on the cover,

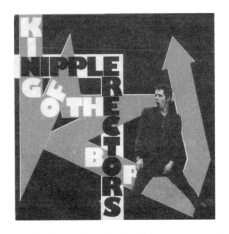

A drape-jacketed Shane MacGowan on the cover of his 1978 debut single with the Nipple Erectors

with the tagline 'Elvis lives – remember him *this* way'. That was really all anyone needed to say.

As for his former rockin' colleagues, some of them were discovering that there was a new audience opening up for them. Many would play London shows at the Royalty in Southgate, such as Bill Haley, Sleepy LaBeef or Charlie Gracie. Mac Curtis appeared at the Minerva in Southend, as did Ray Campi, and when Sun rocker Warren Smith returned to England in 1978 for a show at the Roxy in Harlesden, his fellow rockabilly Ray Smith showed up onstage unannounced. The two of them even played a show together in Basingstoke during that tour, alongside British outfits like the Riot Rockers and the Flying Saucers. Within two years, both Ray and Warren would have met untimely deaths, but they saw some recognition of their 1950s musical achievements when gigging over here and in France, performing to audiences that knew every one of their songs.

The late 1970s rockabilly revival developed at much the same time that punk rock first hit the headlines, and the energy involved in both scenes had many points of similarity. Labels like Chiswick/Ace were simultaneously releasing records by The Damned while reissuing Sonny Fisher's vintage Texas rockabilly cuts, and The Clash moved slowly but surely from their paint-splattered, zipped-up urban guerrilla clothes to 1950s hepcat threads and greased-back hair within a couple of years. The British tabloid press may have had something to gain from stirring up trouble between rockers and punks, but the ageing hacks who wrote those articles knew damn all about either scene, and cared even less, while the real situation was far more fluid and complex. John Peel regularly played a single on his Radio 1 show in 1978 by a teenage British band called The Jets, entitled 'Rockabilly Baby', which had been recorded for a small label called Soho Records. He also gave a fair bit of airtime to another disc from the same imprint, 'King Of The Bop' by the Nipple Erectors, whose picture sleeve featured lead singer, punk fanzine writer and future Pogue Shane MacGowan dancing in full Teddy Boy gear. Also, as befitted someone who'd had the good taste to sign Gene Vincent to his own record label back in the late 1960s, John would throw in the occasional Blue Caps record alongside the punk and reggae tracks in his playlist.

Boz Boorer co-founded a rockabilly band called the Polecats in London during the punk years, inspired by a mixture of many things he'd heard growing up in England during the 1970s, as he explained to me:

> I sort of discovered Chuck Berry at an early age, and my brother had the *That'll Be The Day* album [soundtrack to the 1973 film]. I was introduced to Tim [Polecats vocalist], 'cause he had a guitar. I loved chart records and chart music, but Chuck Berry had a number one with 'Ding-a-Ling', you know, and at the age of twelve I quite liked the underlying metaphors... So my mate up the road bought a *20 Rock'n'Roll Party Greatest Hits of Chuck Berry*, and we started playing them – it was fantastic. So

after that, when we hooked up with Tim's mate Chris, his two brothers were Teddy Boys, and they had the Crazy Cavan, they had 'Bip Bop Boom' [by Mickey Hawks & the Night Raiders, 1958] on a 45, they had all those *Rare Rockabilly* albums and a few originals, and we listened to 'em. It was all rock'n'roll, all Teddy Boys – I had my hair quiffed up then – but it wasn't rockabilly, we didn't count it as rockabilly, it was the country side of rock'n'roll that we liked. We didn't know what a slap-bass was, and when we realised, we went and got one. And then we started playing, and of course we played things like 'Sunglasses After Dark' [by Dwight Pullen, 1958]. But we also played punk rock and we also went to punk rock gigs.

As the decade drew to a close, there was clearly a full-blown rockabilly revival going on, which merited another *NME* cover, under the headline 'Rockabilly The Kid – The Bop That Just Won't Stop'. The music that many in the industry had thought long gone at the start of the seventies would see an outbreak of renewed activity in the eighties that few even in the rockin' scene would have predicted.

19 STRAY CATS, POLECATS AND BORN-AGAIN HEPCATS

NEW BANDS, NEW AUDIENCE, AND A NEW SPARK FOR THE OLD FLAMES

Although the 1980s in Britain were in some ways a miserable wasteland brought low by mass unemployment, Margaret Thatcher and witless synth-pop horrors, they also turned out to be the best era for seeing the original generation of rockabilly artists performing live over here, while a new set of mostly home-grown young groups began playing the music, some of whom even made the charts.

Over in America, a band who'd also been spending countless hours picking through old rockabilly singles in out-of-the-way places were starting to be noticed, although, like the original rockers themselves, they found that England seemed perhaps more tuned in to their wavelength than some cities back home. These were The Cramps, and they probably had the finest taste in navigating the wilder extremes of America's rockin' past than just about anyone. The fact that they also looked suaver than hell, and turned out, if you had the good fortune to meet them, to be genuinely decent people,

remains one of the wonders of recent musical history.

The Cramps started out in the 1970s playing regular gigs in New York punk clubs like CBGB and Max's, and their set list regularly featured rockabilly covers such as 'Rockin' Bones' (Ronnie Dawson), 'Uranium Rock' (Warren Smith), 'Can't Hardly Stand It' (Charlie Feathers) and 'I Got A Rocket In My Pocket' (Jimmy Lloyd). A superb example of one of their early live performances was captured on film when they played a free gig for the residents of the California State Mental Hospital at Napa on 13 June 1978. It's black & white, decidedly low-fi, the audience wanders in and out of shot in the finest slow-motion stage invasion in rock history, and it's absolutely compelling. Shot for the rough equivalent of a couple of packs of Lucky Strike and a pint of whiskey, it puts to shame pretty much every other live video ever recorded.

A year later The Cramps were over in England, having landed a deal with Miles Copeland's IRS label, which meant they wound up supporting Copeland's brother's band The Police in one of the most ill-matched double bills since Hendrix opened for the Monkees. On 23 June 1979, the band appeared on the cover of the *NME*, with a lengthy feature inside written by Nick Kent. He attempted to provide some background about the history of rockabilly, as well as mentioning that the band's own favoured description of their sound was 'psychobilly voodoo' – perhaps the first public use of a term which would come to be applied to many bands in the 1980s that blended rockabilly with a punk sensibility. Kent knew there was something different about them, and spent most of the article seeking to pin it down:

> The Cramps baulk at being considered reactionaries, fervently believing, on the contrary, that the basic spirit of rockabilly as they both view and practise it is the well-spring of pure rock'n'roll essence. In practice, their sound can be seen as utilizing a similar feel and tension as that of the Ramones. Also like the Ramones, their songs appear, superficially anyway, to sound all very much one of a kind.

Their debut album, *Songs The Lord Taught Us*, had been recorded at the Sam C. Phillips studio in Memphis, with Alex Chilton producing. Alex himself was no stranger to this sort of thing. The Kent article quotes The Cramps as saying of him, 'We've heard he's playing in a band called Panthers Blazing [sic]. He's not singing or writing songs. Just playing on guitar.' The band in question was Tav Falco's Panther Burns, another group that has flown the flag for the true rockabilly spirit from the late 1970s up until the present day. Years later I corresponded frequently with Tav when preparing an article to accompany his superb photographs of Tennessee juke joints and Memphis musicians, and he told me some of his memories of those days:

> At one time Memphis qualified as the murder capital of North America. It is not that there are any fewer killings today, only more killings somewhere else. Five or six homicides remain a daily average. Cold killers beat Piano Red to death in his own bed the first weekend after he'd returned from some dates in Europe with a pocketful of money. The same cold killers that came to Red's house one afternoon while I was videotaping him.

One of the kids pulled out a .32 calibre pistol from under his T-shirt, aimed it right at the camera lens and asked, 'Now d'you want me to shoot you?' Around the same time The Cramps came to town to record, and they were a revelation of how apocalyptic rock'n'roll can be.

Panther Burns and The Cramps played primal double-header shows in Memphis at the Orpheum around that time, and Tav says that the band applied a similar level of mayhem when making their debut album:

In Studio A of Sam Phillips' Recording Service at 639 Madison Avenue, The Cramps took the very same approach to recording, as if they were onstage. After a while one lost count of the chairs, stand-up ashtrays and metal coat racks that Lux twisted, tossed and smashed around the studio in the process of recording a single track. Nor can one forget the confrontations between Lux and the studio engineers – who had radically different ideas on how to capture their performance onto tape, and who were even less understanding of his leaping about on the tops of amplifiers, piano lids and Leslie cabinets during the course of a take.

Songs The Lord Taught Us was released in 1980, at the start of a decade when synthesised sounds and stadium bombast would largely rule the airwaves. Yet this also turned out to be an era that began with various second-generation rockabilly bands storming the UK charts, while the trickle of original 1950s acts making the journey over to play for the hepcat audience rapidly turned into a full-scale invasion. Soon there would also be little need for bands to play on inappropriate bills, as a separate rockabilly gig circuit developed, with its own major events

100% ROCK N ROLL   ONLY 95p   NO. 2

now DIG this

IN THIS ISSUE:
A JERRY LEE LEWIS
SPECIAL
ALSO:
BUDDY KNOX
RECORD REVIEWS
AND MUCH MORE

Issue No. 2 of Now Dig
This, 1983

such as the Hemsby weekenders or the mid-1980s all-dayers at the Birmingham Powerhouse. For news, it was no longer necessary to rely on the mainstream weekly music press, since first-class specialist magazines such as Adam Komorowski's *New Kommotion* (founded 1976) and Trevor Cajiao's *Now Dig This* (founded 1983) provided detailed information about all facets of the scene and the history of the music, while showing the original artists who were starting to come over a fitting measure of respect.

ROCKIN' ON *TOP OF THE POPS*

As for the mainstream charts, it was a common enough sight to see bands whose own music bore no relation to rockabilly or rock'n'roll either adopting 1950s haircuts and clothes, while suits available from shops like Johnson's in World's End, Rock-a-Cha in Kensington Market and shoes from Robot in the

King's Road were regularly being worn by all sorts of people in the pages of new rock/lifestyle magazine *The Face*. The look was everywhere, and it was becoming harder to separate the genuine rockabillies from the fashion victims. As a musical style, it could be thrown in for flavour on one or two tracks of an album, just as reggae had been picked up and put down by all kinds of bands during the punk era. A prime example would be the song 'Messed Around', a convincing slap-bass rocker recorded by Squeeze on their 1981 album *East Side Story*, which was also released as a single in the US.

Rockabilly was so well established in Britain by 1981 as one of the country's recognised youth movements that London Weekend Television devoted an entire programme in their *20th Century Box* series to explaining its distinguishing features. By this stage it was clear that many old-school Teds had little time for the largely younger rockabilly fans, and the feeling was sometimes mutual. Whereas the classic Teddy Boy clothing was based around an Edwardian drape jacket, and the Teds themselves pre-dated the arrival of rock'n'roll in England by roughly half a decade, the new rockabilly crowd tended to dress more like the original Memphis rockers themselves, often wearing vintage fifties US clothing bought at Flip in Covent Garden, which had been importing huge amounts of it since 1978.

Rockabilly was certainly all over the UK media by that stage, and in the Top Ten. The Stray Cats had come over from Long Island in the summer of the previous year, rightly figuring that London was a better bet. For a month or so they were sleeping on the floor of their publicist's office in the West End, but success came very fast. They landed an *NME* cover feature only six weeks after their arrival (before even signing a record deal or releasing a single), which carried the misleading strapline 'Stray Cats – How Yankee Quiffabilly

Put The Bop Back In Britain'. In actual fact, the band had come to this country precisely because the rockin' scene was far stronger here than anywhere else in the world, and, like The Cramps, the Ramones and Blondie before them, they went from playing small clubs in New York to major venues in London, with sympathetic crowds and lots of column inches in the music press.

Britain already had plenty of rockabilly and rock'n'roll acts – long-time trailblazers like Crazy Cavan & the Rhythm Rockers, the Flying Saucers, Shakin' Stevens or CSA, or newer outfits like Whirlwind and The Polecats, while Matchbox reached the UK Top Twenty in 1979 with a song called 'Rockabilly Rebel', and scored further hits in 1980. Even a mainstream chart act like Queen had used a complete rockabilly pastiche sound for their 1979 hit 'Crazy Little Thing Called Love'. As far as the press were concerned, however, the Stray Cats had the major trump card of being American. Still, as anyone who saw their early gigs will tell you, they could certainly deliver the goods. On 20 November, just as their Dave Edmunds-produced debut single 'Runaway Boys' was climbing up the charts, I stood down at the front of their show at the University of East Anglia, in Norwich, taking pictures of their blistering live performance. Listening to them sound-check earlier in the evening, it was also quite something to hear nineteen-year-old Brian Setzer casually throwing in note-perfect snatches of Cliff Gallup's guitar solos from various 1956 Gene Vincent recordings between numbers, just for the hell of it.

The Stray Cats, like many of the newer bands, used an upright bass, rather than the electric which some older groups were still attempting to use for rockabilly. Without the slap and the accompanying click of a double bass, half the authentic sound is missing, no matter what you do. It was this that gave

'Runaway Boys' its distinctive pulse, and yet to hear 'king of the Teds' Sunglasses Ron tell it on a *20th Century Box* programme, the Stray Cats and the newer fans were the beginning of the end:

> In this country it's gone right down. Very few of the old clubs are left. What there are, they're getting over-run by these youngsters out there – punkabillies, or whatever they are, you know. A lot of people like myself who are still about just don't bother any more, it's just not worth the effort. You can go there and mix, but when you get up and you jive with your wife, and you get a dozen kids who are pogo dancing around you, you think, what's going on?, you know. Are we listening to the same kind of music? ... Let 'em have their own do and let them have their music there, but for Christ's sake let us have our music, you know? There's not enough of our lads left ...

The Stray Cats at UEA, Norwich, November 20, 1980 – photo by the author

Max Décharné

THE RISE OF THE ROCKABILLY WEEKENDERS

In the spring of 1981, I, along with my college friend Anton
Vent, blagged my way into the grandly titled International
Rock'n'Roll Weekend Hop at Ladbroke's Caister Holiday
Centre, Great Yarmouth, Norfolk – an event which blazed the
trail for the nearby Hemsby rock'n'roll weekenders that arguably
became the most important regular rockabilly gathering in
the world. I still remember the feeling of walking into the
main hall at Caister that day and seeing the huge crowd, their
hair and clothes exactly right for 1956, with a band onstage in
matching white vintage dinner jackets and a line of the classic
original Sure 55SH Unidyne vocal microphones stretched out
in front of them. Around the walls were clothing and rare
record stalls, at one of which I found a bootleg of the legendary
Million Dollar Quartet sessions at Sun, which were still half
a decade away from their legal release. I took a lot of black &
white photographs, and we went backstage and interviewed
whoever was around. That turned out to be The Jets – three
brothers from Northampton whose 'Rockabilly Baby' single I'd
picked up after hearing them on John Peel's show in 1979 – and
a cracking US outfit called Buzz & The Flyers, who were mates
of the Stray Cats and had come over to the UK presumably
looking for similar opportunities.

We also met that band with the white dinner jackets, who
turned out to be The Stargazers. They'd been in existence only
a couple of months, and took us back to their chalet for what
turned out to be the first interview they'd ever done. I hadn't
been involved in many myself, and proved it beyond question
by putting the tape machine on top of the fridge for the whole
thing, so that when I got home I discovered it had recorded
plenty of the electronic hum of the appliance and pretty much
nothing of the conversation. Years later, when my band The

Flaming Stars started, I wound up on the same label as The Stargazers, called Vinyl Japan, which issued a fair amount of rockabilly and neo-rockabilly in the 1990s.

The man who introduced the latter-day Stargazers to Vinyl Japan in 1991 was another key player in the rockabilly revival, Boz Boorer, guitar player with The Polecats. I caught a fine Polecats show in 1981, and was knocked out that they did a version of Hal Harris's 'Jitterbop Baby'. They had three singles which made the Top Fifty that year, mixing fifties covers such as Jimmy Carroll's 'Big Green Car' (originally from 1958) with rockabilly versions of glam rock material like T. Rex's 'Jeepster' or Bowie's 'John I'm Only Dancing' – an effective technique also employed by Dave Phillips & the Hot Rod Gang, with their rockabilly cover of the Northern Soul classic 'Tainted Love' (1983).

Into this 1980s world where rockabilly outfits were signed to major labels – The Polecats on Mercury, Stray Cats on Arista, The Jets on EMI – came the strongest wave yet of visiting original 1950s rockabillies, often after some tireless UK promoter had spent years tracking them down. On 2 March 1984, former US Decca artist Roy Hall passed away, and Sun rocker Onie Wheeler died two months later, onstage at the *Grand Ole Opry*, yet the same year saw other Sun artists appearing in England: Carl Mann toured with the Dave Travis band, Charlie Feathers returned, appearing at Bristol Town Hall, and in 1985 Eddie Bond and Huelyn Duvall were among those who came over to play. On the very last day of that year came the tragic death of Ricky Nelson and his band in a plane crash. Three months later, at Hammersmith Odeon, I saw The Cramps play their cover version of Ricky's 'Lonesome Town' – which had featured on their *Gravest Hits* EP back in 1979 – as a tribute to the man himself. The support act that night was The Stingrays, one of the new breed of psychobilly bands who'd made a reputation playing shows at places like the Klub Foot, just down the road in Hammersmith. Bal Croce, the singer, had even been on the cover of the music paper *Sounds,* as one of the figureheads of the movement. Little did I know that I'd wind up in a band called the Earls Of Suave with half of the Stingrays five years later, and that we in turn would be opening for The Cramps.

DIG THAT DIGITAL DISC

By 1986, original rockabilly recordings had started showing up on the new CD format, although the record industry as a whole seemed scared to death of vintage recordings. I remember tracking down the CD section of the giant Virgin Megastore on Oxford Street at the end of 1985, hidden away upstairs in a tiny room and filled almost entirely with over-produced stadium rock product. CDs were supposed to deliver 'perfect sound quality', and so most of the major labels had decided that what the public was crying out for in the new format was the complete works of 1970s acts like Barclay James Harvest and Genesis. The sole CD I could find with any connection to the rockin' scene was a copy of the live *Smell Of Female* album by The Cramps. A few months later, when Charly Records decided to stick a toe in the water, they rounded up some decent Sun material – a Jerry Lee Lewis collection called *Ferriday Fireball,* some Carl Perkins Sun tracks titled *Dixie Fried,* plus a useful various-artists compilation, *The Best Of Sun Rockabilly.* Yet they didn't put a 1950s image of these people on the cover, preferring instead to use a modern picture of Carl in his toupee, out of seeming embarrassment at the age of the performances.

Still, the original rockers kept on coming in '86: Texas rockabillies Sid & Billy King played the 9th Rock'n'Roll Jamboree, at the Powerhouse, Birmingham, supported by vintage London outfit the Chas McDevitt Skiffle Group; three

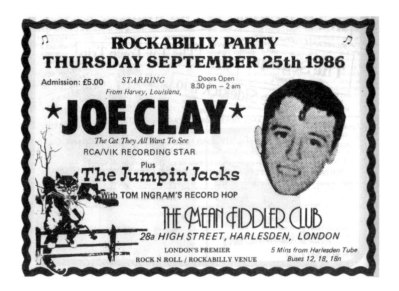

months later the recently discovered Joe Clay appeared at the same venue, making his UK debut; Janis Martin played the Clay Pigeon in Harrow; Big Al Downing showed up at the 8th International Weekend Festival in Weymouth; Louisiana rocker Johnnie Allan toured the UK; and I caught a fine set by Buddy Holly's original band The Crickets at Dingwalls in Camden Town.

All the above activity was made possible by the work of promoters like Paul Barrett (originally Shakin' Stevens' manager), Colin Silcocks (organiser of the Birmingham Powerhouse Jamborees), Willie Jeffrey (the man who finally located Joe Clay), Ian Wallis and rockabilly deejay Tom Ingram. Of course, some of the punters occasionally wrote to the rockin' press to complain about the arrangements for these shows, but that in itself was something of a high-risk occupation. In May 1987, *Now Dig This* printed a letter from promoters Johnny Hale and Paul Barrett responding to questions about whether original Gene Vincent drummer Dickie 'Be-Bop' Harrell would be able to make the upcoming '1958 Blue Caps' visit to England, which ended with the sentence 'And if this isn't good enough for you, well, I suggest that you crap in your hat, pull it over your head and call it curls.'

The artists themselves generally have nothing but good things to say about the UK promoters and the audiences they encountered. Sonny Burgess – born in 1931 and still touring the world with the Pacers – told me he first came over in 1986 to play a festival organised by Paul Barrett, and credits the European rockabilly revival of the 1970s for reawakening interest in the whole genre:

> If it wasn't for all you folks in Europe, England especially... When this stuff started coming out in the seventies, I guess it was, they came over here and bought a bunch of records from Tom Phillips, that's Sam's brother. He had the distribution. Bought them for a dollar a piece. Wish I'd have been smart enough to buy them. You folks over in Europe discovered 'em, and that's why we're still playing.

I met Sonny in 1987, when he appeared at the Mean Fiddler in Harlesden – the nearest thing to an honest-to-goodness juke joint you were likely to find in West London – and he signed my original Sun 45 of 'We Wanna Boogie'. He'd just played a phenomenal show in which the entire crowd joined in on the backing vocals for 'Ain't Got A Thing', and his own lead guitar work was every bit as fine as on his 1950s recordings. I also met another remarkable rockabilly guitarist and singer that year, Ronnie Dawson, when he played in Birmingham on a double bill with Joe Clay. That venue also saw the UK debut of Detroit rockabilly Johnny Powers, who had been enjoying a successful career in other aspects of the music business, and suddenly was offered the chance to come over and play his 1950s material to a new audience. Johnny, like other original rockabilly artists who could still deliver the goods, went on to become a regular and very popular visitor to the UK. Inspired by the response, he also then wrote and recorded some of the finest new material in the rockabilly style produced by any of the original 1950s artists, including songs such as 'New Spark (For An Old Flame)' (1993) and 'I Was There When It Happened' (2002). Recalling that first visit, he told me: 'Willie Jeffrey and Ian Wallis were the first guys to bring me over… I had to learn all my songs over again. I didn't even have a guitar. This was a place called Birmingham, the Powerhouse. It was cool.'

20 STILL A LOT OF RHYTHM IN THESE ROCKIN' BONES

The incredible resurgence of interest which had developed in the UK during the decade following Hank Mizell's surprise 1976 entry into the national charts with 'Jungle Rock' was probably far beyond the wildest dreams of the original band of record collectors who'd made the trip over from here to Memphis and all points south in the 1960s, looking to pick up copies of old singles by the likes of Jack Earls, Alvis Wayne or Orangie Ray Hubbard. These performers were mostly names from the past, about whom virtually nothing was known: all there was to go on was the music, which still leapt out of the grooves, undimmed and wild. In the interim, because of the research work put in by the likes of Escott & Hawkins, Ray Topping, Bill Millar, Rob Finnis, Adam Komorowski, Trevor Cajaio's diligent crew at *Now Dig This* and Billy Miller and Miriam Linna at *Kicks* magazine – interviewing numerous 1950s artists, songwriters, club promoters, producers and former label owners – a picture had slowly been building up of the true nature of the explosion of rockabilly talent which had appeared in the wake of Elvis's Sun recordings. Hell, they'd even tracked down and unmasked The Phantom.

Then there was West Virginia wildman Hasil Adkins, who'd been located by Billy and Miriam from *Kicks* in the mid-1980s. They formed their own label, Norton Records, in 1986,

Ronnie Dawson

just in order to release *Out To Hunch,* an album of some of the hundreds of songs Hasil had been recording in his trailer home all these past years. Billy told V. Vale and Andrea Juno how he initially encountered Hasil's music: 'I first heard "Haze" in the '70s when I found a copy of "She Said" ... Then a friend showed me "Chicken Walk" and I went, "Wow – this guy made *two* records?"'

Having finally made contact and begun releasing Hasil's records, Billy and Miriam discovered the particular delights of having the man himself as a house-guest at their place in New York:

> **MIRIAM:** He eats more meat than any other human being we've ever met; he carries around Vienna sausages in his pocket. 'What would you like for lunch?' 'Meat.' 'Any special kind?' 'Meat.'

BILLY: Many years ago Miriam ran into Andy Warhol – he was standing on a street corner, and she said, 'Stay right there!', ran into a deli, got a can of Campbell's soup and had him autograph it. We had it on a shelf in our house for years. Then Hasil stayed at our house, and I said, 'Haze, I'm going out for a while; there's plenty of food in the fridge.' I came back and asked, 'Did you have lunch?' and he said, 'Well, I just fixed myself a can of soup.' You guessed it…

By 1987 even people such as Sun wildcat Jimmy Wages or Alabama legend Al Ferrier were visiting Europe for shows, although Al, like Hal Harris and many other former rockabilly artists, would eventually find religion in 1996 and turn to recording gospel music. Ferrier later described his conversion in an interview with Steve Kelemen, adding: 'I was a drunk and a bad man while in the music scene and liked to fight and get into lots of trouble.' Yet the crowds in England still wanted to see some sign of the teenage rebels that these people had been several decades earlier when they'd cut their songs, rather than newly converted gospel singers, and a great many were able to oblige.

ROCKIN' WITH WANDA

Wanda Jackson, who'd been born again along with her husband Wendell back in 1972, still manages to deliver the rockabilly goods at every show, pausing for a minute to talk about her conversion and then launching into a cover of Hank Williams' 'I Saw The Light'. As news of the rockabilly revival reached her, she became aware that UK audiences were asking repeatedly for an old song of hers called 'Funnel Of Love' (1960), which had never been a hit back in the rockin' era, but was regularly featured by The Cramps during the 1980s. Lux and Ivy from The Cramps eventually appeared on one of Wanda's albums, *Heart Trouble* (2003), and Wanda told me that they specifically requested that they play on a version of 'Funnel Of Love'.

This crossover between the younger rockin' outfits and the 1950s originals had been going on for many years by that stage. It was something happening a long way removed from the mainstream music charts and the bright shiny world of MTV homogenisation, but you'd be hard put to find any mention of it when reading the music histories of those times. The 1990s, for instance, had a lot more going on in the UK than the media-generated hype of Britpop, and not every musician was queuing up to get an imitation Beatle haircut and go to 10 Downing Street to shake a deferential hand with Tony Blair.

RONNIE DAWSON – FROM TEXAS TO TOE RAG STUDIOS

Way over on the other side of town, Liam Watson had started his groundbreaking vintage recording studio Toe Rag in an old warehouse in Shoreditch in 1991, using an eight-track desk and favouring live-in-the-studio sessions which had a great deal in common with the working methods of Sam Phillips or Liam's own hero, Joe Meek. This is the place where Ronnie Dawson came in 1994 to record his comeback album, *Monkey Beat*, for the English record company No Hit. It was run by Barney Koumis, who'd started the label after meeting Ronnie and reissued a great compilation of his early material, entitled *Rockin' Bones*. In 1995, Koumis then opened the Sounds That Swing record shop in Camden Town, which, with the closure of the long-running Rock On record store around the corner, became the prime location for finding new and used rockin' vinyl in London.

In 1991 I was in two different bands at the same time: Gallon

Drunk, and also the Earls Of Suave, whose 1992 debut single covered Sanford Clark's 'A Cheat' (1956) and Charlie Rich's immortal Phillips International cut, 'Who Will The Next Fool Be' (1961), and was the first piece of vinyl to emerge from the new Toe Rag studios. I played drums in the former band and keyboards in the latter. The press took a shine to Gallon Drunk, and we were frequently described as a rockabilly band, generally by people who wouldn't have recognised a Charlie Feathers record if a crate of them fell on their head. Fair enough, the clothes and the haircuts looked that way, and the band's debut single had been a cover of Bill Allen's 1958 monster 'Please Give Me Something', which we took great pleasure in playing at live shows across Europe, the US and Canada, but we weren't remotely trying for an authentic rockabilly sound, and there was just as much of Machito, Bo Diddley, early Stooges or Suicide going on in the mixture. Nevertheless, something of the spirit was there, just as it was in many of the more sixties-influenced garage bands that eventually found their way to Toe Rag.

If you can pin it down at all, the common ground which went all the way back to the early days at Sun was a shared belief that music shouldn't be too clean or too planned, and that good mistakes happen in the heat of the moment when recording. As Nick Lowe used to say, when recording the early Stiff singles at the eight-track Pathway Studios in the mid-1970s, 'Bash it down and we'll tart it up later', which is the kind of philosophy that would certainly have struck a chord with Sam Phillips. Indeed, as Boz Boorer from The Polecats reminded me recently, when we were talking about the Malcolm Yelvington gig we'd both attended at the Clay Pigeon in Harrow back in 1988, one of the other people in that small room, enjoying the show, had been Nick Lowe.

As an example of how the various strands of musical

influence could blend together, consider the string of five gigs which The Cramps played at the Town & Country Club (now renamed The Forum) in London, leading up to Halloween 1991. There were different support bands each night, including Billy Childish's band Thee Headcoats, Dave Vanian's Phantom Chords (who used to do a killer version of Eddie Dixon's 'Relentless', from *The Loveless,* the 1982 biker film starring Robert Gordon) and Dallas's finest, Ronnie Dawson, singing 'Rockin' Bones' and 'Action Packed' while looking about twenty years younger than his real age. The Earls Of Suave opened the show for Ronnie and the Cramps that night, and the following evening Gallon Drunk preceded The Cramps, so I had two shots at the event, which remains one of the most enjoyable I've ever been involved with. The second night, being Halloween, Lux appeared onstage out of a coffin, and carrying a skull.

ROCKED OVER ITALY, ROCKED OVER SPAIN...

Then, of course, there was Morrissey, who recruited his post-Smiths band from the ranks of North London's rockabilly musicians, with Boz Boorer acting as his musical director from 1991 up to the present. As a member of Gallon Drunk, I gigged with Boz across the US and Canada when we were the support act on Morrissey's *Your Arsenal* tour (during which we also did a solo show at the Whiskey A Go Go on Sunset Strip, supported by one of the new US rockabilly outfits, Big Sandy & the Fly-Rite Trio). A year or so earlier, Boz had led a reformed Polecats on a tour of Japan, at the instigation of Tetsuya Nakatani, the founder of the Vinyl Japan label.

First time I went over was the end of '88... I don't know how it came about. I was at a record fair, and he [Tetsuya] kept buying Polecats records – as many as I could find, he'd buy them – and then he said, 'Have you ever thought about doing a new album?' And I said, 'Well, only if we can come and play' – bit of bravado – and he went, 'All right'. So we did an album, which was basically all the rockabilly songs we'd ever played that we'd never recorded, and he formed Vinyl Japan. That was the first record he put out.

That there was a serious collector's market out in Japan was very obvious when Tetsu first took me over there in 1990, playing drums for my friend Nikki Sudden, where we were met by people who had mint copies of pretty much everything that Nikki had ever released. Tetsu's shop, simply called Vinyl, remains one of the best-stocked vintage record stores I've ever seen: copies of the first Velvet Underground LP with

Morrissey & his band with Gallon Drunk, backstage at Pacific Amphitheatre, California, 1992 (l-r: Morrissey, Joe Byfield, Mike Delanian, Gary Day, Spencer Cobrin, Max Décharné, Boz Boorer, James Johnston)

the peelable banana sticker on the front still unpeeled; early Rolling Stones albums signed by all of the band including Brian Jones; you name it, it seemed to be there. Tetsuya recorded many fine albums by vintage and new rockabilly groups over the coming years, and brought a fair number of them over to play.

By the mid-1990s, labels like this and the shows they were promoting were part of an international network which had built up, almost entirely removed from whatever the mainstream music industry was pushing that particular year. In business terms, the 1990s in the UK consisted of trends like grunge, shoegazing, acid house and rap, giving way to Britpop, drum & bass and a seemingly endless supply of witless manufactured boy and girl bands, during which time the Top Twenty as it had existed for decades pretty much ceased to have any meaning whatever. Yet this was only part of the story, and in the parallel rockabilly world, things continued to follow their own rules, regardless of outside trends.

In the 1990s, the flood of original rockabillies touring the world continued unabated – among others, I saw Sun artists such as Billy Lee Riley, Carl Perkins and Johnny Cash (newly popular with the mass market after his *American Recordings* series began in 1994), not to mention catching Jerry Lee again and playing a show with Link Wray. Just as the newer bands like The Polecats and Restless had been heading over to Japan, others like the excellent Welsh rockabilly band The Rimshots travelled out to Australia, Finland and all across the US. Meanwhile, there were many remarkably authentic bands such as Swedish rockers Wildfire Willie & the Ramblers, who since 1986 had been performing material that could easily have been mistaken for original 1950s recordings. By now there was a worldwide circuit for rockabilly bands of several generations to play on, and rockin' labels appeared in countries such as Germany, Sweden and Spain, looking for new material by older and newer artists. In 1998, British promoters Barney Koumis and Tom Ingram decided to start promoting weekenders in Las Vegas, booking a line-up at the Gold Coast Hotel that featured a variety of 1950s acts, including rockabilly originals such as The Collins Kids and Ronnie Dawson, bringing the European rockabilly revival back home in more ways than one. Many European fans made the trip over for the shows, and continue to travel for the wide variety of rockabilly events which are now staged across the US.

Although rockabilly now has an audience in numerous countries, because of the crossover between rockabilly and country music, some performers who've recorded both in their careers find that they are asked more for the wilder material in certain nations than in others. Wanda Jackson – who scored a string of country hits in the 1960s, and also branched out by singing in German, reaching the charts over there with 'Santo Domingo' in 1965 – told me how her set list varies these days depending on the location:

> Well, for me it's country music, in Germany. They know my stuff, and they like it when I sing it – 'Party' and 'Fujiyama' – but they love the country stuff. In France, all they want, all they *know* of me, is rockabilly, so I don't have to put much country in. In Germany, mostly country; Scandinavia, all rockabilly. England was a bit confusing to me… [On an early visit, at the Wembley Country Music Festival at the start of the 1980s] I just figured it was all country, but then I started getting requests: 'But you've gotta do "Fujiyama Mama", please do "Mean Mean Man".' I said, 'I thought this was a *country* festival' [laughs].

HELLO CLEVELAND

Trying to pin music down into separate categories has always been a tricky business, but one of the more contentious developments in recent years has been the founding of the Rock'n'Roll Hall of Fame, now based in Alan Freed's old stomping ground, Cleveland. Every year since 1986 they've inducted a handful of nominees, and the difficulty comes with the prominent use of the words 'rock'n'roll' in the name. Sure, the opening year saw the rightful inclusion of Elvis, Little Richard, Chuck Berry, Jerry Lee Lewis, Buddy Holly, Fats Domino, The Everly Brothers and Sam Phillips, and the following year Ricky Nelson and Carl Perkins and Roy Orbison were among the inductees. Yet what exactly was going through their heads that it took until 1998 to get around to a giant rock'n'roll pioneer like Gene Vincent, years after the likes of Bobby Darin (1990), Cream (1993) or The Grateful Dead (1994)? If the last three are rock'n'roll, then the genre is so wide as to be meaningless. It's a measure of the particular tastes of the nominating panel that the sole person to have been inducted three times in different categories is Eric Clapton, while Scotty Moore, the man who laid down the rockabilly guitar blueprint, made it through the selection process only in the year 2000.

Small wonder that in 1997 the Rockabilly Hall of Fame was established in Nashville by Bob Timmers, and their first inductee was Gene Vincent. Their huge website, rockabillyhall. com, contains a formidable amount of information about rockabilly performers past and present. Then there's Terry E. Gordon's invaluable and ever-growing website 'Rockin' Country Style' (rcs-discography.com), probably the most comprehensive attempt to categorise and document the first wave of 1950s rockabilly activity, providing a searchable listing of tens of thousands of records by any performers active between 1951 and 1964 whose work falls into the rockabilly category, complete with label shots, song samples and other information. With the advent of Gordon's website, it became possible to date many obscure recordings which had appeared over the years on countless compilations like the long-running *Bison Bop* series or the numerous LPs issued by the Collector Records label, many of which offered just the briefest of details. It's fair to say that the average rockabilly enthusiast now has far more access to the music itself and to the story behind its creation than at any time in the past.

Of course, many of the first generation of rockabilly performers are now no longer with us. The 1990s alone saw the loss of Carl Perkins, Charlie Feathers, Hank Snow, Buddy Knox, Bobby Helms, Johnny Carroll, Jean Chapel, Charlie Rich and Groovey Joe Poovey, to name just a few, and in more recent times I've written obituaries in *Mojo* magazine for pioneers such as Janis Martin, Andy Starr, Cordell Jackson, Ronnie Dawson and Sonny Fisher. Just in the past year, during the writing of this book, we've lost Billy Lee Riley, Herbie Duncan, Dale Hawkins, Jim Dickinson and Lux Interior, but these are all people who very much made their mark and whose work will continue to find new listeners. In most cases, the original performers had seen a greater appreciation of their early recordings in their final years than in all the decades beforehand.

Far from being a genre of music which burned brightly for just a few years in the mid-1950s, rockabilly has proved itself to be a primal force, which has now retained its power and its ability to keep drawing a new audience for more than half a century. As for Elvis, you could probably build a fair-sized house out of all the books that have been written about him since he died, yet he remains an enigma, despite it all. The spark he lit up in all those young rockabilly musicians with his Sun recordings and his early tours across the South shows no sign of fading, but if you're asking what it was that marked him out as different from everyone else, before or since, let's leave the last word to the only surviving man who was there in the studio alongside The Hillbilly Cat, Scotty Moore, talking to Arjan Deelen: 'He had a rhythm in his voice, he just had a natural thing about that. He could hear a song, and he knew what he could do with that song. And nobody else could do it. They're still imitating him today but they just can't do it.'

Elvis leaves the building, August 1977

ACKNOWLEDGEMENTS

Many thanks to my agent, Caroline Montgomery at Rupert Crew Ltd, for believing in this book from the beginning, and for really helpful feedback on the text. Grateful thanks also to my editor John Williams, whose suggestions really gave the book a new pair of fins, some racing wheels and a boss set of tailpipes. A raised glass and a warm thank you to Pete Ayrton, Anna-Marie Fitzgerald, Rebecca Gray, Niamh Murray, Ruth Petrie and all the fine people at Serpent's Tail/Profile for catching the rockabilly fever.

I'd also like to thank the following people for their kindness, assistance, support or inspiration: Abigail Adams, Roger Armstrong, John Beecher, Jakub Blackman, Boz Boorer, Sonny Burgess, Trevor Cajiao, Ted Carroll, Bobby Crafford, Bal Croce, Del at Jeteye Music, Johnny Dickinson, John Donnelly, Colin Escott, Tav Falco, Vicki Fox, Wendell Goodman, Terry E. Gordon, Ant Hanlon, Martin Hawkins, James Intveld, Wanda Jackson, Miriam Linna, Hettie Lott, Memphis Mike, Billy Miller, Doreen Montgomery, Scotty Moore, Claire Munro, Stewart Pannaman, Gail Pollock, Johnny Powers, J. J. Rassler, James V. Roy, Mark & Karen Rubenstein, Ann Scanlon, Neil Scaplehorn, Jim Snively, Cathi Unsworth & Michael Meekin, and Andrew Weatherall, not to mention all the countless people over the years for their tireless work compiling rockabilly reissues or interviewing numerous original artists who are no longer with us.

Warmest thanks to Margaret & Geoffrey, Derek & Fiona, James & Eleanor for seeing it through all the way to Memphis.

Above all, here's to Katja, for everything.

BIBLIOGRAPHY

BOOKS

Alan Betrock, *The I Was a Teenage Juvenile Delinquent Rock'n'Roll Horror Beach Party Movie Book: A Complete Guide to the Teen Exploitation Film: 1954–1969*, London: Plexus, 1988

Beverly G. Bond & Janann Sherman, *Memphis in Black and White*, Mount Pleasant, SC: Arcadia Publishing, 2003

Louis Cantor, *Dewey and Elvis: the Life and Times of a Rock'n'Roll Deejay*, Champaign, IL: University of Illinois Press, 2005

Johnny Cash with Patrick Carr, *Cash: The Autobiography*, San Francisco: HarperSanFrancisco, 1997

Alan Clayson, *Only The Lonely: The Life and Artistic Legacy of Roy Orbison*, London: Pan Books, 1990 (first published 1989)

Robert M. W. Dixon & John Godrich, *Blues & Gospel Records, 1902–1943*, Chigwell, Essex: Storyville Publications, 3rd edn, 1982

Bob Dylan, *Chronicles, Volume One,* London: Simon & Schuster, 2004

Colin Escott, *Hank Williams,* Boston: Little, Brown & Co., 1994

——*Tattooed on Their Tongues: a Journey through the Backwoods of American Music*, New York: Schirmer Books, 1996

Colin Escott, ed., *All Routes Lead to Rock: Legends of Early Rock'n'Roll*, New York: Schirmer Books, 1999

Colin Escott & Martin Hawkins, *Catalyst: The Sun Records Story*, London: Aquarius Books, 1975

——*Good Rockin' Tonight: Sun Records & the Birth Of Rock'n'Roll*, New York: St Martin's Press, 1991

——*Sun Records: The Brief History of the Legendary Record Label*, New York: Quick Fox, 1980

Ken Garner, *The Peel Sessions*, London: BBC Books, 2007

John J. Goldrosen, *Buddy Holly: His Life and Music*, London: Panther Books, 1979 (first published 1975)

Robert Gordon, *It Came from Memphis: the Unturned Roots of Rock and Roll*, London: Secker & Warburg, 1995

Britt Hagarty, *The Day the World Turned Blue: A Biography of Gene Vincent*, Poole, Dorset: Blandford Press, 1984 (first published 1983)

John A. Jackson, *Big Beat Heat: Alan Freed and the Early Years of Rock & Roll*, New York: Schirmer Books, 1991

Jay B. Leviton and Ger J. Rijff, *Elvis Close-up: Rare, Intimate, Unpublished Photographs of Elvis Presley in 1956*, London: Century Hutchinson, 1989

Kip Lornell & Tracey E. W. Laird, *Shreveport Sounds in Black and White*, Jackson, MS: University Press of Mississippi, 2008

Randy McNutt, *We Wanna Boogie: An Illustrated History of the American Rockabilly Movement*, Hamilton, OH: HHP Books, 1988

Greil Marcus, *Mystery Train*, London: Omnibus Press, 1977 (first published 1975)

Bill C. Malone, *Country Music USA: Revised Edition*, Austin, TX: University of Texas Press, 1997 (first published 1968)

André Millard, ed., *The Electric Guitar: A History of an American Icon*, Baltimore, MD: The Johns Hopkins University Press, 2004

Scotty Moore with James Dickerson, *That's All Right Elvis: The Untold Story of Elvis's First Guitarist and Manager, Scotty Moore*, New York: Shirmer Books, 1997

Ed Naha, *The Films of Roger Corman: Brilliance on a Budget*, New York: Arco Publishing, 1982

Robert K. Oermann, *America's Music: The Roots of Country*, Atlanta, GA: Turner Publishing, Inc., 1996

Tony Palmer, *All You Need Is Love: The Story of Popular Music*, London: Futura Publications Limited, 1977 (first published 1976)

John Repsch, *The Legendary Joe Meek: The Telstar Man*, London: Cherry Red Books, 2004 (first published 1989)

Pete Silvester, *A Left Hand Like God: The Story of Boogie-Woogie*, London: Omnibus Press, 1990 (first published 1988)

John L. Smith, *The Johnny Cash Discography*, Westport, CT: Greenwood Press, 1985

John Swenson, *Bill Haley*, London: Star Books, 1983 (first published 1982)

V. Vale & Andrea Juno, *Incredibly Strange Music, Volume 1*, San Francisco: Re/Search Publications, 1993

Ian Wallis, *American Rock'n'Roll: The UK Tours 1956–72,* York: Music
    Mentor Books, 2003

Joel Whitburn, *Joel Whitburn's Top Country Singles
1944–1988: Compiled Exclusively from Billboard,*
    Menomonee Falls, WI: Record Reasearch, inc., 1989

Charles White, *The Life and Times of Little Richard, the Quasar
of Rock,* London: Picador, 1985 (first published 1984)

Peter Coats Zimmerman, *Tennessee Music: Its People and Places*, San
    Francisco: Miller Freeman Books, 1998

Mark Zwonitzer with Charles Hirshberg, *Will You Miss Me When I'm
Gone? The Carter Family & Their Legacy in American Music,* New
    York: Simon & Schuster, 2004 (first published 2002)

ARTICLES, SLEEVE NOTES, ETC.

Paul Ackerman, 'Diskeries in Race for R&R Country Talent', *Billboard,*
    12 May 1956

'An open letter to the industry from Jerry Lee Lewis', *Billboard*, 19 May 1958

Lou Anderson, 'Girls! Beware Of Elvis Presley's Doll-Point Pen',
    Confidential, January 1957

'Are You Businessmen?', *Billboard*, 22 June 1959

Geoff Barker, sleeve notes to *Four Rock'n'Roll Legends: Recorded Live in
London*, April 1977', Harvest, 1978

——sleeve notes to *When Rockabilly Ruled OK?*, Cherry Pie Records, 2008

'Be Bop A Lula'/'Woman Love' – record review in *Billboard*, 2 June 1956

John Beecher, sleeve notes to *Long Blond Hair,* Roller Coaster Records, 2008

Bo Berglind & Claes Olofsson, sleeve notes to *Jimmy Patton: Ya! I'm Movin'*,
    Star-Club, 1999

'Bill Haley Rocks At Wembley', *NME*, 29 July 1972

'Blue Suede Shoes'/'Honey Don't' – record review in *Billboard*, 16 February 1956

Bob Bernstein, '"Bandstand" Sociology But Not Entertainment', *Billboard,*
    12 August 1957

'Bob Neal: Managing the Hillbilly Cat', *Rockville International,* June 1973

'Brewery Sets "Ranch Party" deal', *Billboard,* 5 August 1957

June Bundy, 'Current Factor in Music Business is Diversification', *Billboard,*
    7 July 1956

Tony Byworth, sleeve notes to *Capitol Country Music Classics: The 1940s*, Capitol Records, 1991

Trevor Cajiao, 'Carl Perkins: The Man Behind The Music, Pt. 1', *Now Dig This*, No. 54, September 1987

——'Ten Years On… Remembering Ricky', *Now Dig This*, No. 153, December 1995

——'The Beat! The Beat! The Beat!', *Now Dig This*, No. 137, August 1994

——'Yakety Yak', *Now Dig This*, No. 69, December 1988

Trevor Cajiao & Mickey Downey, 'May 1958', *Now Dig This*, No. 2, May 1983

Dave 'The Chopper' Campbell & Larry 'Eegah' Harrison, 'Everything's Arch!', *Kicks,* No. 6, 1988

'Can't Hardly Stand It'/'Everybody's Lovin' My Baby', record review in *Billboard,* 6 October 1956

Roy Carr, review of 'Eddie Cochran: On The Air', *NME*, 4 November 1972

——'Junkyard Angels: The Original Greasy Trucker', *NME*, 1 June 1974

——sleeve notes to *Elvis: The Sun Collection*, RCA, 1975

Rose Clayton, 'Celebrate Peabody's Return With Music', *Billboard,* 19 September 1981

Howard Cockburn, sleeve notes to *Radio Rockabllies, Narvel Felts and Jerry Mercer,* Rockstar Records, 1988

——'The Charlie Feathers Enigma', *Now Dig This*, No. 90, September 1990

Howard Cockburn and Trevor Cajiao, 'An Interview With Terry Noland', *Now Dig This*, No. 91, October 1990

Jim Cole, Eddie Bond, Hayden Thompson & Billy Miller, sleeve notes to *Wildcat Jamboree! Rockabilly Radio Broadcasts from the Dixieland Jamboree, Corinth, Mississippi, 1958–59*, Norton Records, 2005

Stuart Colman, sleeve notes to the box set *Eddie Cochran: Somethin' Else, The Ultimate Collection*, Bear Family Records, 2009

'Cool Love'/'Do You Miss Me?' – record review in *Billboard*, 5 August 1957

'Country Musicians Fiddle Up Roaring Business', *Life*, 19 November 1956

'Country Thrush Scores Pop Hit', *Billboard,* 3 October 1960

'Crossroads Sues Mother Of Moppet', *Billboard,* 12 August 1957

Clifford Davis, 'Charlie Belts Out The Beat', *Daily Mirror,* 6 August 1957

——'Hot Spot! When Charlie Gracie Hit The Strings', *Daily Mirror*, 12 August 1957

——'Where There's Hope (Bob), There's Life', *Daily Mirror*, 3 March 1958

Hank Davis, Colin Escott & Martin Hawkins, sleeve notes to the box set *Jerry Lee Lewis: The Sun Years*, Charly Records, 1983

Arjan Deelen, 'Scotty Moore Interview', 28 March 1998, scottymoore.net

Deke Dickerson, 'A Technical Appreciation of Gene Vincent's Recordings' in the box-set *Gene Vincent: The Road Is Rocky*, Bear Family Records, 2005

'Distributor News', *Billboard*, 19 May 1958

Patrick Doncaster, 'On The Record', *Daily Mirror*, 20 June 1957

Larry Donn, 'Rockabilly Days', *Now Dig This*, No. 149, August 1995

Jim Downing, 'Wills Brothers Together Again: Bob Back with Heavy Beat', *Tulsa Tribune*, 4 January 1958

Marc Ebner, 'Wild Man Blues', *Dallas Observer*, 18 June 1998

Bill Ellis, 'Music's Kingmaker', *Commercial Appeal*, 14 August 1999

'Elvis: A Different Kind of Idol', *Life*, 27 August 1956

'Elvis Presley: King Of Western Bop', *Your Record Stars*, 1956

Colin Escott, sleeve notes to *Johnny Burnette Trio: Rockbilly Boogie*, Bear Family Records, 1989

——sleeve notes to *Onie Wheeler: Onie's Bop*, Bear Family Records, 1991

Tav Falco, 'Road To Memphis', full text of essay for *Mojo* article, 2003

Charlie Feathers, sleeve notes to *Charlie Feathers Volume 2*, Feathers Records, 1979

'Feathers Trio Signed', *Commercial Appeal*, 22 August 1956

Rob Finnis, sleeve notes to *Gene Vincent Cut Our Songs*, Ace Records, 2004

——sleeve notes to *King Rockabilly*, Ace Records, 2001

——sleeve notes to *Wanda Jackson: Queen of Rockabilly*, Ace Records, 2000

Roger Ford, 'Charlie Feathers', *Not Fade Away*, No. 16, 1980 (reprinted from *Rock'n'Roll Collector*, 1969)

Jim Gibbins, 'How Fabulous is Fabian?', *Picturegoer*, 10 October 1959

Charlie Gillett, 'Jerry Lee: A Case Of Too Many Cooks Spoil The Rock', *NME*, 10 March 1973

Derek Glenister, 'Jerry Lott: The Phantom Speaks', *New Kommotion*, No. 24, 1980

'Go Get The Shotgun, Grand'pa' – record review in *Billboard*, 30 March 1959

'Grandpaw's A Cat'/'Baboon Boogie' – record review in *Billboard*, 17 November 1956

Dick Grant, 'Jean Chapel', *New Kommotion*, No. 22, 1979

Nat Green, 'American Folk Tunes', *Billboard*, 14 April 1945

'Greenback Dollar, Watch & Chain'/'Foolish Heart' – record review in *Billboard*, 5 August 1957

Peter Guralnick, 'Charlie Feathers', *New Kommotion*, No. 22, 1979

Johnny Hale and Paul Barrett, Letter – 'A Right To Reply', *Now Dig This*, No. 50, May 1987

Bob Hall, sleevenotes to *'Some Piano Player, I'll Tell You That' The Piano Blues Volume Twenty: The Barrelhouse Years 1928–1933*, Magpie Records, 1984

David Hammond, 'Back Comes the Ballad', *Picturegoer*, 7 September 1957

——'Calypso Gets the Big Boost', *Picturegoer*, 9 March 1957

——'Calypso? It Won't Rock the Cats', *Picturegoer*, 13 April 1957

Martin Hawkins, sleeve notes to *The Complete Meteor Rockabilly & Hillbilly Recordings*, Ace Records, 2003

——'Malcolm Yelvington', *New Kommotion*, No. 22, 1979

'He's A Real Gone Guy'/'Maybe' – record review in *Billboard*, 2 February 1957

Derek Henderson, sleeve notes to *Gene Vincent & the Blue Caps: The Lost Dallas Sessions 1957–58*, Dragon Street Records, 1998

'Jimi Hendrix, Speaking For Himself', *Rolling Stone*, 9 March 1968

'Hep Cat Update', *Kicks*, No. 7, 1992

'High School', *Billboard*, 9 June 1958

'High School Confidential'/'Fools Like Me' – record review in *Billboard*, 19 May 1958

David Hinckley, 'Rock Revival Promoter, Richard Nader, Dead At 69', *New York Daily News*, 2 December 2009

Jan Hodenfield, 'Rock and Roll Revival', *Rolling Stone*, 29 November 1969

'How Long'/'Daydreams Come True' – record review in *Billboard,* 14 January 1956

'I Need A Man'/'No Matter Who's To Blame' – record review in *Billboard,* 20 October 1956

'"…I'm Just a Solid Mess of C-o-n-tusions," Cries the Newest Song Hit', *Life,* 11 June 1956

'In a Spin', *Memphis Press-Scimitar,* 28 July 1954

'Jock Showcasing of New Talent Keeps Wax Fresh', *Billboard,* 26 January 1957

Robert Johnson, 'That Something Has Captivated Fans Over U.S.', *Memphis Press-Scimitar,* 5 February 1955

'Jungle Rock'/'When I'm In Your Arms' – record review in *Billboard,* 10 November 1958

Steve Kelemen, 'Al Ferrier', rockabillyhall.com

Ken Kennamer, 'Presley Creates Musical Storm Here', *Lubbock Avalanche-Journal,* 12 April 1956

Nick Kent, 'The Cramps: Tales Of American Gothick', *NME,* 23 June 1979

'King of Western Bop Due Here Thursday', *Amarillo Globe-News,* 9 October 1955

James D. Kingsley, 'Mr Phillips Met the Appliance Salesman at 706 Union Ave.', *Billboard,* 23 May 1970

Barry M. Klein, 'Bond On Bond, Buford & The "Pink & Black" Days', rockabillyhall.com, 28 September 1999

Adam Komorowski, sleeve notes to *Barbara Pittman: Getting Better All The Time,* Charly Records, 2005

——sleeve notes to *We're Gonna Rock, We're Gonna Roll,* Proper Records, 2005

Dave Laing, 'Obituary: Sam Phillips', *Guardian,* 1 August 2003

Spencer Leigh, 'Obituary: Charlie Feathers', *Independent,* 9 September 1998

——'Obituary: Janis Martin', *Independent,* 6 September 2007

——'Obituary: Sam Phillips', *Independent,* 1 August 2003

'Lester Bihari Sets New Meteor Label', *Billboard,* 20 December 1952

'Lewis Reset On Steve Allen Show', *Billboard,* 5 August 1957

'Like Wow'/'Dangerous Doll' – record review in *Billboard*,
22 December 1958

Miriam Linna, 'Runnin' Wild With Ron Haydock', *Kicks*, No. 7, 1992

——'Wow! Sparkle!', *Kicks*, No. 6, 1988

'Little Lovin''/'I'm Ready If You're Willin'' – record review in *Billboard*,
26 May 1956

Michael Lollar, 'Photographer Sensed Star Quality As Soon As He Met
Young Singer', *Commercial Appeal*, 16 August 2002

'Love Me'/'Whisper Your Love' – record review in *Billboard*,
29 February 1960

Michael Lydon, 'Carl Perkins', *Rolling Stone*, 7 December 1968

Michael McCall, 'Nashville Cats: A Salute to Hargus "Pig" Robbins',
countrymusichalloffame.com

'Many Fine Surprises Await Katz Patrons', *Commercial Appeal*,
9 September 1954

'Memphian On Frolic', *Commercial Appeal*, 30 July 1954

Bill Millar, sleeve notes to *Dale Hawkins: Rock'n'Roll Tornado*, Ace
Records, 1998

——sleeve notes to *Rare Rockabilly Volume One*, MCA Records, 1975

——sleeve notes to *Rare Rockabilly Volume Two*, MCA Records, 1977

Bill Millar, Ray Topping & Adam Komorowski, 'The Major Bill Smith
Story', *New Kommotion*, No. 23, 1980

Lacy Mitchell, 'Elvis, Johnny Cash, Conway Twitty, Sonny Burgess Played at
King of Clubs', *Batesville Daily Guard*, 16 July 2008

Chris Morris & Melinda Newman, 'Sun Records Founder Sam Phillips, 80,
Dies', *Billboard*, 9 August 2003

John Morthland, sleeve notes to *Okeh Western Swing*, Epic, 1982

'Movies Reach for Pens as Juve Disk Stars hit Top 10', *Billboard*,
13 April 1959

'NBC Readies Steve Allen As Sub For "Comedy Hour"', *Billboard*,
21 April 1956

Stanley Nelson, 'Haney's Big House', *Concordia Sentinel*, 26 November 2007

Jim Newcombe, 'Wildwood Boogie', *Now Dig This*, No. 41, August 1986

Simon O'Hagan, 'Meet The Man Who Discovered The King – And Sold Him For $35,000', *Independent*, 2 July 2000

'Obituary: Sam Phillips', *The Times*, 31 July 2003

'Oh! I Like It'/'Weary Blues From Waitin'' – record review in *Billboard*, 27 September 1954

'Okie's In The Pokie'/'Lonely Nights' – record review in *Billboard*, 26 September 1960

'Oldies & Revival Shows Fill A Void For "Rough, Direct Music"', *Billboard*, 22 July 1972

'Ooh, Watcha Do!'/'Randy' – record review in *Billboard*, 14 April 1958

'Owen Bradley Seeking The New; Views The Old', *Billboard*, 7 August 1961

'"Ozark Jubilee" Is All For R&R Says Si Simon', *Billboard*, 21 April 1956

John Pearce, 'Jerry Lee, Rockin' It With Frampton, Gallagher, Lee', *NME*, 17 February 1973

'Philip Morris C&W Shows To Continue', *Billboard*, 16 December 1957

John Pilgrim, 'Obituary: Johnny Duncan', *Guardian*, 20 July 2000

Joseph Pirzada & John Michael Heath, sleeve notes to *The Beginning of Elvis Presley: The Birth of Rock'n'Roll: Volume 1, 1953–1954*, Memphis Recording Service, 2005

'Prep Disks to Unveil Pop LP Line in July', *Billboard*, 6 April 1957

'Presley On Pan But Cash Keeps Rolling', *Billboard*, 16 June 1956

'Presley To Sing On Radio Show Saturday Night', *Commercial Appeal*, 14 October 1954

Mark J. Price, 'Akron Teen-Agers Shared Stage With Rockabilly Legends', *Akron Beacon Journal*, 2003

'R&B Is Broadway's Current Lullaby', *Billboard*, 16 February 1957

Eric Random, 'Here He Is… Presley: The New Svengali Of Song', *Photoplay*, November 1956

Ben Ratliff, 'Obituary: Charlie Feathers', *New York Times*, 11 September 1998

'"Rock, Rock, Rock" Jumbo Size Disk Talent Package', *Billboard*, 8 December 1956

'Rock Your Baby'/'Sinful Heart' – record review in *Billboard*, 3 November 1958

'Rock-A-Bye Boogie'/'I Forgot More Than You'll Ever Know' – record review in *Billboard*, 20 June 1953

'Rockin' In The Graveyard'/'No Date' – record review in *Billboard*, 22 June 1959

'Rock'n'Roll Rolls On'n'On', *Life*, 22 December 1958

John Rolls, 'Big Chief Rainwater: He Bring Six Gamps!', *Daily Mirror*, 11 April 1958

——'Just A Few Dry Lines From Manchester', *Daily Mirror*, 30 April 1958

Tony Rounce, sleeve notes to *Crudup's Rockin' Blues, Arthur 'Big Boy' Crudup*, RCA International, 1985

Anne Rowe & Arlene Fillinger, 'Elvis Came, He Sang and He Conquered', *St Petersburg Times*, 8 August 1956

Wayne Russell, sleeve notes to *Boogie Woogie Fever*, Charly Records, 1982

——'Tragedy (You Bet!) The Story of Thomas Wayne', *Now Dig This*, No. 90, September 1990

Bill Sachs, 'Folk and Talent Tunes', *Billboard*, 24 December 1955

——'Folk and Talent Tunes', *Billboard*, 28 January 1956

——'Folk and Talent Tunes', *Billboard*, 4 August 1956

——'Folk and Talent Tunes', *Billboard*, 1 December 1956

——'Folk and Talent Tunes', *Billboard*, 14 April 1958

'Sam Phillips To Go Global With New International Label', *Billboard*, 5 August 1957

Ben Sandmel, sleeve notes to *Charlie Feathers*, Elektra Nonesuch, 1990

Dave Sax, sleeve notes to *That Real Hot Boogie Boy: Wayne Raney, The King Anthology*, Ace Records, 2002

'Sholes Has Last Laugh As Presley Rings Up Sales', *Billboard*, 21 April 1956

David Simmonds, 'Gene Vincent: The Last Interview', *Now Dig This*, No. 175, October 1997

Sing, Boy, Sing – album review in *Billboard*, 13 January 1958

'Skull and Cross Bones'/'Rock-a-Bop' – record review in *Billboard*, 17 November 1956

'Steve Allen To Relax At 8 On Sundays', *Billboard*, 16 June 1956

Tony Stewart, 'Rock'n'Roll Never Passed Away: It Just Ran Out Of Time', *NME*, 10 April 1976

'Sullivan Chalks Up Top Viewer Count', *Billboard,* 13 October 1956

'Talent Topics', *Billboard,* 6 November 1954

'Tape Recorder Sales Jumped 50% in '55', *Billboard,* 16 February 1956

'Teen-Age Hops Best Disk Talent Pay-Off', *Billboard,* 25 November 1957

'The Fool'/'Lonesome For A Letter', record review in *Billboard,* 26 May 1956

'The Train Kept A-Rollin''/'Honey Hush' – record review in *Billboard,* 13 October 1956

'Three Months To Kill'/'Little Boy Blue' – record review in *Billboard,* 30 June 1958

Adrian Thrills, 'Stray Cats: How Yankee Quiffabilly Put The Bop Back In Britain', *NME,* 30 August 1980

'Throngs On Hand for Big Opening With Special Sales, Entertainment', *Memphis Press-Scimitar,* 9 September 1954

'Tiny Teen's Big Song Hit', *Life,* 12 December 1960

'Tongue Tied Jill'/'Get With It', record review in *Billboard, 23* June 1956

——record review in *Cash Box, 16* June 1956

Ray Topping, sleeve notes to *Gulf Coast Grease: The Sandy Story Volume 1,* Ace Records, 1996

——sleeve notes to *Kings of Rockabilly,* Ace Records, 1980

——sleeve notes to *Rockabilly Party,* Ace Records, 1978

——sleeve notes to *Shreveport Stomp: Ram Records Volume One,* Ace Records, 1994

——sleeve notes to *Shreveport High Steppers: Ram Rockabilly & Hillbilly,* Ace Records, 2001

Andrew Tyler, review of *Suzie Q: The Best Of Dale Hawkins, NME,* 11 August 1973

Tony Tyler, 'Don't Knock The Rock', *NME,* 29 July 1972

Jack Warner, 'The Road to Rhythm with Gene Maltais', *Kicks* No. 6, 1988

'Wax Pact Snap For Gal With Right Talents', *Billboard,* 7 August 1954

Matt Weitz, 'Action Packed', *Dallas Observer,* 13 March 1997

——'Rock'n'Roll High School', *Dallas Observer,* 3 July 1997

Jann Wenner, 'Johnny Cash and Country: The Spiritual Core of Rock & Roll', *Rolling Stone,* 25 May 1968

Max Décharné

'Whole Lotta Shakin' Goin' On'/'All By Myself' – record review in
      Billboard, 8 October 1955

'Will You, Willyum'/'Drugstore Rock'n'Roll' – record review in *Billboard*,
      28 April 1956

Bill Williams, 'The Sounds Of Texas', *Billboard*, 21 November 1970

Robert Wilonsky, 'Good at Being the Best', *Dallas Observer*, 18 March 1999

——'Good Rockin' Last Night', *Dallas Observer*, 6 January 2000

——'Legendary Stardust Cowboy', *Dallas Observer*, 15 October 1998

——'The Late, Great', *Dallas Observer*, 9 October 2003

Chris Woodford and Dave Travis, 'Porky For President!', *Now Dig This*, No.
      50, May 1987

'You Rocked When You Shoulda' Rolled'/'The Killer' – record review in
      Billboard, 8 December 1958